How to catch
Alaska's
Trophy
Sportfish

How to catch
Alaska's Trophy Sportfish

Christopher Batin

Photos by Christopher and Adela Batin

Foreword by Homer Circle

Illustrations by Adela Batin

Alaska Angler™

Published by Alaska Angler Publications

Fairbanks, Alaska

How to Catch Alaska's Trophy Sportfish and Hunting in Alaska: A Comprehensive Guide are part of the Alaska Angling and Hunting LibraryTM, which is dedicated to providing only the very finest in Alaska fishing and hunting literature.

Cover on trade edition: Adela Batin with a 56-pound king salmon she caught on the Kenai River, Alaska. It was the 1981 IGFA world record for the 30-pound-test line class.

Published by Alaska AnglerTM Publications
P. O. Box 83550, Fairbanks, Alaska, 99708
(907) 456-8212

First Edition, April 1984
Revised Edition, January 1988

Book and cover design: Adela Ward Batin
Typography and production: Award Design, Fairbanks, Alaska

Library of Congress Cataloging in Publication Data
Batin, Christopher, 1955—
    How to catch Alaska's trophy sportfish
    Includes index.
    1. Fishing--Alaska. I. Title
SH464.A4B3

Library of Congress Catalog Card Number: 84-070673
ISBN 0-916771-03-2 (Trade Edition)
ISBN 0-916771-01-6 (Limited Edition)

Produced in the State of Alaska
Printed in the United States of America

This book is dedicated

To my wife Adela,
To the life-giving energy
that has brought our two souls together,
To turning dreams into reality,
And to those who take their passion
And make it happen.

Table of Contents

Fishing for lake trout in the Lake Clark region.

Homer Circle unhooking a large, Arctic grayling

Foreword

The only man I know with a name almost as crazy as mine is Chris Batin. And Chris Batin is the only man I know who is crazier about Alaska fishing than I. He eats it (I've seen him go hungry to do it), sleeps it, lives it, and writes about it with loving finesse.

I've been fishing Alaska since 1960, tetched on both its freshwater and saltwater species, and fished with many of its finer fishermen. Each had a specialty such as certain salmon species, Arctic char, pike, trout, halibut, flounder, etc. Chris Batin has the unusual distinction of being enamored with and expert about all of Alaska's species.

You get to know a fellow man rapidly and well fishing in remote country. During the days I spent with Chris I observed numerous things, like: he was the last one out fishing, usually after everyone else had retired after a rigorous day's outing.

And he'd be the first one up, standing there on the shore, changing lures, probing to see which species he could entice to take the plug or fly. His desire is not simply to catch fish but to learn, and write, all he learns so others can share in his enjoyment.

On our fly-ins to outback rivers and lakes I watched him first look after newcomers to make certain they were properly geared and fishing the right spots for the fish they sought. Satisfied, he would settle for secondary spots and invariably catch the biggest fish.

Upon returning home I wrote Tom Paugh, editor of *Sports Afield* magazine and said: "Just returned from Alaska where I learned a heap about fishing from a young man named Chris Batin. If you need anything authoritative on Alaska fishing I suggest you contact him. Chris Batin IS Alaska fishing!"

Well, you'll see as you read his book. His love for the fish comes through hand-in-glove with his empathy and concern for their well being. If you plan to go to Alaska, or already live there, read this book thoroughly and you fish it better. If you never go to Alaska, read this book and you'll learn things about fishing that will be helpful wherever you live.

Now married to Adela, I hope the Batins live almost forever so I can return to enjoy Alaska's fabulous fishing with them!

Homer Circle
Angling Editor
Sports Afield magazine
January, 1984

Acknowledgements

A book of this magnitude could not have been accomplished without the help of individuals, companies, and lodges who, over the years, have helped directly and indirectly in a variety of ways.

I would first like to thank my wife Adela, for sharing with me the countless fishing trips and for her long hours in preparing this book; mentor and friend Dave Bowring, who tolerated my greenhorn writing questions for all these years; Dave and Kay Richey, who put the bug in my head of doing a book of this magnitude; Homer Circle, for his always appropriate philosophy and instruction; Evan Swensen, for his support in the early years; Silver Stanfill, for her much appreciated comments and suggestions in reviewing this script; and Jill McMahon for her assistance in production.

For a variety of help, thanks to: Alan Swensen, Lee Langbehn, Richard Gardner, Bob Certain, Ron Kahlenbeck, Larry Mitchell, Mike Ticconi, Jerry Romanowski, David Doering, Bob Batin, Bill Batin, Joe Batin, Greg Shotts, Ned Pleus, Glenn Clawson, Frank and Wilma Kempl, Ken and Carol Guffey, Steve Mahay, Harry Gaines, Reggie Gates, Lorrie Schuerch, Stan Stephens, Bruce and Don Mallory, Bertil Laxhed, Rolf Smedman, Ake Stena, Olle Mattsson, J.W. Smith, Vince Guzzardi, Dave and Tam Ketscher, Phil Klobertanz, Dan Rodey, Jay Cassell, Jim Bailey, Jack Brown, P.J. Gesin, Gerry Siebert, Dick George, Larry and Sheary Suiter, Jean and James Price, and Alaska Department of Fish and Game biologists.

Thanks to the lodges, fishing guides, and charter services that have assisted this research: Mahay's Riverboat Service, Tyee Airlines, Sourdough Outfitters, Tanada Lake Lodge, Camp Denali, Tuwalaqua Lake Lodge, Van Valin's Island Lodge, Lake Clark Wilderness Lodge, Painter Creek Lodge, Stephan Lake Lodge, Central Charter Booking Agency, Ketchum Air Service, Freebird Charter and Fish Camp, The Fish House, Paul Pearson, Stan Stephens Charters, Walrus Charters, and Waterfall Resort.

And special thanks to the companies that have provided me with tackle and gear: Yakima Bait Company, Marathon Rubber Company, Luhr Jensen, Bill Norman Lures, Bass Buster, ABU-Garcia, Juhl Associates, Manns Bait Co., Shakespeare, Sheldon's Inc., Acme Tackle, Berkley and Co., Cortland Line, Sunset Line and Twine, Lou J. Eppinger Mfg. Co., Maxima Fishing Line, Scientific Anglers, Uncle Josh Bait Co., Dupont Stren, True Turn, Sampo Swivels, Gapen's, Heddon Lure Co., Fred Arobagst/Fin Baits, Lowrance, and Mountain View Sporting Goods, Anchorage.

And last, but certainly not least, I thank my Mom and Dad for instilling within me a love for the outdoors, and most of all, for teaching me about the God who made it for all of us to enjoy.

To any person, lodge, or company that I've forgotten in this listing, my apologies and heartfelt thanks and appreciation.

Christopher Batin

Chris Batin fighting it out with a wilderness stream chinook. Bill Batin photo.

Introduction

There is no better place than Alaska to catch trophy sportfish. Forty-pound king salmon are common, sockeye salmon enter streams and rivers by the millions, and deepsea halibut can reach weights of up to 400 pounds. Yet, despite the seemingly endless number of fish within the state, trophy fish in Alaska are not easy to catch: A lure or technique that catches small fish simply won't tempt the larger ones. It often takes a different technique, presentation, or lure—or a combination of all three—to entice trophy fish to strike.

This book contains a wide selection of methods, tips, and fish-catching secrets that have worked for me and other trophy fishermen throughout the state. Do not use this information to rape a watershed of its large fish. If anything, I hope these words and photos instill within you not only confidence in catching trophy sportfish, but also a sincere desire to learn about and appreciate their personalities, lives and habits. This one-on-one interaction between man and fish is what trophy sportfishing is all about.

However, a fish doesn't need to break a record or meet certain weight and length standards to be a trophy. Alaska has over 375,000,000 acres of land and water where a wide variation in fish sizes and populations exist. For instance, in the Aleutian Chain, a 2-pound Dolly Varden is considered a trophy fish, while the same size fish caught in the Bristol Bay Area is considered a youngster. A crimson-colored, 6-pound spawning sockeye may rank as a first-rate trophy to some anglers, while a delicately speckled cutthroat trout caught from a high-mountain lake may be held in higher esteem than a lunker king. And of course, there are trophy sportfishermen who release their catches, and keep nothing but their memories of wilderness mountains, tidewater glaciers, and bubbling alpine streams pure enough to drink from. In Alaska, whether or not a fish is a trophy rests in the eye of the beholder.

In gathering material for this book and my fishing articles for various magazines, I've logged over 20,000 hours fishing lakes, streams, and saltwater throughout the state. I've experienced Alaska like few people have. But this book is not a know-it-all, follow-it-by-the-rules bible. Rather, consider it an enticement...an invitation to experience the best sportfishing in North America. With that, come with me on an Alaska fishing adventure, to witness firsthand through my experiences the special qualities of this land and her fish. If by reading this book, you catch a trophy fish or appreciate Alaska's fish resources just a bit more, then I'll feel my efforts have been worthwhile.

Christopher Batin
Fairbanks, Alaska
January, 1984

King
Salmon

CHAPTER 1

King Salmon

At the turn of the century, East Coast writers often referred to the king as an "imposter salmon." To them, the king was a freak of nature with merely a superficial resemblance to the only real salmon, their Atlantic salmon. Easterners argued that the king—with its mammoth physique and brute mannerisms— couldn't begin to match the Atlantic's regal mien and pristine elegance. However, over the years, anglers have learned that whatever aristocratic qualities the king lacks, it compensates for with its Spartan-like aggressiveness, gargantuan size, and lure-smashing power. And that's just for starters. A big king can sizzle a drag for a mile or more, mangle an extra-strong, 6/0 treble hook into a useless clump of wire, and display in its aerial acrobatics an anger that can intimidate the most stouthearted trophy fish angler.

Yet despite the ravages this fish inflicts upon lures, muscle and mind, anglers still love him. Why? Because Alaska king salmon are the largest in the world. It isn't the 10- to 30-pounders that deserve the credit here. Salmon this size are often tossed back as if they were smolts. The celebrities are the 50- to 90-pound mutated giants that resemble a byproduct from some genetic mishap. To catch a fish this size—one whose tail drags the ground after you heave it over your shoulder, or one with a mouth large enough to stick your head into—is considered the ultimate achievement in the salmon sportfishing realm. Catching a trophy king, however, is more than having plenty of luck and en-

Dave Doering battles a Talkeetna River king salmon. The fish struck a Super Duper fished along a freshwater/glacial water breakline.

durance. An angler or guide must also be intimately familiar with the king's history, lifestyle, habits, and behavior.

The king salmon (Oncorhynchus tshawytscha) is also known as chinook, tyee, blackmouth, tule, quinnat, or spring salmon. "Hog" and "soaker" are slang terms used to describe kings over 60 pounds. Yet *king* best describes this fish, both in stature and appearance. The saltwater king is deep-bodied, with an iridescent, blue-green coloration on its dorsal surface. Its side flanks are a bright silver. The pearly white of its belly extends from the lower operculum to the base of the anal fin. It has black, irregular spotting on its dorsal fin and on both lobes of its caudal fin. Kings also have black gumlines. These are what distinguish small kings from cohos. In contrast, spawning kings can be dark red to copper, with heavy black pigmentation in some strains. Males are colored more intensely than females, and are also distinguished by their "ridgeback" condition and their hooked kypes.

Life History

The evolution and history of the king salmon are as stately as its name and appearance. Biologists theorize the king evolved from Atlantic salmon stocks over one million years ago. These early salmon migrated across the Arctic Ocean and thrived in the Pacific until the polar ice cap and Bering Sea land bridge formed, preventing their return. According to Charles Darwin, species that become isolated acquire unique characteristics. And the king did just that, changing little from its final evolutionary adaptation during the Pleistocene era.

The king prospered to the extent that early Indian tribes based their religion upon the fish. The Chinooks, an Oregonian tribe after whom the fish was named, believed the king was a supernatural being that ascended the streams for man's use, died, and after the natives returned the well-picked bones back to the sea, resumed its original form and returned the following year. Later, the king salmon became important in international trade. Historical documents show that as early as 1787, the Russians traded Alaska king salmon to the English for Hawaiian produce. On the homefront, Native Alaskans and early settlers traditionally utilized the king salmon as food for both humans and dogs. Because of its past and present importance in subsistence, commercial, and sport fisheries, the king has earned the distinction of being Alaska's official state fish.

Kings on their spawning migration enter Alaska streams as early as late May. A general rule is that the earlier a fish enters freshwater, the farther it will travel upstream. It is common for kings to migrate several hundred miles to their freshwater spawning sites. Yukon River kings hold the distinction of traveling the greatest distance: over 2,000 miles in less than 60 days. Equally remarkable is that these kings don't feed during this time. Instead, large deposits of body fat and oil nourish them on their upriver journey and enhance the development of eggs and milt.

Upon reaching the spawning area, females dig a redd in relatively deep water; in the Kenai River, that's water between 3 and 9 feet deep. Despite the male's quivering actions and slight courting nudges, the female pays little attention to him during nest building. She will, however, drive off other females venturing too close to her redd. After the nest is dug, the female drops into the pit with the dominant male, and sometimes with one or more subordinate males. The female will release from 4,000 to 12,000 eggs, which are immediately fertilized by the males. This process is repeated until the female has released all her eggs. The spawned-out female continues to dig nests for several more days: Her actions become more haphazard as her internal organs begin to fail. Both sexes die soon after spawning.

The eggs take 7 to 12 weeks to hatch, depending upon the locale and water temperature. The alevins take from 2 to 3 weeks to absorb their yolk sac, at which time they emerge from the gravel to feed on zooplankton and crustaceans. One to two years later, they outmigrate to sea as smolts.

Growth is phenomenal during the king's ocean life phase. Young kings feed on herring, sand lance, bottomfish, cod, crabs, and squid, and often double their weight during a single summer season. Sexual maturity is reached between two and seven years of age, triggering a spawning migration. This migration usually starts in winter, so that the fish arrive at their natal stream in late spring or early summer. However, biologists do not fully understand how this return migration is accomplished.

Kings are born orphans and die childless. They have no

opportunity to learn from their parents. Yet the king travels across broad expanses of the North Pacific, away from land masses that might provide clues to their location. Celestial navigation appears to be an unreliable means of guidance for fish on a definite time schedule, as weather is often stormy and overcast during spawning migrations. Salmon biologists have suggested that possible migratory cues include polarized light, or the most accepted theory, a chemical sensitivity to the earth's electromagnetic forces.

Once the king nears its natal watershed, its olfactory nerves take charge. Studies show kings possess an acute sense of smell, capable of detecting five parts of a substance in a million parts of water. This explains how kings can locate the "scent" of their natal stream while still several miles out at sea, and thus how they can often migrate to their exact place of birth.

Size

There is one main reason why the king is my favorite salmon. It is a BIG fish! The current state record is a 96.4-pound Kenai River fish caught in 1985 by Les Anderson. A 126-pound king was taken in a fish trap near Petersburg, Alaska in 1949. This fish had a length of 53½ inches, a girth of 38½ inches, and a tail spread of 17½ inches! And divers examining spawning beds on the Kenai River found a spawned-out king they estimated to be well over 100 pounds! I can only marvel when I think of how early man pursued this fish with his three-pronged spears and fishhooks whittled from the legbone of a mastodon. Yet today, with sophisticated tackle and the combined experience of generations of anglers, we are still trying to decipher the secrets of catching these huge salmon.

During the past 10 years, my contributions to the lore of the king are the specialized techniques and philosophies which I have used to catch 1,004 fish weighing more than 30 pounds, topped by 76-, 70-, and 69-pound giants. I've learned that the tactics used by most anglers today are adequate for catching the small 10- to 30-pound kings. But lunker salmon seem to develop an increased susceptibility to lockjaw with their ever-increasing size, and catching them with any consistency requires patience and a thorough knowledge of both fresh and saltwater fishing techniques.

An angler strains to hold up a 74-pound Kenai River king. Second-run Kenai River kings are the largest strain of king salmon in the world.

Techniques

Saltwater

The best saltwater fishery for trophy king salmon is the Deep Creek-Anchor Point fishery. Deep Creek is located on the east shore of Cook Inlet, at Mile 137 on the Sterling Highway. It has been called Alaska's fifth largest city on Memorial Day weekend. And for good reason. Hundreds of resident and non-resident anglers come here to catch big kings. And their efforts don't go unrewarded. From mid-May through mid-July 1980, over 5,000 kings were taken from this saltwater fishery. The May run of fish consists of 20- to 50-pound kings heading for the Kenai and upper Susitna tributaries. The late-June, early-July run is made up of second-run Kenai River fish that range from 40 to 90 pounds. While a boat ramp is available at Deep Creek, most anglers launch their car-topper and trailered boats off Cook Inlet beaches. After that, it's a matter of finding the breakline (fish attracting structure) that kings are using and the trolling technique to put those fish into the boat.

Deep Creek kings are concentrated into definite migration routes by Cook Inlet tides, which are the second highest in the Northern Hemisphere. These routes hug the Kenai Peninsula shoreline from Anchor Point to the mouth of the Kenai River. Their corridor width varies with tidal activity. A heavy outgoing tide concentrates kings near the bottom and from 75 to 100 yards out from shore. On an incoming tide, fish can be found at any depth, but they are most frequently caught near the bottom and from 5 to 75 yards from shore. Over the years, I've experimented extensively with both lures and bait in this fishery. The three types that have produced over 80 Deep Creek kings for me in the past 10 years have been bait herring, spinners, and spoons.

Bait

Quality herring is a must when fishing for Deep Creek kings. Because the bait will be working slowly in the current, kings have a chance to scrutinize it before striking. It should be shiny, firm, and look good enough to eat. A bait that is waterlogged, with scales falling off and the flesh cut in several places will not draw many strikes. I remember

Quality herring is necessary to catch trophy saltwater kings. Flesh should be firm with few scales missing. Keep bait frozen until ready for use.

fishing Deep Creek with such a bait for several hours one May evening. Anglers all around were catching kings. And friend Larry Mitchell had just fought and landed a sleek 42-pounder. Yet with so many kings in the area, I wanted to see if quality of bait really made a difference. After Larry hooked his second fish, I terminated the experiment for the day and rigged up with a silvery blue, unmarred herring. I dropped my rig into the water and within five seconds a bone-jarring strike had me shouting with excitement. The fish was a wild one, screeching

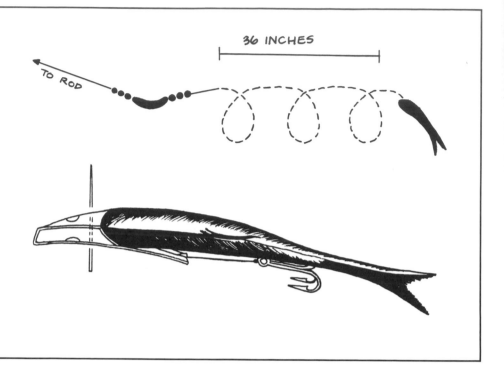

36 INCHES

TO ROD

A Herring Aid is a bait harness that imparts a spin to the herring. The amount of curve put in the bait by the harness determines its rotation speed. Kings prefer a slow, lazy spiral: Two to three revolutions per 36 inches is best.

across the inlet on what seemed to be a one-way ticket to China! Friend Mike Ticconi kicked the outboard into high gear and chased the big fish down. From his boat, Larry cheered us on. I struggled to hold the rod high as the king kicked in its afterburners. I was shouting to Mike for more power from the 7½ horse motor, Mike was yelling "Fish On!" in a rage of excitement, and Larry had just opened a brew in a toast to such a magnificent fighting fish.

A half hour later, with the outboard sputtering in the salty air, Mike eased the net around the 44-pounder and hauled it aboard. I was convinced. Always use prime, 6- to 9-inch herring for large kings.

Once you have a supply of herring, a proper rig to fish it is necessary. Although there are several on the market, I favor the Herring Aid bait harness because of its simplicity in design and effectiveness in catching big kings. I prefer to adjust the Aid so the herring works in a wide slow spiral: About 2 to 3 turns every 36 inches is best. Attach the leader that comes with the Aid to a 1½- to 3-ounce keel sinker; use the lighter weight for trolling closer to shore,

How to Catch
Alaska's Trophy Sportfish

and the larger for deep water. Fish the lure on a slow troll from 30 to 50 yards behind the boat while slowly trolling a zig-zag pattern parallel to the beach. If you have a graph recorder, locate the point where the sloping shoreline of the inlet immediately begins to flatten. In Deep Creek this is the only structural breakline for several miles, and can easily be found and studied on a minus tide. On an incoming tide, kings use this breakline as a migration corridor. I'll often record kings within 15 feet on either side of this structure, and nowhere else.

Another important structure that attracts migrating kings is a freshwater breakline, for example, where the lighter-colored freshwater from Deep Creek gradually mixes with the darker saltwater of Cook Inlet. Kings hatched from Deep Creek will follow this breakline until they enter the creek. Fish bound for other watersheds may mill around this breakline for several minutes to several days. They are attracted by the freshwater, even though it may not be from their natal watershed. I never underestimate the attractiveness of a freshwater breakline to a big king, especially if suitable holding structure is nearby. Twin Falls, located several miles down the beach from Deep Creek, has only a small freshwater breakline that attracts kings. Yet the surrounding bottom structure has large boulders, holes, and channels that allow fish to weather the tidal changes. This is an excellent area to fish on both an incoming and outgoing tide.

After you've found a structural or freshwater breakline and trolling into the current, give your herring some fish-attracting action. With rod in hand, twitch the herring about 12 to 18 inches forward every 30 seconds. This imparts a darting movement to the already rotating herring. My experimentations have shown this action is a major factor in triggering kings to strike. They will usually strike when the herring is dropping back.

Spinners and Spoons

There are three lures I recommend for fishing off Deep Creek: Tee Spoons, 1-ounce HotRods, and Mepps Giant Killers. I fish these lures with the same trolling techniques I use with the Herring Aid. However, I usually use a 1½-ounce keel sinker with the Tee Spoon and HotRod, and go to 2-ounces when fishing the Mepps. When using a downrigger, it's often necessary to trail the lure 7 to 10 feet behind the downrigger weight to allow for proper lure action. During slack tide, I've found a hootchie/dodger or flasher combo works extremely well when trolled slowly at mid-depth or at night.

Large kings are reluctant to chase a lure very far unless it has come-and-get-it charm. Always strive to fish a lure in the most tantalyzing and erratic manner possible. To do this I troll shoreline structure at the slowest possible speed, allowing my lure to flutter enticingly in the current, just above bottom cover. This technique allows the king to home in on the lure. That's why I polish all spoon and spinner blades to a high lustre. There's not a better dinner bell than "flash" for a big king. If the lure finish is worn, or the water is turbid, I attach a strip of prism tape for greater reflection.

Saltwater fishing for Deep Creek kings may not offer you the wilderness fishing experience found in other parts of the state. But at Deep Creek you can fight the "king" of sportfish in a no-holds-barred contest sure to make you want to return each year for more.

Freshwater

Once kings enter freshwater, they acquire different characteristics than those they had in saltwater. Being a cold-blooded species, the king matches its body temperature to the river. And it is blood temperature that determines the salmon's rate of metabolism, and consequently its readiness to strike a lure.

I've found that when the water temperature is below 48 degrees, freshwater kings will be sluggish and slow to respond to visual stimuli. Then, they generally hold in deep pools or at the mouths of rivers, showing little interest in anything other than holding their places in the current. Low water temperature makes catching big kings difficult.

Persistence and precise fishing technique are the keys to success in low water temperatures. A lure must constantly be worked across the salmon's kype before an interception is triggered. I refrain from saying strike, because cold-water salmon usually swim slowly up to the lure and mouth it ever so lightly. This action is triggered only when a slow wobbling plug or attractor bait is fished in front of the salmon for long periods of time. A good analogy would be your telephone ringing at 3 a.m. The constant ringing may trigger an aggravation response. Perhaps curiosity will

Alaska kings have outstanding stamina and strength. After traveling for over 100 miles up a silty glacial river, this king is still full of battle. The fish jumped five times and took over 20 minutes to land.

This 54-pound king fell for a large Kenai Special. Size of lure, color, and action are three important factors that anglers must consider when fishing for freshwater kings.

move you to answer the phone, or maybe the desire to chastize the caller.

A cold-water, lethargic king will likewise strike a lure out of aggravation, curiosity, or simply to relieve its senses of an irritating object, i.e. a lure. Therefore, to be most effective, the lure should be large—over 3 inches for plugs, and 5 inches for attractor lures—to provoke a response. At this time small lures are unproductive, as they don't have enough mass to sufficiently aggravate the fish. I've often had to work cold-water fish holding in deep pools or along migration routes for 20 minutes or more before triggering a response. If you can't turn a fish after a half hour of effort, try another location. But always give any lockjawed salmon another dose of aggravation by fishing these same holding areas later that day. I theorize that aggravation accumulates in fish and is not lost over a period of time. The more you aggravate cold-water salmon, the closer you'll get to making that fish inhale your lure.

By contrast, water temperatures over 48 degrees seem to rejuvenate lethargic salmon. In warmer waters, salmon are

How to Catch
Alaska's Trophy Sportfish

more prone to aggravation, and will wander throughout a stretch of river, like a kid exploring a new playground. They'll investigate every movement and flash in their vicinity and often strike for a variety of reasons. Since a king's digestive system atrophies after the fish enters freshwater, it cannot feed. Yet they aggressively strike properly fished lures. Why? Some say that this response is left over from their sea-going feeding habits; some say curiosity; while others insist the aggressive nature found in most predatory fish causes the king to attack and ingest maimed or injured baitfish, and lures. The most bone-jarring strikes do occur when you trigger the aggravation response in warm-water kings. These strikes have almost always been verified as aggravation responses by the hook being buried in the kype or upper jaw. When a king is mad, it will nip or grab a lure. On the other hand, if a king is merely "cleaning house" or inhales a glob of eggs fished stationary on the bottom, the fish will be hooked in the back or bottom of the mouth. Of course, there are exceptions to this.

Lure size is not as crucial in water over 48 degrees. However, for warm-water kings, again I recommend large lures because they enhance the aggravation process. Also, large lures can take the punishment big kings dish out. Small lures generally disintegrate after the first strike.

Use large lures when fishing glacially silted waters such as the Kenai. Where visibility is low, a big salmon needs every opportunity to see the lure drifting through its territory. This is especially true for drift fishing, when you only have one pass at the fish. Large lures not only provide more surface mass to aggravate a fish, but also tend to stay near the bottom where trophy kings are found.

Lure color is equally important. On cloudy days or when the sun is at a low angle, even the strongest sunlight is relatively weak. Light is greatly diffused once it penetrates the river currents, and becomes even weaker in glacial waters. The fluorescent colors and metallic finishes are extremely visible to fish in these low light situations. Over 98 percent of my king catches have been on these two color types. Solid fluorescent colors also are useful in clearwater streams where light penetration is not a problem. On the other hand, a flashy metallic lure may spook fish, especially those holding in shallow water. I've also found these same principles apply to fly patterns.

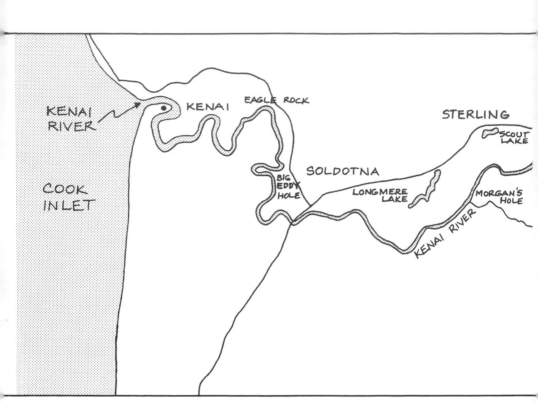

The Kenai—River of Big Kings

The most popular trophy king fishery in the world is the Kenai River. Sportfishing for big kings in the 85-mile long, glacially-fed Kenai first became popular around 1973. Now it has grown to be the largest sportfishery in the state. Over 100,000 man-days of effort are concentrated there annually, not only on 30- to 90-pound king salmon, but also on rainbow trout, Dolly Varden, sockeye, coho, and pink salmon. Yet most of the effort is spent by anglers trying to catch a trophy, if not a world-record king salmon. And the Kenai allows them two opportunities to do this.

Most river systems in Alaska have only a single run of kings. But the Kenai River is unique in that it has two. The first in-migration occurs from mid-May through June; most fish enter Kenai tributaries by June 25th. The kings in the Kenai's first run are generally small, ranging from 20 to 50 pounds, with a 30-pound average.

Early-run fish have a tendancy to "mill around" in the main river and tributaries before spawning. Research studies of tagged fish indicate this "milling around" lasts 24

How to Catch
Alaska's Trophy Sportfish

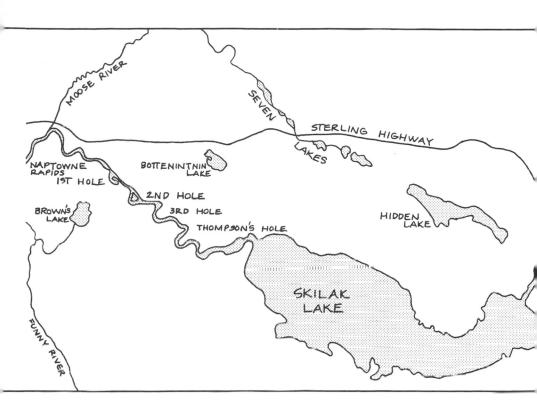

days. That's 24 days a fish is available for catching—before it enters a tributary or passes Kenai River Mile 54—an area that has been traditionally closed to fishing. These early-run fish are more energetic because they are not quite ready to spawn. Consequently, there are two responses that can be triggered: investigative or curiosity, and aggravation. When early-run kings are migrating upstream, they are often playful, swimming up and down river, becoming reacquainted with their freshwater environment. They are curious and will investigate numerous objects bouncing downriver, including lures. They may follow a lure 10 yards or more before grabbing it. Fish investigate or "feel" objects by mouthing them. This mouthing is often lightning fast. Because fish can spit out a lure in a flash, the angler should be ready to strike quickly at any movement in the line or rod tip. My experience has been that in the Kenai, only first-run fish exhibit curiosity responses to lures.

As spawning time nears, however, the fish lose their energetic drive. An object that once piqued their curiosity

The 85-mile Kenai River flows through both semi-wilderness and populated areas. Excellent fishing can be found along its entire course.

King Salmon

A guide wrestles ashore a large 58-pound Kenai River king for an angler. Quality, heavy-duty tackle is a must for catching large kings from this watershed.

is now a threat to their spawning or holding territory. A king exposed to the repeated "trespassing" of a lure into its area becomes aggravated and strikes the lure. Aggravation or territorial responses to a lure are immediately before or after the fish have entered a Kenai tributary to spawn.

Second or late-run kings have completely different migratory habits and personalities. They migrate into the Kenai the last week in June and during the month of July. Because they enter the river ready to spawn, second-run kings have neither the energy nor the heightened curiosity of early-run fish. They are extremely territorial the moment they enter the river. They become loners that seek out migration routes and resting areas removed from other salmon such as sockeyes or pinks. Unlike first-run fish, second-run kings will spawn in the Kenai rather than the river's tributaries. The reason is evolutionary adaptation at its finest. In late spring, Kenai tributaries have plenty of water from melting ice and snow. First-run kings can spawn safely in this abundant runoff. However, summer

Migration Facts

• Kings move faster through high-velocity areas of the Kenai River, such as Naptowne Rapids, than through calmer sections of river. Early-run fish average 1.5 miles per day through such sections, while late-run chinook average .98 miles per day. In normal currents, males usually travel upstream the fastest; up to 18 miles per day. Females average 9 miles per day. According to the results of radio telemetry studies, kings are most likely to migrate during late afternoon and early evening.

•• Researchers have found that almost 50 percent of the kings will use a riverbank as a focal point in establishing holding areas or migratory pathways. This doesn't mean that kings travel along the shallow-water breakline of the Kenai as coho or sockeye do. Rather, kings were found to stay within 15 to 60 feet of the bank or some type of shoreline structure. They were also found to hold at or migrate through areas where vegetated islands are present.

• Tagged, second-run fish were available to anglers for 12.8 days. Fish spend an average of 18.4 days at the spawning site before dying. With a good percentage of these kings spawning in the Kenai from Mile 10 to 21, it's easy to understand why the lower river receives the most fishing pressure. Kings do not select spawning areas below Mile 10 during the month of July.

• Research has turned up some surprising facts regarding king salmon behavior. Radio telemetry studies of Kenai kings show that they occasionally migrate up to Mile 30 before they turn around and head back out to sea. And even more surprising, the king may be evolving into a repeat spawner. Studies show that Kenai kings often fail to respond to the natural urge to reproduce and continue their life as loners, far beyond their normal life span. These fish are called "leatherbacks" because the color and texture of their aging skin resembles a dark brown leather. Here are a few U.S. Fish and Wildlife Service case histories that prove how unique the Kenai king is:

• Following an upstream movement to Mile 24.1, fish 81-27 on June 22 migrated downriver where it was last detected at Mile 18.7 on July 6. This fish was subsequently harvested by gill netters on the west side of Cook Inlet.

• A king was radio-tagged at Mile 12.5. For the next 10 days, biologists could not locate the fish with telemetry. Fish apparently re-entered the Kenai and was later detected at Mile 6.5.

• King 81-31 was tracked to Mile 45.5 on July 21. The king then descended past an automatic counter on July 26. It was later harvested in a Cook Inlet net, apparently spawned out.

Researchers also found that early-run kings that stay in the Kenai are extremely nomadic. Two examples are:

• A king was tagged at Mile 12.2 before descending to Beaver Creek (Mile 10.2) for 18 days before resuming upstream migration.

• After biologists tagged a king on May 26, the king moved upstream to Mile 16.5. On June 3, it was found downriver at Mile 8. Subsequent upstream migration occurred to the Killey River.

Kenai River guide Larry Suiter (right) hefts up the author's 70-pound, second-run king. The fish struck a Magnum Tadpolly back-trolled through a run.

heat often reduces these tributaries to mere trickles of water. This low water would subject second-run kings to predators and injury. Thus, it's possible that the second-run kings' larger size evolved so that they could cope with the rigors of spawning in the Kenai's swift, mainstream currents.

Whether fishing the first or second run, the foremost concern of any angler or guide is to find the major migration routes and spawning locations of these fish. It's an annual chore, as water currents constantly change the bottom structure. However, channels and spawning areas are likely to be found along stretches of gravel-bottom riverbank near shoreline, behind riffles and large rocks, at the mouth of a tributary, through deep channels, and along the perimeter of islands. Catching a big king becomes a matter of using lures that are equally effective in triggering either its curiosity and/or aggravation response. I have found that plugs, Spin-N-Glo/hootchie combos (Kenai Special), and salmon eggs fall into this category.

34

Plugs

Plugs are excellent lures for Kenai River kings. They can dive deeply in either fast or slow currents, and they have an intense wobbling action that greatly aggravates big kings. Plugs are ideal for fishing confined or snag-filled areas where big salmon like to hold.

Perhaps the plug's most appreciated quality is that it's easy to fish. Toss it out into the current and it works almost automatically. There is no messy bait to handle, no precision casting, nor bottom-bouncing tricks to learn. While the plug may be easy to fish, its salmon-catching effectiveness depends upon the person operating the boat. And there is not a more skilled plug fisherman/boat handler than Kenai salmon guide Larry Suiter.

While Suiter fishes several types of lures, plugs account for a majority of his big kings. He fishes plugs with a method known as backtrolling, drop-back fishing, or plug running. This method requires longlining several plugs from 15 to 50 or more feet behind the boat. Rather than each angler working a plug through the currents, the river current works the plug automatically. Water pressure against the lure's planing lip causes the plug to dive down to a few inches above the riverbottom. While backtrolling, the plug dives into the riverbed and bounces back up, an action that greatly aggravates territorial kings. A guide can fish up to five plugs on five rods, with each rod in a rod holder. Suiter "fishes" all the plugs by using enough engine power to keep the boat stationary with its bow in the current. He steers the boat from side to side, while slowly dropping back in the current. Thus, the line of plugs sweeps across a section of river. Suiter allows the boat to slip several feet in the current and repeats the procedure. The result is a thorough coverage of bottom structure and a very effective way to provoke a king to strike. All the angler must do is wait for the rod to dip sharply, grab the rod, and set the hook.

Suiter's favorite plugs are simple: the Hot Shot or Magnum Tadpolly. Both are excellent lures, yet the Hot Shot requires modification to stand up to the ravages of Kenai kings. Suiter replaces the factory hooks with extra-strong treble hooks. He also epoxies the screw eyes that anchor the hooks into the plug. Due to its internal anchoring system, the Tadpolly doesn't require these modifications. The J-Plug is also an excellent big king lure, along

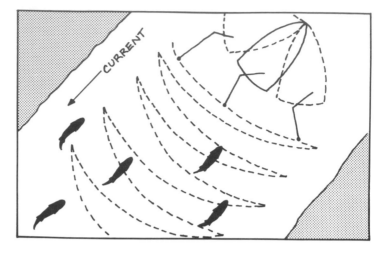

Proper backtrolling technique requires the boat to work the plug(s) in a side-to-side motion while slowly slipping downstream. Planers and attractor baits can also be fished with this method.

with the shallower running Flatfish, which is a good choice in low water conditions. All are effective, yet each has an action that is slightly different than the other. I usually let the kings decide which plug type they prefer most.

Time of year and water turbidity will dictate the best color. For instance, a nickel-plated plug is an extremely effective color at any time except for late May—early June. At this time, the early-season king run coincides with the in-migration of millions of flashy, wiggly hooligan. Kings quickly become immune to flash and ignore lures with a metallic finish. Solid colors such as fluorescent red, fluorescent green, fluorescent yellow and chartreuse are productive colors until the hooligan either enter the Kenai tributaries or die.

Throughout the rest of the season, try the above color combinations in addition to chrome, chrome/chartreuse, chrome/flame, red, metallic blue, and gold. Suiter has experienced substantial success by painting up lures in color combinations not available from the factory.

When fishing plugs, use a rod with a sensitive tip. The plug's wobbling vibrations travel up the line to the rod tip, which will pulsate in time with the plug. A plug's action triggers the strike response in a king like no other lure. A king will usually grab the plug and quickly rocket downriver with it, causing the rod to snap sharply downward and the reel's drag to screech in deafening protest. It's a sound I consider music to my ears. Yet there

A Kenai Special is a popular lure for catching lunker king salmon. Many variations exist, but all have four basic elements: Spin-N-Glo body, hootchie skirt, attractor beads, and extra-strong single or treble hooks.

always seems to be one lazy king that will inhale the plug and for several seconds do nothing else but hold in place. During those seconds your sensitive rod-tip is still. Therefore, any hesitation in the lure's rhythm is cause for a hook-set.

Spin-N-Glo/Hootchie

The Spin-N-Glo/hootchie lure is one of the most unnatural looking lures I've ever used. It consists of a cork body with rubber wings, two or more fluorescent beads on a wire shank, an Okie Drifter or Lil Corky for added attraction, and a plastic, tentacled hootchie skirt hiding a 6/0 hook. I believe this lure's uncanny effectiveness in hooking large kings is due to its ugliness. Kings strike it with a force intended to put something out of its misery. As a result, the only thing in misery at the end of the battle is my fightin' arm. Yet it's an affliction I'll suffer with an ear-to-ear grin.

A Spin-N-Glo/hootchie (locally referred to as a Kenai Special) is best fished with a sliding sinker in calm, spawning pools, while backtrolling down migration channels, or when drift fishing a section of river. The Kenai Special is also a good choice to bottom-bounce through snag-filled structure or at the head of mid-river pools located behind large rocks or other structure.

When fishing a relatively calm pool near the main current, or a migration route adjacent to islands, your objective is to get the lure to the bottom of these structures with a one- to three-ounce, slip-sinker rig. Ensure the Special is holding slightly above bottom in current fast enough to twirl the Spin-N-Glo. Once the lure is working properly, put the rod in the holder and wait. It's not easy to keep patient when waiting for a huge Kenai king to strike a lure fished in this manner. But it's a very effective method of fishing, as my wife Adela and I discovered when fishing Super Hole on the Kenai River several years ago with guide Larry Suiter.

It was almost 5 a.m., and Alaska's July sun shone as brightly as it would at noon. We had cast out some modified Specials to the head of Super Hole. As I sat down with a cup of coffee, I smiled. Several king salmon broke the river's surface. The run was on.

I watched my rod tip for any indication that a big king was mouthing my lure. Expecting that a small tap would signal a strike, my mind went haywire for a moment when Adela's rodtip crashed downward from its 50-degree position in the rod holder. The drag screeched so loudly I thought it would explode as Adela jumped up and struggled to remove the wildly bucking rod. She set the hook with all the strength she could muster while standing on one foot. The other was propped firmly against the gunwale after a sudden surge by the fish nearly pulled her overboard.

Adela didn't need any electronics expert to tell her she was plugged into a live wire of a king salmon. The reddish-silvery fish charged out into the mainstream of the Kenai in a series of jolting acrobatics.

Larry had already disengaged the rope from the hog line, (a row of fishing boats) and quickly fired up the engine to chase down the rampaging salmon. The salmon was a tactician in river warfare. Several times the fish sounded under the boat, forcing Adela to thrust the rod tip in the water while scurrying to the other side. Twenty minutes— and what seemed to be a gallon of sweat for each of us— later, Adela fell back into her seat as Larry struggled to hoist the 56-pound king into the boat. The hooks on the Spin-N-Glo were twisted at right angles, and would have snapped off with another good run. We motored back to the Hole where I caught a silvery 34-pounder. Since, I've been an advocate of fishing Specials for Kenai kings.

Some veteran king salmon guides, such as Harry Gaines, prefer to add a small chunk of cured salmon eggs to the tre-

Kenai guide Harry Gaines baits up a Kenai Special with a glob of salmon eggs. A popular big king bait, salmon eggs can either be fished by themselves or with an attractor lure.

ble of the Special. Gaines says that the added scent of the eggs triggers kings to strike the lure much more readily than a Special fished without eggs. Another popular theory is the kings are trying to perpetuate the species by mouthing the eggs and expelling them back into the gravel. (Free-floating eggs are usually eaten by sculpins and other fish, in addition to becoming diseased.) I believe eggs are effective because they increase the mass of the lure, they help to keep it on the bottom, and because their scent disguises human scent. Studies of Kenai kings show that human scent greatly alarms them. So if you don't like fishing with eggs, at least use a commercially prepared scent to mask any human odor on the lure.

Jet Planers

When fishing Specials, especially when anchored in main channels or when backtrolling through rocky stretches of river, don't use the easily snagged lead weights. Instead, use a diving device known as a Jet Planer to take the Special down to the bottom and keep it there.

The Jet Planer rig works on the same principle as a diving plug: The planer is designed to dive in response to water pushing against it. And it is as easy to fish as a plug. Tie your Kenai Special to a 20- to 40-inch, 25-pound-test leader. Attach the free end of the leader to the snap swivel just below the air chamber of the planer. Sharpen your hooks and you're ready to fish.

Backtrolling the planer or fishing it from an anchored boat in fast current is also easy. Throttle the boat's motor fast enough to hold the boat, bow facing upstream, stationary in the current. Float the planer/Special rig to the structure to be fished. Close the reel's bail and the planer will dive. The planer keeps the lure in the salmon's low

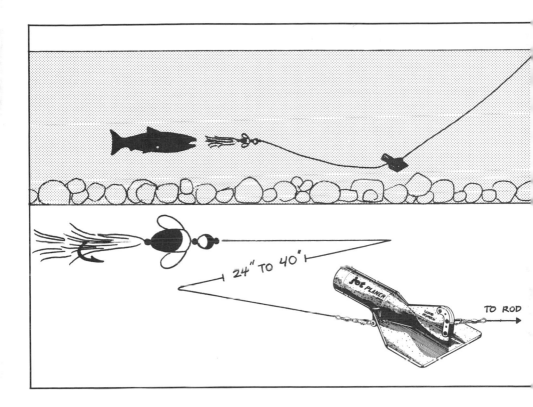

angle of sight by maintaining it in a horizontal attitude above bottom at all times. Fish this rig the same as you would plugs, using the backtrolling maneuvers described earlier in this chapter.

The planer can also be used to fish eggs, spoons, spinners, and other lures. Unless you're an experienced king angler, it's best to keep the rod in a holder while backtrolling or anchored. Salmon will often play with a lure or bait before striking. These "nibblings" often prompt the inexperienced angler to prematurely set the hook and possibly spook the salmon. Adjust the rod in the holder so that it is set at a 30- to 40-degree angle. Salmon strikes are lightning fast and can come at any time. Set the hook only after the rod tip has straightened out. I sit within two feet of my rod at all times. I've seen many anglers miss strikes because they were in the bow of the boat having a cup of coffee with the guide rather than watching their rod. A Kenai king may only give you one chance to catch it. Make the most of it.

A Jet Planer/Kenai Special rig. Use this popular trophy king lure when backtrolling, while anchored in current, or in snag filled lies where casting presents a problem.

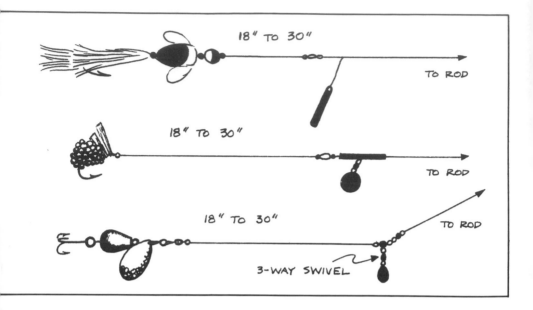

18" TO 30"

TO ROD

18" TO 30"

TO ROD

18" TO 30"

TO ROD

3-WAY SWIVEL

Drifting

Three types of drift rigs are popular on Alaska's snag-filled rivers and streams: From top: Dropper line/pencil lead with a Kenai Special; sliding sleeve with a round lead and eggs/yarn; and a 3-way swivel with bell-shaped lead and Cherry Drifter. Weights can be used interchangeably with lures.

There are times when you need to hold the rod in your hands: That's when drifting a Kenai Special through a migration channel or spawning hole. A drift can be done in two ways: Bottom bouncing the lure from an anchored boat or shore, or bottom bouncing the lure from 15 to 50 feet behind a drifting boat. Jet Planers do not work well with this technique. Therefore, pencil sinkers, sliding sinkers, or drop-line rigs are preferred for keeping your lure on the bottom. Attach just enough lead so that the lure intermittently hits and misses the bottom while drifting: Too much lead and your rig will snag easily; too little and it'll float above the strike zone. I usually carry a variety of sinkers weighing from 1 to 3 ounces.

When drifting, your line is being dragged over rocks and snags. Therefore, it's important to use at least 25-pound-test, abrasion-resistant line. Some anglers prefer 40-pound-test; others favor braided Dacron. It's a matter of personal preference. The longer the leader, the more frequently you should check your line for abrasion. I make a point of checking my leader after every drift. A tiny nick in the line is all a big king needs to make his escape, especially when you begin muscling the king to the landing net.

One last tip. Because kings often strike a lure softly on a drift, it's important to keep your hooks "sticky sharp." A

How to Catch
Alaska's Trophy Sportfish

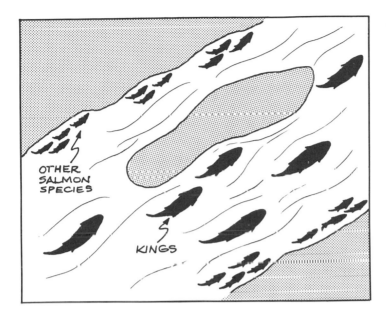

OTHER SALMON SPECIES

KINGS

Experienced drift fishermen know that Kenai kings can be found anywhere throughout a river, while other salmon species cling toward the slower side currents. However, research shows that islands, underwater gravel bars, mid-river obstructions, and deep pools and channels regularly attract and hold large kings.

hook must have a point that will stick in your thumbnail under slight pressure. If it doesn't, either sharpen it or don't fish it.

When kings are in a soft-strike mood, attach a piece of Velcro around the base of the hootchie skirt. The loops of Velcro catch on the sharp teeth of a king and keep the hooks in the king's mouth for an extra second or two. This should be long enough for you to respond with at least one, but preferably two hooksets. And there are more advantages to using Velcro. For example, after a 15 minute fight on the slow currents of Deshka Creek, I landed a 32-pound king, fresh from the sea. I was astonished to find my hook had broken. The Velcro skirt entangled in the king's toothy jaw was a most effective "hook." It took five minutes for me to free the lure. I've been a believer in Velcro ever since.

The Kenai king is a difficult fish to catch. Unless you've fished the river for several seasons, I suggest hiring a reputable guide to show you the ropes before trying to catch a king on your own. In 1983, over 56 percent of the Kenai's sport-caught kings were taken by anglers who had employed the services of a guide. By hiring a guide on your initial trips, you'll save time and money in the long run with possibly more fish and a better understanding of the Kenai king.

Clearwater Rivers and Streams

Fishing the Kenai River is a memorable and exciting experience, especially after you've fought and landed a 70-pound-plus trophy. Yet it can't match the excitement of fishing for big kings on an isolated wilderness stream. Why? Because water levels are usually low enough for the angler to see the reddish hulks of 30- to 55-pound kings migrating from pool to pool. The excitement of stalking, casting to, and hooking one of these fish is angling excitement sans pareil!

My first experience with stream kings took place 10 years ago at Montana Creek, an east-side tributary of the Susitna River. Very few anglers fished the creek because it was closed to the taking of kings. However, an Alaska Fish and Wildlife Protection officer stated that catch and release fishing for kings was permitted, and that very few anglers were taking advantage of this. As my brother Joe and I walked through the woods, we were confident in having the mouth of the creek all to ourselves.

Walking into the clearing near the mouth of the creek, we were amazed to find a middle-aged angler sprawled out on the gravel bar. His hat covered all but the lower half of his whiskered face. Nearby was an open tackle box, void of lures.

I nudged Joe in the ribs. "Do you think he's dead?"

The form suddenly stirred to life. "I might as well be!" the man bellowed. He slowly sat up and arched his back, as if to relieve it from a muscle spasm. Halfway through his stretch, he slapped at and flicked a mosquito off his arm. "Yep, those things are enough to make a man die from exhaustion," he commented while shaking his head.

"We noticed the mosquitoes were thick this year," I replied.

The man shook his head and pointed to the water. "Not the darn bugs. Those king salmon!" he bellowed again. "Last night, I hooked over 20 of those monsters. Now I'm just an office clerk from the Northeast where the biggest fish we have are bass. But these salmon are somethin' else. I've been fighting them for over 12 hours. They ripped my lures apart and snapped my line as if it were spider web. My rod guides are grooved and my muscles feel like they've been taken through a shredding machine. But I'll tell you one thing," he whispered as he hunkered closer to us. "I ain't never had so much fun in all my life."

It took Joe and I only a half hour to race back to the car, grab our fishing gear and return to the mouth. The angler was gone, but he had given us enough advice to experience the same ailments that plagued him. We didn't have to wait long for our first dose.

The steady pulse of my spinner was cut short by a quick strike. I soon experienced the first exception to the law, "For every action there is an equal and opposite reaction." I halfheartedly set the hook, but the action that followed was far from equal. The rod was nearly torn from my hands! I immediately contracted a case of the wide-eyes as a bronzed form of 45, 50, 65 pounds, maybe more, exploded horizontally out of the water, its tail pulsating wildly. I had hooked one of those lunker kings that spend several years longer at sea than their smaller 30-pound cousins.

The salmon's teeth snapped angrily at the flapping spinner blade as the fish re-entered the water. The king im-

The battle antics of large kings are unpredictable. This fish weighed over 70 pounds and took only 12 minutes to land on 25-pound-test line. However, it's not uncommon for Kenai kings to cover a mile or more of river and take up to two hours to bring to net.

45

mediately surged 100 yards upstream, non-stop. I strained my tackle to its max trying to stop the runaway fish, yet my harnessing effort proved futile, despite the fact that my shoes were buried to their tops in the soft sand. The salmon kept on going.

The salmon soon stopped its surging, sounded to the bottom of a deep pool and refused to budge an inch. I welcomed the rest. By now the amazement of hooking such a large fish had worn off. I was enjoying the battle and found it challenging to fight a fish so powerful and skilled in the use of current and obstacles. I had to constantly guess its every move.

My determination and fighting strategy paid off. Half an hour later, I wrestled the fish into the shallows. Thinking the fish was tired, (because I was exhausted) I eased the tension on the rod. The move proved to be a terrible mistake. The salmon sprayed the shallows with icy water from a wildly flapping tail and quickly disappeared into the current. I fell back on the gravel shoreline, my broken line dangling in the wind. I looked through water-speckled eyeglasses at Joe, who was just beginning to grunt it out with a large king. It was the beginning of a fine and pleasant addiction to the sport.

I've found that kings are much easier to catch in shallow rivers and streams. Sometimes you might see them porpoise, a graceful, leaping action ridding them of marine parasites and perhaps helping to loosen eggs and milt in preparation for spawning. Or they can usually be located before a cast is made, appearing as subdued red forms lying in pools. Streams also make it easier for anglers to spot snags and play their fish accordingly.

On the other hand, finding stream chinooks when none are showing calls for a thorough knowledge of fish holding structure. Such locations (tail of riffles, undercut banks, deep pools or slight changes in stream gradient) usually have good current flow with high oxygen content, and adequate water depth to protect fish from predators.

Once you've located a holding area, the stalk is made. Keep as close to the bank as possible, and avoid any sudden movements while inching within casting distance of the fish. If you spook a fish and it bolts upstream, the chances of relocating that particular salmon are nil. If it bolts downstream, however, wait a few minutes. Often a salmon will move back to its original holding spot.

Utah taxidermist Thurm Preece is happy about his 52-pound Clear Creek king. The fish was tagged (disk below dorsal fin) by Alaska Department of Fish and Game biologists to help determine the destination of salmon entering the Susitna watershed.

If a fish has been caught from a pool recently, stay there and fish it that much harder. Something about the frantic movements of a hooked salmon excites other fish in a pool, and very often they are moved to strike lures at such times. Fellow chinook angler David Doering and I discovered this fact several years ago on an isolated stream flowing into the Talkeetna River. We had caught and released a few fish between 20 and 30 pounds, but had not found any of the truly heavy kings we knew were in the river. I cast my spinner upstream and had a heavy strike followed by a violent head shaking that is typical of a large chinook. The fish began to swim erratically through the school of kings in the pool, causing the other fish to move nervously throughout the stream. Before Dave could retrieve his lure out of the way of my fish, another huge salmon grabbed it and we had a double header going. Luckily, Dave's fish moved off downstream, and we were able to keep the two battling kings apart. Twenty minutes later, neither of us had landed his salmon, and the remaining fish in the pool were swimming around our hooked kings, obviously very excited.

We finally landed our fish, mine a mediocre 40-pounder compared to Dave's 55-pound heavyweight. The remaining salmon were so worked up that they wouldn't let us rest. Almost every other cast brought a jarring hit, and after another two hours and five more salmon, we finally quit fishing, our arms and wrists literally too sore to continue the carnival. This is not an isolated case; I've often seen it happen when schools of large kings are in the same pool. It's just a matter of time before your lure's action triggers one fish—and from then on it's a matter of having enough lures and tenacity to battle king after muscle bending king.

I've experimented with hundreds of lures under a variety of conditions on stream kings. I've had the opportunity to watch individual fish react to various types, shapes, patterns, and colors of lures. I recommend:

•In streams less than 5 feet deep, fluorescent-bladed Mepps spinners in sizes 3 to 5 are my most consistent producers. In deeper streams and small rivers, I favor a Giant Killer with a fluorescent red blade. The heavier Killer seems to stay down in the often swirling currents of deeper rivers.

•A king will rise from its lie and inhale a spinner more

A 60-pound-plus king does an aerial cartwheel for angler Lee Langbehn (right). The salmon required 16 casts with a fluorescent orange Krocodile before striking. The fish broke off after a 30-minute battle.

often than any other lure. So with a spinner you can fish several inches out of the strike zone and still be fishing effectively, whereas other lures would probably be ignored.

•An angler can feel a larger spinner blade working at all times. Therefore, whenever the thrumming stops is cause for a hook set. A spoon exhibits a similar—yet not as intense—vibration.

•Spinners and spoons with a feathered dressing will draw more strikes over a period of time than unfeathered lures.

•When fishing large rivers, such as the Mulchatna, from shore or on a float trip, large spoons such as HotRods and Krocodiles in silver or chartreuse with red dots have produced the largest kings for me. One of the best features about a spoon is that it can be fished without the skillful manipulation required for fishing spinners. A tight line is all that's needed. Because so little surface area is exposed to side pressure, a spoon tends to hold better than other lures in deepwater currents. It also swings around in the current much more slowly than other lures.

Whatever lure you use, it's important to cast quickly yet accurately. Anglers often use the excuse that salmon are on or off the bite. I don't believe it. Any salmon will strike your lure if you present it both in a proper manner and enough times to trigger its aggravation response.

One of the best techniques I've developed for big kings starts in mid-cast. The second before the lure enters the water, sweep back the rod to strip off a few extra feet of

Most off-the-shelf lures can't withstand the ravages of a large king. Always replace thin, wiry hooks with extra-strong single or treble hooks that can penetrate and hold in a king's bony, tooth-filled mouth.

line. Check any excess runoff with a thumb for a level-wind or a forefinger on a skirted spinning reel. This allows for the lure to drop straight down without immediately crossing in the current. Once the lure has drifted slightly above and to the far corner of the salmon lie, take the slack up and start the lure across the current on a course that will intercept the front row of salmon. It's important to have the spinner working several inches above bottom and slowly moving across current WELL BEFORE it reaches the salmon. This allows the fish plenty of time to see the lure, and initiates the aggravation response that triggers a strike.

As long as the spinner stays close to the bottom and doesn't travel across current too quickly, you can vary the lure's action through speed of retrieve or rod angle. A king will often strike a lure if you speed up the retrieve before it crosses the salmon's kype. If your spinner doesn't work directly into the intercept zone, (which for king salmon, is within 8 inches of its kype) continue to slowly fish out the

How to Catch
Alaska's Trophy Sportfish

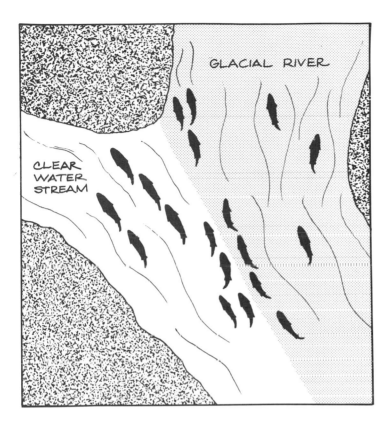

GLACIAL RIVER

CLEAR WATER STREAM

A stream mouth emptying into a glacial river is an excellent place to catch large kings. Fish will follow the freshwater/glacial water breakline and either enter the stream, mill in the area, or continue upriver. If conditions are right, it's not uncommon to hook 20 or more kings a day from this type of structure.

cast before making another. You might need several trial casts before you find the optimum angle for the retrieve.

In waters where you can't see fish, learning to interpret the various signals from a king will help you to decide what technique to use. For instance, a heavy strike and miss may indicate that the fish grabbed your lure halfheartedly. This is often a signal to use a larger spinner blade. A flutter across the line often indicates the lure could have been moving too quickly above the fish, or that the salmon could have smacked it with its tail. These reactions are not uncommon for lures that miss the intercept zone. Whatever the reason, you know the fish are interested and curious. Refine the presentation and you'll eventually hook a salmon.

A favorite technique responsible for vicious strikes is a diagonal retrieve through a school of kings. Cast a No. 4 spinner upstream and to the far side of a school of holding salmon. After the lure has touched bottom, immediately buzz the spinner downstream, taking care to work the lure so that it passes directly through the outer third of the salmon school. A hesitation in retrieve—before the lure reaches the school, yet in sight of the salmon—seems to be the spark that ignites a king's anger. I've had spinners so mutilated from this technique that the only thing salvagable was the spinner blade itself.

Fly Fishing

Fly fishing for kings calls for the same basic strategy used when fishing spinning gear. You have to find migration routes, trigger aggravation responses, and use large, fluorescent flies—tied with materials that undulate in the water. Follow these pointers if you wish to hook kings successfully on fly gear.

First, position yourself so that you must cast upstream at a 45 degree angle to the fish or school. Drift a weighted attractor pattern down through the depths until it is within several feet of the lead salmon. Ever so gently twitch the fly across current while still maintaining its downstream drift through the school. A strike will usually occur immediately after a twitch.

Another effective technique is to work a fly through the outer edge of a school. Once it reaches the fish, slowly raise the fly toward the surface by lifting the rod tip, stopping only when the fly has surfaced. I've seen kings charge from the opposite side of the pool to strike a yellow Marabou Muddler fished in this manner.

In deep pools or runs, fish with weighted patterns and extra-fast sinking lines. Since it's often difficult to impart the proper action to flies in 7 to 10 feet of water, you'll have to fish a fly on a collision course with a salmon, forcing the fish to intercept, rather than strike at, the fly. A systematic fan cast starting at the head of a run and continuing in six-inch to one-foot increments to the tail of the pool has proved to be an effective casting pattern for me. The object is to saturate an area with the fly, and heighten the salmon's territorial aggressiveness. With a fly, the resulting strike is often barely detectable. Whatever the technique, persistence and consistency in presentation are the key factors in provoking stream kings to strike.

I favor large, gaudy patterns for kings, especially those tied with fluorescent marabou, FisHair, and tinsel materials. In clearwater streams, I recommend chartreuse,

fluorescent green, and fluorescent red marabou flies. In clear water/bright light conditions, kings can see a fly coming for quite a distance. The undulating effect of the marabou fly drifting downstream seems to be responsible for triggering many strikes.

On cloudy days or in deepwater haunts, I consider action less important than pattern density. Thick-bodied fluorescent bucktail streamers and yarn flies in chartreuse, fluorescent orange, pink or yellow with a silver body have proved very effective. Polar bear hair, because of its sheen and translucent qualities, is an excellent material to use in place of white bucktail.

In deep water, kings may require repeated slow drifts through an area before they'll strike. In areas with low concentrations of kings, 20 to 30 casts before the first hookup are not uncommon. Where fish are abundant, strikes come much easier. (Fly fishing information in the sockeye chapter provides more details on factors that induce strikes.)

A large stream chinook surfaces to eye this flyrodder. Brush-free sections of bank or gravel bar adjacent to runs or holding pools make it easier to run down big kings.

Equipment

Large, attractor patterns, tied with fluorescent materials are effective for clearwater kings. In murky water, stick to fluorescent patterns with a greater density.

One of the most important aspects of trophy salmon fishing is having the right tackle selection. Most anglers new to the sport and to Alaska fishing conditions cannot imagine the sort of punishment these huge fish inflict on even heavy tackle. Large kings can chew through plugs as if they were putty, snap wire leaders and heavy-action fishing rods as if they were toothpicks, and deplete a year's supply of lures in a matter of hours.

I always carry a minimum of two rods when fishing for kings. On the Kenai, I prefer a 6½- to 8-foot medium-heavy to heavy-action boron or graphite rod fitted with an Ambassadeur 6500 or 7000 level-wind reel filled with 20-to 25-pound-test high-visibility monofilament line. On streams and small rivers, I favor a 6- to 6½-foot, medium-action boron spinning rod with a matching reel capable of holding 150 yards of 17-pound-test, high-visibility monofilament line. I prefer short rods for streams because unlike the heavy-action types, you can cast them all day without fatiguing your casting arm. The boron filaments also give these rods solid hook-setting power, critical in hooking and landing a heavy chinook. My fly rod recommendation is a 9½-foot, 10-weight graphite rod equipped with a multiplier reel with a stout drag system. Carry a variety of sink-tip, full sinking, and lead core shooting heads to cover the myriad conditions you'll encounter on Alaska's wilderness king salmon streams. Use just enough line to do the job. Don't overkill.

Fighting Techniques

I've never had much trouble hooking chinooks. The main point to keep in mind is to strike with an upward sweep of the rod so the barb is driven into the fish's kype. This provides a solid hookup and, because the kype is especially sensitive, seems to make the salmon fight their hardest. Many anglers go wrong by handling their fish incorrectly once a hookup is made. And even if you are perfect from hookup to net, you're going to lose a large percentage of these monsters. That's just the way it is when you fish for oversize Alaska kings.

Here's a few methods I've found helpful when playing these fish. After the initial strike, you have a second or two before the king starts its charge. Use those seconds to drive home the barb a second and third time. Don't try to force the salmon out of making that initial run; freshly hooked kings are at their strongest and it's useless to test your tackle against raw muscle—muscle will win every time. Stand your ground and let the reel's drag do the work. Try not to give the fish much more than 75 yards of line at a time. Remember, the shorter the line between you and the king, the more control you have.

Once the fish stops in midstream to sulk, which most big salmon do, it will take the strength of Hercules to get it moving again. This is when I chunk a small stone just downstream from the salmon's position, hopefully to get it moving upstream against the current. Just be sure you have both hands on the rod when the stone hits, or your fish may take off, rod and all but without you. If you need to move a salmon heading for a snag, lower your rod to waist level and fight the fish with the rod length parallel to the ground. This method is known as the Dynamic Draw and is extremely effective in handling big fish on light tackle. The principle is that a fish is easier to control when lateral force is applied rather than the steady, vertical pressure imparted by holding the rod tip high overhead.

Gilling a large king can be risky. Ease the fish to hand, but be prepared for sudden surges and acrobatics. Watch out for those sharp teeth!

Vertical pressure tries to "break the fish's back" and does little in terms of control. It does, however, keep the hook buried in the upper roof or jaw. If the Dynamic Draw is used with heavy tackle throughout a fight, rather than when needed, chances are the hook will rip through the softer side tissues of the fish's mouth.

Once that salmon finally comes close, keep cool and avoid any sudden moves that might trigger another burst of energy. Have a buddy net the fish, preferably with the fish swimming into the net, or if by yourself, gently slide one hand inside a gill flap, avoiding those sharp, canine-like fangs.

If you're thinking about fishing for Alaska's huge king salmon, now is an excellent time. King salmon stocks have been holding at stable levels since the 1970s, and in some watersheds, have reached all-time record highs. Passage of the 200-mile commercial fishing limit for foreign vessels, along with a series of mild winters, have helped considerably. Kings can now complete their 4- to 7-year

maturation cycle in food-rich coastal waters.

Alaska summers offer 21 hours of daylight per day beginning in mid-June, when the runs of really big kings are reaching their zenith. Then you have more time than you can use to battle these bruiser kings. But, I can only fish for so many hours before my wrists and arms ache and I have to stop. Only after I've settled down on a comfortable log overlooking the stream does my heartbeat slow and feeling return to my fighting arm. Then I can leisurely reflect upon the challenge of king fishing. White cottonwood seeds drifting out of a blue sky, the fragrance of dew-covered fireweed on an early-morning breeze, or the gurgling serenade of a mountain stream pure enough to drink from are a few of the many things that enhance this sport for me. Other locations offer sights equally grand. Indeed, fishing anywhere in Alaska can be grand. But only a king salmon offers tremendous power and non-stop excitement: It is without question North America's most challenging trophy freshwater sportfish.

Netting is the safest way to land a trophy king. Always work the fish to the netter and avoid any unnecessary movement that can spook the salmon. After capture, turn the sides of the net rim skyward to enclose the king in the net.

Where to go for King Salmon

Southeast

Fishing in Southeast Alaska is saltwater trolling only. Freshwater fishing is prohibited.

Admiralty Island
Point Retreat
Pybus Bay

Juneau
Auke Bay
Barlow Cove
Outer Point
Piling Point
Point Arden
Point Bishop
Saginaw Channel
Scow Bay
Tee Harbor

Ketchikan
Bell Island
Blank Inlet
Clover Pass
Mountain Point
Point Alava

Vallenar Bay
Waterfall
Yes Bay

Petersburg
Cape Straight
Frederick Sound
Scow Bay

Sitka
Sitka Sound

Wrangell
Greys Pass
Zimovia Straights

Yakutat
Eleanor Cove
Khantaak Island
Monti Bay
Point Carrew
Redfield Cove
Sawmill Cove

Southcentral

The largest strain of king salmon in existence hail from the Kenai River during the month of July. Fish can reach 90 pounds, with 60-pounders an every day catch. A guide is recommended. The Deep Creek saltwater fishery allows access to Kenai River-bound kings while they are still in saltwater. Late June through mid-July is the peak of this fishery. However, large kings can be caught as early as late May near Twin Falls. For trophy kings on a fly rod, try one of the Susitna tributaries such as Clear Creek, the upper Deshka or the Talachulitna River.

The Gulkana River has fish up to 50 pounds.

Cook Inlet/Kenai Peninsula
Alexander Creek
Anchor Point
Anchor River
Clear Creek
Deep Creek
Deep Creek saltwater fishery
Deshka River
Kenai River
  Eagle Rock
  Killey River (mouth of)

Morgan's Landing
The Pillars
Poacher's Cove
Sunken Island
Thompson's Hole
Torpedo Creek
Ninilchik River
Talachulitna River

Copper River
Gulkana River

Southwest

The Kanektok has some of the largest kings in this region, reaching up to 55 pounds.

The Karluk River is the only king run readily accessible to Kodiak anglers. The run peaks the first week in July.

Alagnak River
Goodnews River
Kanektok River
Kvichak System
Mulchatna River
Naknek River
Nushagak System
Togiak System
Wood River System

Kodiak
Karluk River
Red River

Interior

Fish in this region run up to 50 pounds.

Chatanika River
Chena River
Salcha River
Yukon River

Silver Salmon

CHAPTER 2

Silver Salmon

Silver salmon are the most malevolent fish found in Alaska. They are bullies, wantonly picking fights with any fish, object or thing that threatens to invade their territorial boundaries. Even their spawned-out and dying pink and sockeye salmon cousins are not exempt from silvers' war-like aggression. Yet silvers' behavior toward their fellow fish is meek compared to the savagery ignited when a lure is cast into their watery domain. Here's a scenario happening hundreds of times each season:

The ever-watchful eyes of a dime-bright silver scan the changing swirls of current, following the spoon as it flutters down into the pool. An intercept response, honed through years of being a fierce predator in both fresh and saltwater, is triggered. The silver's tail muscles propel the fish upstream. Gills flare as its whitish mouth opens and snares the wobbling spoon. A hooked kype and sharp teeth chew spasmodically on the metal and plastic lure as the silver turns forcefully in the current and heads back to its holding pool. Then, when the salmon feels the sting of the hook, it erupts in fury, its tail undulating in powerful strokes shooting the fish skyward.

Flared gills and open jaws strain air and water as the form shatters the tranquil surface of the stream. The silvery flanks twist and snap with a power that atomizes the river water in all directions. The aerial contortions and acrobatics continue—five, six, seven times—before an underwater slug-out takes place. Sizzling runs through schools of smaller Dolly Varden cause them to flee upstream in a panic. The rage of this hot-headed fish continues to boil the river as it quickly twists the line around a snag, and with several stout headshakes, abrades the line

Chris Batin prepares to unhook a 12-pound coho. Always handle to-be-released salmon carefully to avoid injury to the fish. Handle fish by grabbing the tail with one hand, while supporting the belly or head of the fish with your other hand.

and breaks free.

It's obvious the Alaska silver doesn't practice the dueling etiquette that princely grayling or midge-feeding rainbows follow. Yet anglers the world over view such rough-house behavior and belligerent attitude as being most proper and acceptable at any time, day or night, especially in large, healthy doses on an 8-weight fly rod!

The silver or coho (Oncorhynchus kisutch) are the second largest of the five species of Alaska salmon. Although there are fewer coho than chum, pink, or sockeye salmon, they are nevertheless one of the most sought-after salmon— in both fresh and saltwater fisheries—because of the acrobatic nature and sizzling runs they exhibit once hooked.

The coho is widespread throughout Alaska, occurring from the Dixon Entrance in Southeastern to Point Hope in the Chukchi Sea. The Yukon River extends the fish's range laterally across the state, with migrating fish entering the river in early summer. These coho reach their spawning grounds in the Yukon some 3 to 4 months and 1,200 miles later.

Fresh-from-the-sea coho are handsome fish. Their stocky form is compressed into a streamlined shape with small scales that shine with the lustre of buffed platinum. Dorsal surfaces can vary from a metallic blue to an emerald green. Small, black dots are present on the back and usually on the upper lobe of the tail, but these are not as darkly pigmented as a chinook's. Also, the gums and mouth of the silver are gray to white, while a king has a black mouth and gums.

In their spawning dress, males have dark green heads and dorsal areas with maroon or red flanks and pronounced, hooked kypes with large, sharp teeth. Females exhibit the same basic patterning, but are less brightly colored than males.

The weight of a mature coho varies according to run and locale. Fish from the Susitna drainage rarely exceed 8 to 10 pounds, while Prince William Sound, Kenai Peninsula, and Kodiak fish range between 12 and 20 pounds. The current Alaska state record is a 26-pound, 35-inch fish caught in Icy Strait by Andy Robbin in 1976. However, larger fish are not uncommon. Commercial netters occasionally catch almost yard-long coho weighing over 25 pounds.

Life History

Coho return to spawn between July and November; the northern-most fish usually enter freshwater before the southern-most populations. The upstream migration into their natal streams may be triggered by rising water levels and water temperatures.

Once coho have entered freshwater, adult fish will often school up in pools, lakes, muskeg, or beaver ponds. There they wait for several weeks until they're sexually ripe. For spawning, they move into shallow tributaries with clean gravel riffle to spawn. The female picks the spot to deposit her eggs and digs a redd with a series of powerful sweeps of her tail. At this time the female is extremely territorial and aggressive toward other females and oftentimes males. While the redd is being dug, the accompanying male usually waits slightly downstream and to one side; that is, when he is not chasing off and fighting with other males for territorial and spawning rights.

After a brief courtship, the female hovers over the redd and deposits anywhere from 2,400 to 4,500 eggs, which are immediately fertilized by the male. Then the female moves upstream and digs a new redd, using the gravel from the second redd to cover the eggs in the first. This spawning ritual continues intermittently for several days, or until the female has spent all her eggs. Both sexes die after spawning.

The eggs develop during the winter months, and hatch in early spring. The sac fry remain in the gravel, utilizing their egg yolk material, before emerging in May or June.

The young fry quickly school up in shallow areas along the stream shoreline and feed mainly on terrestrial insects. They soon establish individual territories which they defend from other juvenile coho with aggressive displays and "nipping." The juveniles grow rapidly during the summer months and begin to feed heavily on larger food items, especially other fish. Studies of Alaska's Chignik Lake show that young coho are serious predators of sockeye salmon. Coho eat more than seven times the number of sockeye fry than Dolly Varden consume. Coho winter from 2 to 3 years in freshwater before outmigrating to sea as smolts in the early spring.

While coho from lower Pacific Northwest streams use a coastal migratory route, Alaska fish seem to spread out into the food-rich Gulf of Alaska and Bering Sea. Studies

The crew of the Y-Knot assists an angler in landing a large coho caught on the hootchie/ herring rig.

indicate that a large number of Southeast Alaska coho move north along the coastline until reaching the vicinity of Kodiak Island, where they follow the Alaska Gyre until they return to their stream of origin. This cycle usually takes about 1 year to complete.

Once at sea, a coho's diet is over 70 percent herring, needlefish, and other fishes; the remainder, crustaceans and planktonic forms. The coho populations that feed strictly on crustaceans do not attain the larger sizes exhibited by the pisciverous types. Big, ocean silvers are meat-hungry fish, and it's been my experience that bait herring is hard to beat when it comes to taking advantage of that appetite.

Techniques

Saltwater/Bait

Herring is the bait preferred by anglers in the Seward Silver Salmon Derby, and by ol' charterboat skippers who would rather set fire to their boats than use anything else. Such faith is not unfounded. Big silvers, especially those experienced in escaping commercial netters, will ignore all types of hardware. Yet they will home in from great distances to attack a herring, especially one fished in a tight, spiraling pattern.

I've found that the Herring Aid bait harness best accomplishes this task. It is a tapered plastic form that fits over the head and gills of a herring, and is held in place

How to Catch
Alaska's Trophy Sportfish

with a toothpick and a single treble hook. The device does away with all the mess and fuss of rigging, filleting, and sewing bait. Those procedures take too much time when coho are on the feed and want that bait NOW!, not five minutes later. And unlike other types of harnesses and home-made rigs that have the tendency to change pitch and form while being fished at fast speeds, herring fished with an Aid rarely require any doctoring or attention. I once rigged an Aid for Prince William Sound coho and fished it for 2½ hours before it was put out of action by a 14-pound hen fish.

An angler battling an acrobatic, Alaska Peninsula coho. Cut herring, shrimp, or salmon eggs are extremely effective in taking these salmon in intertidal areas, as well as from upstream lies.

I like to adjust the Aid so that it drops into a sharp roll from 12 o'clock and completes the spin within 9 inches. My experimentations show that the depth of the spin makes a big difference also. A 5- to 8-inch spiral attracts and hooks more coho because the fish can capture the bait more easily. A wide, fast spiral often causes coho to strike wildly at the bait; then they lose interest and swim off. In other words, lure action is the key to triggering a coho's intercept response.

The best way to describe the importance of this principle is to compare it to an alarm clock ringing in a room where you're watching t.v. The noise is aggravating, annoying; it elicits your immediate response. You get up and shut it off. However, the barely audible 'drip...drip' of a kitchen faucet would probably not cause such a reaction. A tightly spiraling herring is like the alarm clock. Because of their territoriality and aggressive nature, coho are easily trig-

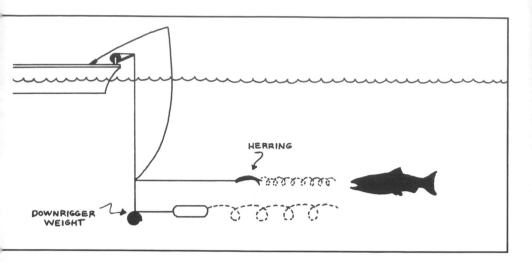

HERRING

DOWNRIGGER WEIGHT

For deepwater coho, attach a flasher directly to the downrigger weight for added flash and less drag on the main line.

gered into action by the "noise" and appearance of a bait fished in this manner. On the other hand, a small lure or a slowly spinning bait has the same effect on coho as the dripping kitchen faucet does on our t.v. viewer. Coho may investigate and strike after several passes with the lure. But with big coho, it's triggering that aggressive nature with the first pass that's so important. You may not get a second chance, especially during a salmon derby when flashy baits are everywhere and the migrating coho are on a short fuse, ready to explode by striking the nearest bait.

Use only frozen, individually-packaged herring. They exhibit a good sheen and streamlined shape, and have good scale retention. Avoid herring with loose or missing scales, mushy flesh or those sold in a frozen clump. I prefer a 5- to 7-inch bait. Keep it on ice until ready for use. Once the Herring Aid is rigged, I usually like to add a few "final touches" that further enhance the bait.

A veteran coho skipper out of Kodiak believed in applying liquid scent to both lures and bait. At first, I scoffed at the idea. But over the years, I came to realize the accuracy of the old man's observations about scent. Scientific research has established that most salmon have an acute sense of smell. From my own personal experience, I've learned that scent doesn't make a bit of difference when fish are reacting instinctively to visual stimuli. Yet at other times, scent may be the only way to make fish strike. Since I make a point of covering all bases when fishing, I always rub a drop or two of herring oil—available from most

How to Catch
Alaska's Trophy Sportfish

tackle shops—onto the bait. As my bait has not been cut or damaged in any way to release fish oils, the scent I add helps simulate the fright hormones secreted by a wounded or spooked herring. This trick is equally effective for king salmon.

Finding the Fish

Coho are top-water fish: Most are hooked within the first 50 feet of water. After they enter the mouths of bays, inlets, and straits, they usually stay directly beneath the surface, or oftentimes soaring above it. Known as porpoising, this leaping, jumping behavior is meant to loosen milt and eggs. Of course, some anglers say the fish are getting rid of sea lice before entering their natal waters. I like to believe the fish are happy. After all, if you hadn't "spawned" in four years, and knew that tonight was the night, you'd probably jump for joy also!

There are times when coho change their top-water habits, especially during or immediately after the commercial fishing season. I'm sure that nets spook coho and push them into deeper water. In 90-plus feet of water—unheard of depths from which to catch a coho—I've hooked fish that have survived the gauntlet of fishing nets. Yet as the commercial fishing pressure increases, coho instinctively begin to run deeper to perpetuate their species. So there's only one serious way to pursue saltwater coho. Use a graph recorder to help pinpoint the location of these schools, and a downrigger to get the bait down to them.

Fishing the scented Herring Aid is deadly with a downrigger/graph recorder set-up. Once I locate a school of coho, I take out a No. 2 rotating flasher and attach it to a 16-inch wire leader. I clip this directly to a 7-pound downrigger weight instead of tying it to the main leader assembly as called for in most saltwater trolling books. Next, the release clip is attached from 1 to 3 feet above the downrigger weight, and the main line with the bait adjusted so that it fishes from 4 to 5 feet behind the downrigger line (see illustration). The rig has all the attractiveness of a flasher set-up, yet without the excess drag a flasher creates when tied directly to the main line. This allows you to fish a lighter line, which in turn allows for better action for the bait. This rig has proven its effectiveness at all depths, and I recommend it strongly, especially when rough water keeps fish down.

Hootchies and Dodgers

When coho are feeding heavily on shrimp and squid, they often ignore a herring. Several years ago, I had the opportunity to witness how much coho actually preferred these two food items.

Skipper John Trent had just idled down the engines of the *Elise* as we entered a small cove on the western side of Resurrection Bay. Hundreds of gulls and cormorants were squawking and diving into the green waves of the cove. Obviously they were enjoying some sort of feast. I found out what was on the menu when I watched a large cormorant pop to the surface, crunching on a large shrimp.

"See that cormorant over there?" asked John. "That shrimp it's eating is all the proof I need. Get those lines in the water...fast!"

The water boiled furiously to our left as we maneuvered for a pass. I was so engrossed with watching the activity that I failed to see my rod tip quiver ever so slightly. Yet John's eyes caught it at once. Just as he was forming the words "Fish on!" I caught a glimpse of the buckled rod and immediately reacted. I jumped up, grabbed the rod with both hands, and buried the steel, maybe a bit too enthusiastically. John caught me, straightened me up, and said, "Set 'er again."

I complied and felt the fish reach for sky. The salmon was short, stocky, and extremely energetic. My reel whined in high gear and kept on whining as I struggled to hold the rod tip high. The salmon sounded and immediately switched into reverse, catapulting itself several times across the calm waters of the cove.

"Now this is fishing," I thought to myself. I looked up and was surprised to see two other members of our party also busily fighting acrobatic coho. John shook his head and said, "With fishermen like you guys on board, I should be in the commercial fishing business."

"It's all your fault, John," I grunted as the net reached out for my coho. "You showed us how to use these hootchies."

Indeed he had. At first I thought a hootchie was a nickname for an intoxicated dog. In actuality, a hootchie is a rather interesting looking lure, resembling the squid or shrimp found in abundance in Alaska waters. A hootchie has no action of its own, and must be trolled behind a

A popular trolling rig consists of a diving planer, optional rubber snubber, flasher or dodger, and a herring/hootchie combo. Use a dodger when fishing a hootchie by itself.

dodger or flasher in order to be effective. However, as my coho pegged the scale's needle at 14 pounds, there was no questioning the effectiveness of this lure. An hour later, we netted our ninth salmon and called it quits. Nearby boats fishing with herring were still trying to hook their first coho.

Since, I've always carried a supply of hootchies in my saltwater tackle box. As squid and shrimp are generally deepwater creatures, hootchies are best fished from a downrigger or diving planer. The lure's erratic action is what triggers strikes, and the degree of action depends upon the length of line between dodger and lure. When fishing from 0 to 20 feet, I like the fast, erratic display a 10- to 12-inch leader imparts. For deeper coho, I prefer the slower dart of a 16- to 20-inch leader.

When fishing from a downrigger weight for deepwater coho, ensure the release tension is strong enough first to partially bury the hooks of the lure into the bony jaw of the coho. A clip that releases too easily defeats this purpose. The coho should have to twist its head two or more times to trigger the release for the best hookset.

Many years ago, I learned a trick from an avid coho angler who always fished and did well at the various salmon derbies throughout the state. He swore the best lure for sub-surface coho was a Herring Aid with a hootchie skirt draped over its head. It seems the attractive qualities of the flasher and the undulating movements of the tentacles on the hootchie—in addition to the scent of fresh herring—caught fish like no other saltwater lure. Because of its overall attractiveness, this is an extremely good lure to use when fishing unexplored waters.

When fish are in-migrating into bays and inlets, they often stop feeding well before reaching their freshwater streams. Coho concentrated along shoreline structure can be extremely susceptible to various types of hardware. Some of my favorites are ½- to 1-ounce HotRods, No. 4 and No. 5 Mepps Aglia and Killer spinners, white-bodied Rooster Tails, 1-ounce Pixees, silver and bronze FSTs, and No. 4 silver Vibrax spinners.

Coho can often be found in deep water around boat docks, points, creeks, and other shoreline structure. Anglers without boats can catch coho by fishing these structures with large spoons, spinners, or cut herring. (Shoreline tactics detailed in the chapter on pink salmon will work equally well on coho.) However, a trolling or drift-fishing angler has more mobility and can effectively cover the types of shoreline structure migrating coho frequent. Most anglers keep their boats 20 to 100 yards from shore, in water from 10 to 40 feet deep. My personal experiences have been that coho will be near bottom in water 10 feet or less, and within several feet of the surface when shoreline channels are 20 feet or greater.

Under either condition, I prefer to longline a No. 4 or No. 5 prism-scale spinner behind a 1- to 3-ounce, fluorescent-red keel sinker. I move the lure constantly; twitching it, speeding it up and slowing it down by working the rod. The constant change in the lure's attitude and spinner blade rotation invariably triggers vicious strikes from shoreline coho. But usually this technique is effective for no more than a half day: Anglers lack the strength to battle such fish for more than several hours at a time.

Shiny spoons fished along breakline structures on an incoming tide will take large coho, like this 12-pounder.

How to Catch
Alaska's Trophy Sportfish

Rivers and Streams

While fishing for ocean coho is fun, it can't match the action or excitement of pursuing fresh-from-the-sea coho once they've entered their natal streams or rivers. An angler also stands a much better chance of catching a mounting-size freshwater coho in less time and with less hassle than it takes to catch a comparable fish in saltwater. The two riverbanks that channel and crowd big coho together help to eliminate extensive searching. Also, once they re-enter freshwater as mature adults, the coho's aggressiveness is magnified 100 fold. More than once, I've retired to my tent to recuperate from a workout with a coho.

Coho aren't particular about lures. They'll strike salmon eggs, spinners, flies, and plugs—all with equal force. However, coho are often particular about lure presentation. For instance, smaller coho will commonly rise up and attack a fly skittering across the surface. These youngsters have a wider territorial boundary—encompassing both mid-depth and bottom surface areas—than their larger brothers. Big coho, on the other hand, are very territorial over bottom structure. A lure drifted through mid-stream will often be ignored, yet bounce the same lure along bottom, and ol' Hooked Snout will waste no time in smashing it. However, each type of lure or bait has its own unique advantages in getting coho to strike.

Eggs

While I don't like to use salmon eggs, I can't deny their effectiveness on coho. After years of coaxing, Kenai River guide Harry Gaines finally persuaded me to leave the lures at home one September morning and to join him in fishing eggs for coho. It was an experience I'll always remember.

Harry uses a basic slip sinker rig and a snelled hook with an egg loop. Like most egg dunkers, Harry has his own recipe for preserving bait eggs. He favors borax; others prefer cane or brown sugar and borax. He insists that with either preservation method, eggs should be a bright translucent red to be most effective. A small section of cured egg skein, usually measuring 1 inch by 2 inches, is drawn through the egg loop and tightened down. Harry fishes 20-pound-test line and as much lead as it takes to keep the bait stationary in a moderate but smooth current.

An angler grabs at and misses a Painter Creek coho. It's not uncommon to catch 20 or more trophy coho a day from this watershed during August and September.

Coho dislike fast water, and avoid current-free eddies. Undercut banks, or flat sections of gradually tapering riverbed are best bets. Harry anchors the boat in these runs and tosses out the rig about 20 yards. After that, it's a matter of patience.

I've spent hours watching how salmon eggs rigged in this manner work in the current, and how coho respond to them. A section of egg skein usually has several irregular surfaces, causing it to dart and swing in the current. Slowly, the eggs milk into the water, and the current begins to smooth the irregular edges, breaking off individual eggs. This is why action is usually best with fresh eggs. Once the irregular surfaces have been smoothed, the eggs won't wobble enticingly in the current. To a coho, a glob of fresh eggs is like a waving red flag to a bull.

Yet strikes with eggs depend upon the personality of individual fish. Generally speaking, most pickups are light. Coho will nip at, strike, inhale, and spit out a glob of stationary eggs. Your rod tip will dance, vibrate, and wiggle as a result of this indecisiveness. You must not strike too early. On four different occasions, Harry had to warn me about setting the hook too soon. Being a lure fisherman, I struck whenever the rod tip dipped in the slightest. And I lost fish. I learned to wait for the rod spine, rather than tip, to flex. This definite flex indicates the fish has a firm mouthhold on the eggs and is taking them either up or downstream. Only then did I set the hook...and I hooked fish.

What happens is the coho reaches its aggravation point. I've seen fish inhale eggs, exhale them, return to their resting pool several yards downriver, and repeat the procedure one or more times before finally inhaling the entire bait and quickly darting off with it. I've also had fish take the bait immediately, especially when the bait is bouncing downstream. Whether coho intend to help perpetuate the species by spitting the eggs back into the gravel, biologists are unsure. But bottom fishing eggs is an excellent way to hook coho in a pool too deep for spoons or spinners.

Under normal conditions, when water is several feet deep and fish are migrating upriver on the tide, a moving bait is best. Remember, the more action you give the bait, the quicker you'll trigger a coho aggravation response. Eggs fished with a Spin-N-Glo, Glo-Go, spinner, or other attractor and bottom bounced or walked downriver from a

boat draw the hardest strikes.

On larger rivers such as the Kenai, you can substitute drift lures for salmon eggs, or use them together in an effective combination. I like Jensen artificial eggs in spawn sacs, Spin-N-Glos in a clown or peach coloration, and Cherry Drifters with a silver spinner blade. Bottom bounce these rigs down migration channels when fish are swimming upriver on an incoming tide. Or fish them in side eddies, in deep pools, and along snag-filled structure with a Jet Planer.

Kenai River guide Harry Gaines assists an angler in bringing a trophy coho to net. This salmon inhaled a glob of salmon eggs fished stationary on the river bottom.

Lures

Spinners and spoons have been responsible for nearly all of my stream-caught coho. In streams less than 6 feet deep, with a moderate to slow current, I favor a No. 4 or 5 char-

treuse spinner. When water depths are greater than 6 feet, or when currents are too strong to properly fish a spinner along bottom structure, I use a heavy bodied spoon with a good action at slow speeds.

There are several rules to follow in fishing hardware for coho. Position yourself directly across or slightly above the lie. Cast the spinner across stream and to the far side of the structure to be fished. Slowly reel in any slack line as the lure drifts down with the current. As the lure nears the fish, snap it into motion with a flick of the rod tip. Vary the retrieve so that the lure swings around in the current within inches of the first coho—or with a school of salmon, the first line of salmon. Fish spoons the same way, except for the retrieve. Allow the current to work the spoon, rather than imparting any special movements with the rod or reel.

Always try to alternate your retrieves. A slow-fast-slow pattern is good, with a slow-falter-slow retrieve even better. Another trick is to cast directly upstream and buzz the spinner downriver above bottom. Many times I've seen coho streak out of a hole and smash lures retrieved this way. In fact, I like to recommend this tactic to greenhorn coho anglers. The subsequent strike is one they'll remember for some time.

In shallow water streams, you can sometimes see coho stacked up in pools and runs. If you have a steady hand, try lifting the rod tip as the spinner begins to cross in front of the coho. As the spinner begins to rise, a coho is apt to charge after the lure, grab it, and continue coming out of the water, with the lure dangling from its wildly snapping jaw. It's enough to get the ol' strikin' arm to start a twitchin' just thinking about it!

Plug fishing for coho is very productive in deeper waters when spoons or spinners can't fish effectively. The plug techniques discussed in detail in the king salmon chapter work effectively on coho. One other technique, however, bears mentioning: That's a Side Planer/Hot Shot combination.

The Hot Shot Side Planer is a buoyant, surface-planing, five-inch long device that will pull a plug or other lure 100 feet or more away from the bank. In effect, it allows a shore-bound angler to fish a plug in the same manner as boaters do. The Planer can also fish water where boats are not allowed or where boat fishing is difficult. Best of all, it

Krista Melby beaches a feisty coho salmon that struck a fluorescent red spinner buzzed across the bottom. Coho have a reputation for being extremely aggressive, and will battle it out to the end.

Outdoor writer David Doering attempts to net a wildly acrobatic coho for Bob Filiatreau. The water is Jim Creek, located at the head of Knik Arm, which is the northernmost corner of the Pacific Ocean. The creek is a popular fishery due to its easy access and good salmon runs.

lets you position your plug in almost any fish-holding structure, and to fish every square inch of it effectively.

The Hot Shot is an extremely effective lure to use with a Planer. Once you've adjusted the plug to dive straight and true, run 15- to 20-pound-test line from your rod through both the tripper arm and then through the eyelet at the base of the Planer. Tie on a medium-sized barrel swivel to the end of the line. When the Side Planer is tripped, the swivel will act as a stopper, keeping it away from any hooked fish. To the remaining end of the barrel swivel tie a 36-inch length of leader (lighter test than your main line) and to the end of this leader, tie on a Hot Shot, being sure to use the round eye snap provided with each lure.

Hold the Planer in one hand and with the other hand place the plug in the water. Then strip out the desired

How to Catch
Alaska's Trophy Sportfish

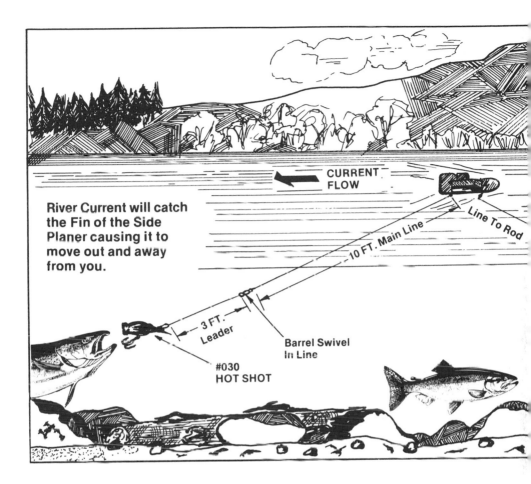

CURRENT FLOW

River Current will catch the Fin of the Side Planer causing it to move out and away from you.

Line To Rod

10 FT. Main Line

3 FT. Leader

Barrel Swivel In Line

#030 HOT SHOT

amount of line to be used between Planer and plug. Most successful anglers use from 15 to 30 feet of line between Planer and plug, rigging short for short drifts or shallow water and long for long drifts or deep water.

Once the desired amount of line has been released, secure the line to the front fin tab of the Planer with four wraps. Snap the locking arm into position. Keeping tension on the line at all times, set the Side Planer in the water. Let out small amounts of line at a time so the river current can catch the fin of the Planer and slowly pull it and the trailing plug away from you and out into the river. Once you've maneuvered the Planer and plug into the upstream end of the water you intend to fish, work the Planer in a zig-zag pattern downstream. If you have a strike, set the hook as you would any other time. The

A Side Planer and Hot Shot allows a bank angler to fish a larger river as effectively as a backtroller. Spinners, spoons, and attractor baits can also be used with this device. Courtesy Luhr Jensen.

Planer acts as a bobber on the strike, giving you minimum friction in the water after the fish is on the line.

While any lure can be used with the Side Planer, I prefer the No. 30 for Alaska coho. Some good color combinations are silver/blue, red, prism-tape dressed models, and green. Try the Side Planer on your next coho salmon outing. It can fill a string quickly.

Fly Fishing

Fly fishing for coho, especially in Alaska's wilderness areas, is a fatiguing sport. Fish migrating upriver by the hundreds are packed into holes and runs like sardines. The tempers of these fish are hot enough to boil lead, and a properly worked fly rarely survives the ravages of three strikes. On one section of a stream within 200 yards of the ocean, I had a series of 24 and again 29 coho hooked and released from the same number of casts. And after those series, what was once a fly box filled with beautiful fly patterns turned into a coffin for mangled flies. But when you fly fish for coho, their destructiveness is something you have to accept!

The same fly patterns and fishing techniques used for king salmon will be twice as effective for coho, the least finicky of all salmon. I use most any attractor pattern. But those tied with bright, fluorescent colors have been consistent producers for me.

The most important point to remember when fly fishing for coho is to concentrate on the fly. I like to dead drift the fly first, and then progress to twitches and full strips across the kypes of the fish. I've taken visitors from the Lower 48, who've never before hooked a salmon, and within 15 minutes after I explained this simple principle, those cheechakos were into tail-dancing coho. Particularly memorable was the visit of a close friend from the East Coast. Mark joined me for several days of fly fishing for coho on the Pasagshak River of Kodiak Island.

Mark was eager to tame these coho, some of the largest in Alaska. Yet as a dry fly purist, he insisted on fishing a fairy-wand rod specially made for large brook trout back East. He had a petite box of salmon flies tied in natural colors such as brown, green and gray—no futuristic or gaudy flies necessary for catching wild coho. And to top things off, Mark brought an ash landing net that couldn't have scooped up a salmon smolt.

J.W. Smith prepares to release an 11-pound silver or coho salmon caught from a wilderness stream near Wide Bay on the Alaska Peninsula. August and September offer the best chance to catch a trophy coho in most regions of the state.

I shook my head and kept my gear packed. Either this was going to be a flop or one of the best fishing lessons I would ever experience. We walked down to a pool and found it dark with fresh-run coho. Mark was excited. He tied on a brown and gray sculpin—which I consider a good trout pattern, but lousy for salmon—and proceeded to lay it out on the water. For half an hour he twitched it through the water, making it appear as lifelike as possible. If those salmon were New England trout, I'm sure he'd have caught most in the pool. I didn't say a word, as this was my opportunity to learn about East Coast trout fishing techniques.

Mark strolled to my observation post under a scrub willow and finally asked for my fly box. Just then, an angler, trying to stop a runaway coho, came running around a corner of the stream. The rampant fish finally pulled over in the pool beneath us and conducted a series of acrobatics that made Mark's eyes bug out. After the angler beached and dispatched the fish, Mark confronted him and managed to sweet talk him out of a chartreuse and blue pattern, heavily laced with tinsel. It was the same pattern the angler had hooked his fish on.

I figured it was time to get involved. I walked down to Mark and advised him to strip the line across the snouts of the fish. He looked back at me, contemptuously. How could I advise such a thing? Such an action would spook the salmon. I was ready to unpack my tackle and show him how it is done when Lady Luck took pity on his stubbornness. His fly line snagged on a rock, causing the weighted fly to sink into the salmon. Unknowingly, in twitching the line several times, Mark had loosened it. A smile crept over my face as I watched a large male inhale the fly and chomp on it. Immediately the fish shot to the head of the pool, made a tight turn to pick up speed, and rocketed downstream, coming out of the water three times in rapid succession.

Joe Maxey with a two-man limit of 9- to 17-pound coho taken from Painter Creek. These fish struck a Pixee spoon with a fluorescent red insert.

Mark fumbled with his reel on the over-stressed rod, while tripping and falling through the shallows in an effort to keep up with the salmon. "OHMYGAWD!" was the only sound that came from his mouth. Gradually, his shocked look became one of sheer ecstasy. However, his ecstasy proved to be short-lived.

The fish ricocheted out of the pool and shot back upstream, with Mark still running downstream. The coho

quickly wrapped the line around a snag, came across river, and swam right through Mark's legs. The tangled line and thrashing fish combined for a mid-stream tackle Vince Lombardi would have been proud of. Shocked by the cold water and sudden fall, Mark reached over and cut the leader. The big coho pouted for a moment, and swam lazily back to its hole.

Mark walked up to the head of the pool, where I was rolling with laughter. His ten-ton silence quickly quieted my mirth. Mark shook his head, emptied his boots, and sat down on a nearby log, where he made a major contribution to the philosophy of salmon fishing.

"Eastern trout fishing enhances life," he said while slowly wringing out his socks. "But with these Alaska coho, life becomes a matter of survival of the fittest."

He slowly stood up, grabbed my 10-weight salmon rod, tied on a 20-pound-test leader and asked, "By the way. Do you have any survival gear in the form of a green and blue fly with silver tinsel?"

Izaac Walton couldn't have said it better.

Where to go for Silver Salmon

Southeast

Three of the best coho streams in Southeast are the Port Banks, Italio, and Situk rivers. Fish can be found entering these waters in September and October.

Admiralty Island
Doty's Cove
Point Retreat

Baranof Island
Port Banks

Haines
Chilkat River
Chilkoot River

Juneau
Cowee Creek
Icy Straight
Montana Creek
Peterson Creek
Shelter Island

Ketchikan
Clarence Straight
Tongass Narrows

Petersburg
Blind Slough
Duncan Salt Chuck
Gedney Island
Petersburg Creek

Yakutat
Italio River
Lost River
Situk River
Tawah Creek

How to Catch
Alaska's Trophy Sportfish

Southcentral

Kenai River coho can reach weights of up to 20 pounds. The Kenai River has two runs: The first in late July and the second in mid-September. Runs peak in most other watersheds in August.

Cook Inlet/Kenai Peninsula
Anchor River
Alexander Creek
Chuit River
Deep Creek
Deshka River
Kenai River
Ninilchik River
Quig Creek
Resurrection Bay
Stariski River
Talachulitna River

Copper River
Eyak River
Valdez Bay
Whittier Harbor

Homer
Barbara Point
Glacier Spit
Mud Bay
Peterson Bay

Southwest

Goodnews River
Igiugig River
King Salmon Creek
Kvichak River
Mulchatna River System
Naknek River System
Nushagak River System
Painter Creek
Togiak River System
Ugashik System
Wood River System

Afognak Island
Afognak River

Kodiak
American River
Buskin River
Karluk River
Mills Bay Beach
Pasagshak River
Saltery River

Northwest

Best time is mid-July and August for coho up to 12 pounds.

Fish River
Niukluk River
Nome River
Pilgrim River
Snake River
Unalakleet River

Sockeye
Salmon

CHAPTER 3

Sockeye Salmon

For decades, anglers journeying to Alaska to fish for sockeye salmon were often viewed as mildly eccentric. Local residents had difficulty comprehending why intelligent people would spend hundreds of dollars on tackle and transportation in order to try to entice such a common, ordinary salmon to strike bits of colored feathers tied on a hook. Most everyone knew that sportfishing for sockeyes was a stagnant activity, as the fish would not strike a lure. Furthermore, the fish was considered a plankton eater, not worthy of serious consideration when yard-long rainbows and sail-finned grayling often inhabited the same stream. Why, the only "sockeye addicts" were the cannery owners who waited for the commercial boats to unload tons of this profitable fish into holding vats at the processing dock!

But as anglers explored the myriad watersheds of the 49th State, they discovered that on certain streams, sockeyes could be taken on select streamer patterns. Stories drifted back of hooked sockeyes performing acrobatic displays that made the esteemed coho resemble a limp dishrag. It wasn't uncommon for a sockeye to strip 100 yards of line on an initial run interspersed with at least a half-dozen aerial cartwheels. And in many areas, sockeyes were the most numerous salmon available with migrations of fish literally knocking each other out onto the bank as they rushed upstream to their spawning grounds.

It was the Pacific Northwest Indians who considered the fish of enough food and bartering importance to name it "sau-kie," meaning "chief of fishes." While the spelling has

A sockeye salmon takes to the air. Large numbers and impressive aerial acrobatics make this salmon a popular freshwater trophy.

changed, the sockeye salmon has not. Anglers are discovering that the sockeye is not only the best eating salmon, but that it really deserves the appellation "salmon-in-chief" of the sportfish realm.

Range and Habits

The sockeye salmon (Oncorhynchus nerka) has acquired a variety of names over the past century. "Redfish" was a term widely used by military explorers to describe the fish's red, flavorful flesh. The nickname "blueback" describes the metallic-blue dorsal surface the sockeye exhibits in saltwater and when first entering freshwater. The landlocked variety is commonly known as kokanee, silver trout, or silver sides.

In Alaska, the sockeye is found in waters from Ketchikan to Point Hope, with Salmon Lake on the Seward Peninsula nurturing the most northerly population. The largest concentrations of sockeyes in the world are found in the Kvichak, Naknek, Egegik, and Nushagak rivers of the Bristol Bay watershed. The number of fish entering these systems is enough to stagger the imagination. For instance, the Bristol Bay sockeye run for 1980 was calculated at 62.8 million fish. In comparison, the recorded escapement for identifiable systems in the Upper Cook Inlet area, which bears the most pressure from Alaska's sportfishermen, was 964,000 salmon of all species. It's no wonder that Alaska is termed the "Sockeye Capital of the World."

Sockeye spawning is impressive, too. This fish outclasses its Pacific salmon cousins with a dazzling display of mating colors. Males have a parrot-green head, a brilliant crimson body, and lighter-hued adipose and anal fins. They exhibit a slightly humpbacked form, although it is not as extreme as the pink's. Like other salmon species, the female sockeyes are generally less vivid than the males, with a reddish-black coloration and a less streamlined form.

Alaska sockeyes return to spawn anytime from June through October. As a general rule, they spawn only in systems having lakes. However, some sockeye populations do spawn in streams without lakes in their watershed.

Females generally deposit between 2,500 to 4,300 eggs in several separate nests. The male fertilizes the eggs as they fall into the crevices of the gravel. Both sexes die several days after spawning.

Hatching occurs between mid-winter and early spring, with the emerging fry showing a strong dislike of sunlight. The majority migrate to a lake where they spend 1 or 2 years feeding on insect larvae and plankton before migrating to sea. In most areas, this outmigration occurs in May or June, when the water temperature reaches 38 to 39 degrees. Biologists have documented that most smolt migrations occur at night, with peak activity being between the hours of 10 p.m. and 11 p.m.

This outmigration is extremely important in the food chain: It provides an enormous food supply for birds and mammals and is one of the best times to catch trophy rainbows, char, Dolly Varden, and pike that also prey heavily upon the smolts. (See the respective gamefish chapters for detailed information pertaining to sockeye smolts as forage food.)

The sockeye smolts that escape predation spend from 2 to 4 years at sea. However, four-year-cycle fish are most prevalent and offer the largest trophies for the sockeye angler.

Kokanee differ from anadromous sockeyes in that they spend their entire lives in freshwater. Established populations of kokanee usually have evolved independently from a particular sockeye run. The greater part of their lives that they spend in lakes is analogous to the saltwater life phase of the sockeye. However, it's not uncommon for kokanee to return to sea, or for anadromous sockeye smolts to remain in freshwater. Kokanee reach sexual maturity from 2 to 7 years, at which time they'll spawn at the inlets or outlets of lakes. All kokanee die after spawning.

Size

When anglers first hook into a sockeye, most are astonished at the head-shaking, aerial displays from a fish that weighs from 6 to 10 pounds. In areas with a run of large sockeyes, it's not uncommon to catch 10- to 12-pound trophies. A sockeye in this weight range has the meanness and sheer power that can match a king salmon twice its size. My fighting arm is grateful that they don't attain the weight of those few Kenai chinooks exceeding 80 pounds. Modern tackle simply wouldn't be able to hold them.

The current Alaska state record for sockeye is a 16-pound fish caught from the Kenai River in 1974 by Chuck Leach. In 1978, I set a new Mepps and annual state record with a 15-pound, 6-ounce sockeye also taken from the Kenai River, about a mile from the mouth of the famous Russian River. However, these weights are quite rare.

Catching a 10-pound-plus sockeye is not difficult. I've caught over 107 exceeding this mark because I've approached the sport from a scientific rather than recreational standpoint. My successes were spurred, in part, by observing the failures of hundreds of people lined up along the banks of the Kenai or King Salmon rivers, where they spent many unsuccessful hours trying to catch their limit of sockeyes. When several thousand fish are in a river, and hundreds of people toss in flies and lures of all shapes, sizes, and dimensions with a wide range of presentations and techniques, and only a handful of fish are caught per hour, the conclusion is obvious. There is more to catching sockeyes than being just a lucky angler in the right place at the right time.

Principles

The Russian-Kenai River salmon fishery is the largest freshwater fishery in Alaska. It is also renowned as one of the few clearwater streams in North America where sockeyes can be caught with artificial flies. Having fished the Russian and other similar—and dissimilar—waters throughout the state, I've concluded that one of the main secrets in catching sockeyes (and the Russian is a good example of this) lies with the nature and layout of a waterway. These features are easy to categorize.

Clear Water vs. Glacial Water

Without question, you'll hook more sockeyes in clearwater streams than glacially silted water. As a rule, sockeyes will not exhibit the aggressive behavior often demonstrated by chinooks or cohos. A sockeye will usually ignore a lure that suddenly pops into view in low-visibility glacial water. However, it will often intercept a fly or lure drifting toward it in a clearwater system. The key word here is *intercept*. A good analogy would be a man catching a baseball, thrown at him without warning, on a clear day. If it is thrown directly at him, he merely opens his hand and catches it. If the ball is thrown too high or

off to one side, it is ignored. Also, the man reacts less readily to a baseball thrown in a fog.

The same principle applies to a sockeye and a drifting lure. The fish will "catch" a drifting lure by simply opening its mouth, *if* it can see the lure coming in plenty of time to trigger that intercept reaction. Often, several casts must be made before this reaction is triggered. And like pitches coming in high, or balls thrown into a fog, lures that are fished in murky water or drifted above and beyond the intercept zone are almost always ignored.

Current Flow

Another factor contributing to a sockeye's intercept response is current flow. Sockeyes milling around in the relatively current-free waters of the Moose River on the Kenai Peninsula are 10 times more difficult to catch than sockeyes holding a few yards off in the stronger currents of the Kenai. My fishing experiences with various slack and fast waters in the Bristol Bay area support this point. Fish holding in the calm headwaters of rivers, lake outlets, and sloughs consistently ignore lures while sockeyes of the same run found in faster, clearwater currents are quite receptive to lures and flies.

Structure

Structure in current also influences sockeye intercept responses, often by reducing territorial boundaries. Waterfalls, channels, fallen trees, rapids, riffles—even sockeyes themselves—all inhibit upstream migration, and you often find fish stacked like cordwood below such structure. Under these conditions, sockeyes can exhibit an aggressive personality resulting in cast-after-cast hookups. But this happens only when you fish the impeding structure properly. Wildlife photographer Ron Spomer, my brother Bill Batin, and I learned this lesson one summer when fishing a clearwater stream south of Homer on the Kenai Peninsula.

We had just been dropped off at tidewater by charter-boat operator Phil Klobertanz. At the mouth of a nearby narrow bay, thousands of sockeye salmon anxiously awaited the high tide to assist them in migrating up a steep stream gradient. Despite the numbers of salmon, we found fishing in the relatively current-free saltwater unproductive. So, we moved to a section of swift-running freshwater a hundred yards upstream.

Joe Batin, the author's brother, gills a large Russian River sockeye. The fish was caught by flippin' to individual salmon in a midstream run.

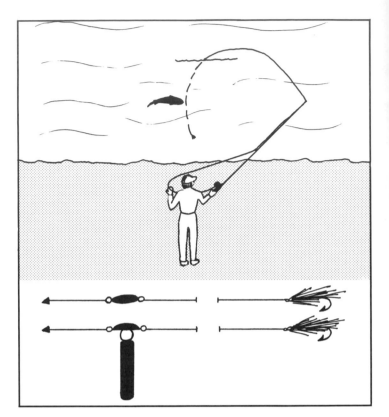

Flippin' is a productive technique when fish are near shore and migrating quickly upstream. This method allows 10 or more casts per minute, and offers excellent depth and drift control. Rubbercore or pencil sinker rigs work best.

Here we found a mass of well-worn, basketball-size boulders that narrowed the stream sharply. The boulders produced a three-foot chute of water connecting the lower stream to the deeper, upstream spawning pools. Sockeyes packed five deep beneath the boiling chute resembled Mexican jumping beans in trying to clear the falls with a series of tail-thrashing leaps. The pool was wide enough for all of us to fish. Yet after a half-hour of effort, we logged only two strikes. Bewildered, watching our lures swirl among the sockeyes, we wondered what could be the key to triggering their intercept response.

It was Bill who observed the clue that solved the puzzle. He watched the sockeyes filter down from the upstream pool—where they were stacked horizontally—to where they held lengthwise behind one another in the narrow channels of the stream. Also, the current in the pool beneath the falls was more circular, while the current flowing through the holding section immediately below the falls was horizontal. I knew from experience that the best sockeye fishing occurs in a horizontal current.

We removed some weight from our outfits and rushed downstream to fish the shallower, yet faster, water. There was no question that the salmon here were perturbed at being compressed by the channel and each other.

We quickly worked our flies through the intercept zone and averaged a sockeye every 10 casts. When the high tide allowed more fish to squeeze into the narrow confines of the stream, we began hooking fish every 3 casts, with frequent runs of a fish a cast. When Phil motored back several hours later, the only things that weren't dragging were the corners of our mouths. If I remember correctly, none of us wet a line for a week afterwards.

Once you have all these conditions—i.e. clear water, moderate to fast current, and structure to compress fish—you will catch sockeyes in the Russian or any other stream. However, proper technique is as important as environmental conditions.

Techniques

Flippin'

One of my most effective techniques for sockeyes is flippin'. While it has long been a popular technique for trout, I first described its salmon fishing applications in an article that appeared in *Alaska Outdoors* magazine. While several variations of flippin' have been in use over the past 25 years on the Russian and Kenai rivers, most anglers are lax in properly executing one or more parts of this technique. Here is my version of a method that has produced more than 670 sockeyes for me over the past 9 years.

Use either spinning or fly fishing gear. When fly fishing, I prefer an 8-weight rod and a sink-tip line with one or more strips of matchbook sinkers wrapped around the main line. With spinning gear, I prefer a 6-foot boron rod, 12- to 17-pound-test monofilament, and—depending upon water conditions—either a ½- to 1-ounce rubbercore sinker attached 18 inches above the fly, or a pencil sinker/surgical tubing rig (see illustration). If I plan on fishing the Russian River, I'll spool up with 20-pound test to permit better handling of the fish. Streamer and attractor patterns work best.

Once you've located sockeyes and have positioned yourself slightly above the intercept zone, strip out 6 to 9

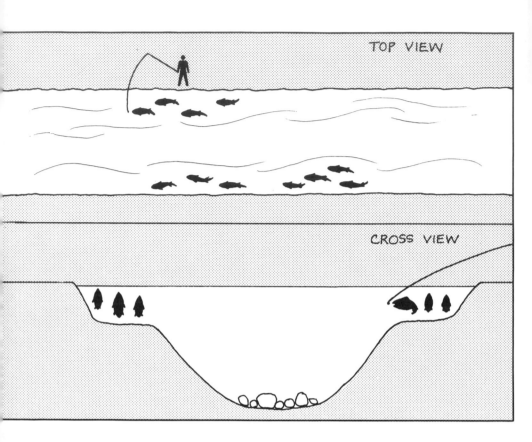

In large rivers, sockeye hold along the edges of fast current often within several feet of shore. Cast upstream and allow the fly to work down the inside edge of the current breakline.

feet of line and gently lob the fly upstream, allowing the cast to take as much of the stripped line as possible. As soon as the fly hits the water, begin following the fly downstream with your rod while inching the fly cross-current by pulling downward on the monofilament or fly line with your free hand. This also serves to keep a tight line, a must for detecting a strike.

If the fly begins to snag bottom, move the rod tip a bit faster or remove some weight. And, if you don't feel the *occasional* "tap-tap" of your weight hitting bottom, slow your cross-current drift by simply moving the rod while holding the line clenched in your free hand.

The next step is the most crucial. You must "aim" the drift of your fly across the salmon's kype. This is much like instinctive shooting. Concentrate on the fish itself, and after a few casts, you'll learn to drift the fly with exact precision. Remember, in order for an intercept to occur, the fly must be drifting both across and down current when it reaches the sockeye's mouth. Flies drifted at dorsal

How to Catch
Alaska's Trophy Sportfish

fin level or bounced on bottom will invariably be refused.

It should take no more than 5 to 9 seconds for the fly to either induce a response or exit the intercept zone. Once the fly has passed through the intercept area, immediately pull the line down as if making a double haul cast, lift the rod tip high overhead, and swing or flip the fly back upstream for another drift.

Once this procedure becomes automatic, work on speed. The cast from downstream to upstream should take no more than a second, which is why flippin' is so effective. When a school of salmon are zipping past, the more times you present the fly to the fish, the better your chances of hooking one. I usually "flip" 10 to 15 times a minute, and have undoubtedly logged more hookups than anglers using the slow-drift method. Too many times I've hooked sockeye on the third and fourth flip. This leads me to believe that repetition is a key factor that triggers the aggravation/intercept response in sockeyes.

Upon any hesitation in the drift, set the hook by lifting your rod tip in one solid motion, while holding the line taut with your free hand. This allows for a solid hook set on spinning reels and prevents the line from wrapping around the reel handle. But the trick to maintaining a tight line during the initial run is to keep the rod tip up and smoothly release line as a fish takes it. Your hand is merely something to *hold* the line. Don't ever attempt to control the fish by grabbing the line or you may receive painful line cuts.

Of course, in deep water, flippin' is impractical. There, you need to use conventional bottom-bouncing tactics.

The first step is to "feel" the bottom structure with the sinker. Mentally map the bottom of the stream by paying attention to the "tap-tap" of the weight bouncing off it. An absence of signal can indicate insufficient sinker weight, strong cross currents, or a depression where sockeyes may possibly be holding.

Once you are familiar with the layout, start a fan-shaped casting pattern at the head of the run and work it toward the tail. If you're using an element rod, a quick flutter usually indicates your sinker has collided with a sockeye, and that fish are present. It also means that you're fishing several inches too high, and need to slow your drift down in addition to getting the fly deeper.

I favor flippin' over bottom bouncing because there's no

mistaking a pickup or intercept. Bottom bouncing requires that the fly do just that: bounce on and over snags, rocks, and oftentimes fish. Bottom bouncing brings too many "false strikes" that are damaging to my nervous system. But once a proper drift pattern has been established with the flippin' technique, there is no touching bottom. The fly is constantly worked through the sockeye's mouth-level intercept zone, 2 to 3 inches above bottom. Then, when the fly stops, it's rare when the angler doesn't yell "Fish On!"

While flippin' minimizes contact with the stream bottom, it's still important for a flipper to check for a frayed line and a damaged fly every 20 casts. And before you retie that fly, check the barb. I distinctly remember the rough time Brooks River sockeyes gave me one year that had me questioning my strike reflexes. Although I could feel the fish striking, I just couldn't hang one. After I conducted a line and fly check on the 20th cast, my face turned as red as some of the sockeyes in the river when I discovered the entire barb had busted clean off. Since, with each line check, I've made it a point to sharpen and closely examine the hook.

Adela Batin with a hen sockeye taken from Tuwalaqua Lake in the Lake Clark Area. Fish were taken at the outlet of the lake by slowly working a wobbler across an underwater gravel bar.

Fly Fishing

There are as many opinions about the proper fly to use for sockeye salmon as there are sockeyes. Of course, no matter what pattern you prefer, it's best if you tie your own or have someone tie them up for you. However, if you are forced to purchase the oversized bucktail creations often sold in stores as Russian River flies, choose the smallest, most sparsely tied flies, as these are much more effective in catching sockeyes than the gaudy creations that catch more fishermen than fish. I learned about the effectiveness of sparsely tied sockeye flies by accident during my second year of fishing for sockeyes on the Russian River.

It was mid-July, and the second run of sockeye had arrived. I had never seen a meaner run of salmon. The fish averaged 10 pounds, were full of salt, and still had sea lice clinging to their metallic-silver sides. The first fish I hooked that morning was a particularly wild one, forcing me to sprint through the streamside willows to keep line on my reel. Not only did I end up losing that fish, but also my only box of salmon flies. To make matters worse, the fly on my line was chewed up badly from that first salmon.

Sockeye Salmon

Yet I had no choice other than to fish it. As the strands of chartreuse bucktail became fewer in number, I began to fish more diligently in an effort to catch a sockeye before my fly disintegrated.

At one point the fly hesitated momentarily and I half-heartedly lifted up on my rod. To my surprise, it was enough to set the hook into an enraged sockeye that immediately wrapped my fingers around the reel handle on its upstream surge. Fearing that I might lose my only fly, I stood my ground and hoped for the best. The fish momentarily succumbed to the steady pressure. After I netted the sockeye, it proceeded to beat me nearly senseless with its tail until I administered the last rites with my priest. Ninety pounds of sockeyes and as many bruises later, my fly finally ended up in the mouth of one red that was still running when my hook snapped. But the lesson proved the point that I still adhere to today: Keep flies sparse for sockeyes.

Over the years, I've dunked every possible color combination and type of fly imaginable. While my findings in this area are still inconclusive, I have determined that contrast and color are two qualities necessary for a fly pattern to produce sockeyes on a regular basis.

My favorite pattern is what I call Sherry's Deliverer, named after a client who absolutely had to win an office bet for the most sockeyes caught in a day. Normally, catching sockeyes wouldn't be a difficult feat. But then the salmon had just recently entered the Kenai River, and fishing was spotty at the mouth of the Russian. The day before, I had decided to combine all the features of my most productive flies into one creation. Using a No. 4 streamer hook, I had tied on a body of flat, silver tinsel, a three-layered wing with polar bear hair on the bottom, fluorescent orange bucktail in the center, and chartreuse bucktail for the top. And with black thread, I tied 5 pieces of peacock herl of various lengths to each side, and added a throat of red calf's tail.

I dread going to the Russian in mid-season. While the fishing is generally good, it is often elbow-to-elbow anglers. But, we didn't even have the benefit of good fishing on the day of the contest. The water was high, and although a few reds were at the mouth of the Russian, the fish were just not biting. However, this didn't deter anglers of all shapes and sizes from trying their luck. As we moved into an open

spot above the ferry, I noticed that several fish were being caught, with a good percentage of those being foul hooked.

It took me several minutes of "bouncing" to determine the bottom structure of the river. We were adjacent to a small gravel bar about 10 feet out. This formed a channel on both sides. After clipping on a one-ounce rubbercore sinker, I instructed Sherry to cast out a precise seven feet above and three feet this side of the bar. On the third cast, she hit the spot. Just as her fly reached the bar, her line twitched and she was into an enraged sockeye. The fish came skyrocketing out of the water, chomping on my newly-tied creation, re-entered the water tail first, and jetted downstream through the maze of lines and people. Several hundred yards later, I managed to net the fish, a sleek 9-pounder.

We returned back to our stretch of bank where my wife

Adela and I proceeded to catch and release six more fish, even as the walls of anglers compacted us closer and closer together. Many tied on green and orange flies in an effort to imitate the pattern we were using, but experienced little success. After Sherry had caught and released several more salmon, including a large, 11-pounder, we gave our last, unmutilated fly to a 9-year-old blonde girl struggling with her Dad's fishing rod. I tied the fly on for her and showed her where to cast. We weren't ten feet up the bank when the rod bucked sharply and the little girl was holding on for dear life, yelling, "Daddy! Daddy! I got one!" Sherry won her contest, and I have used the pattern without fail since.

Before developing this pattern, my single most effective fly consisted of chartreuse yarn with a red-floss head. Another effective producer was a fluorescent purple/chartreuse bucktail. Popular Russian River flies favored by other anglers consist of red/white, black/white, green/white, yellow/red and orange/red bucktail patterns, along with standard West Coast salmon patterns. Patterns using fluorescent materials have always been the top producer in my book. I attribute their success to the fact that they hold their color intensity under a far greater range of weather and water conditions than standard-colors.

Supposing those skeptics who doubt the usefulness of color patterns are right, let's just say for the sake of argument that fish have no color preferences. The "catchability" of a fly, then, lies in the basis of an angler's *confidence* in a particular fly or color. He believes in it and will patiently fish it with the proper technique. Thus, I feel that no color in existence can surpass such an effective combination. Indeed, confidence and patience are two of the most important secrets in catching trophy freshwater sockeyes.

You'll often encounter situations when sockeyes are extremely spooky due to heavy angling pressure, low water, or bright sunlight. Although I've only needed to tie it on twice in 10 years, a No. 6 Spruce pattern has opened the mouths of these anxiety-ridden sockeyes when the bright fluorescent patterns wouldn't connect. It's always wise to carry a selection of dark streamer flies such as muddlers, Woolly Worms, and marabous just in case you run into a school of salmon with a taste for these patterns.

Lakes and Saltwater

Rarely does a lake sockeye offer the fighting display that a fresh-from-the-sea fish can provide. However, the lake spawners can often get extremely sassy near their spawning beds. While most of these fish are disinterested in lures at this time, there are always a few that do exhibit an aggressive attitude, especially toward vibrating lures such as the Gay Blade by Cotton Cordell or the Sonar by Heddon. These lures consist of a lead head and metal body which vibrate rapidly when retrieved.

Homer Circle, Angling Editor of *Sports Afield* magazine, and I experimented with these lures on a record-breaking sockeye run several years ago in the Lake Clark region. Results were impressive, with over 30 hookups on chartreuse, fluorescent red, and black Sonars.

We found it necessary to fish the lure fast enough to see as well as to feel the rod tip vibrating. We also logged more hookups by keeping the rod tip down and at a right angle to the lure. Because they are defending territory, sockeyes tend to hit these lures harder than flies. They'll also spit them out faster if you're not prepared.

In lakes, sockeye will congregate in areas with pea gravel or at the mouths of freshwater inlets. A good way to catch them is to buzz a Sonar or similar vibrating lure across the bottom. This fish was caught from Crescent Lake in the Lake Clark National Park and Preserve.

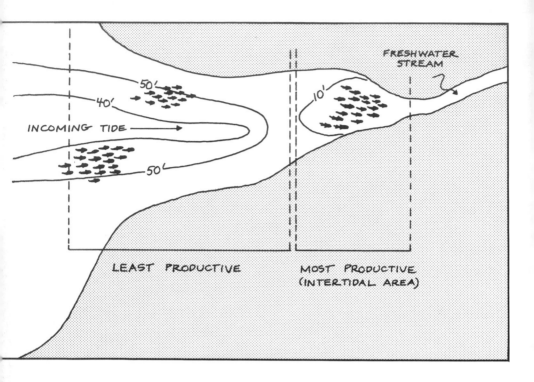

INCOMING TIDE →

50'

40'

50'

10'

FRESHWATER STREAM

LEAST PRODUCTIVE

MOST PRODUCTIVE
(INTERTIDAL AREA)

(above) Sockeye use deep-water channels when approaching their natal streams. As they near the head of an inlet or channel, the salmon will compress into tight schools, which increases their aggravation response. Most hookups come when fishing an intertidal area on an incoming tide.

(opposite page) Saltwater sockeye fishing requires locating schools of these salmon after they enter a bay or inlet on an incoming tide. Work the lure from the head to the tail of the school for best results.

Fishing for saltwater sockeyes is another story. Don't expect frequent success, as this fishery is still in its infancy.

You'll first need to find concentrations of fish. I use a graph recorder to locate sockeyes in bays, at the mouths of freshwater inlets, and in narrow fjords and straits. I've had my best successes at high tide in saltwater bays with freshwater inlets at their head, and deep water sanctuaries ranging from 40 to 90 feet at low tide.

After years of experimentation, I've found that a fluorescent red flatfish or neutral density plug—one that neither sinks nor rises at rest—are my top producers. I prefer to fish these behind a downrigger weight, or by longlining on 8-to 12-pound-test monofilament line in shallow bays. It's imperative to troll at the slowest possible speed: Backtrolling (stern first) is good, rowing better, and a controlled drift is ideal.

A strike under these conditions is usually no more than a line twitch or a brief hesitation in the lure's action. I always prefer to hold the rod rather than using a rod holder. Holding the rod myself makes all the difference in the world between hookups and missed strikes.

How to Catch
Alaska's Trophy Sportfish

Equipment

Here are a few special tips for choosing your equipment for trophy sockeyes.

A medium-action rod, with plenty of backbone and a limber tip to prevent tearing the hook loose from the sockeye's tender mouth, is ideal. I prefer a 6- to 7½-foot graphite or boron rod because of the extra sensitivity they provide. Avoid using rods with butt extentions longer than 6 inches, as they will inflict undue stress on your wrists after a few hours of casting.

For real sport, try fishing for trophy sockeyes on light tackle, but only in wilderness areas. On many of Alaska's sockeye streams, especially the Russian River, light tackle is taboo because a sockeye can run through a group of anglers' lines before you can even yell "Fish On!"

Reels, whether level-wind or spinning, should turn freely with no noticable resistance. Perfect for the type of abuse sockeyes dish out are the medium freshwater spinning reels such as the ABU Cardinal. In heavy currents, I prefer an Ambassadeur 5600 C, a stout performer. In this equipment you have the smooth, strong drags and fast gear ratios important for picking up slack line when a sockeye decides to change directions—which is often!

I prefer 12- to 17-pound, high-visibility lines as they allow me to keep track of my fly or lure through surface glare. The optically brightened blue-green monos don't seem to spook fish as readily as the yellows and oranges. If using Dacron, tie on a monofilament leader. However, keep in mind that while high-visibility lines may not bother sockeyes, they easily spook trout, grayling and other feeding species in Alaska's clear water. Carry an extra spool of clear mono if you intend to fish for these species.

Flyrodders should use an 8-weight rod with heavy-duty guides. I prefer an 8½-foot graphite with a heavy-duty reel seat that can handle a large, single action or multiplier reel with a strong drag system. For sockeyes, a reel should be capable of holding at least 150 yards of 15-pound backing. The Medalist 1495, Supreme, and other similar-sized reels fill the bill nicely. Carry a selection of leaders of varying lengths in 12- to 17-pound test.

I have no doubt that anglers will continue to search for additional methods and techniques to catch trophy sockeyes successfully. In the meantime, I'm going to con-

Virginia Clawson admires her 9½ pound sockeye. The fish struck a chartreuse yarn fly worked quickly through a migration channel. Medium-action tackle allows for quick casts to migrating salmon with a minimum of fatigue.

tinue to have fun trying to find the combination that will take sockeyes under all conditions. I crave getting soaked from their aquatic flips and cartwheels, and as a consequence of all this effort, having a heating pad put on my fighting arm at day's end. While the king and coho traditionally claim the hearts of many anglers, Alaska's large sockeyes will win an angler's respect through performance. In my book, the "sau-kie" is truly the "chief of fishes."

Kokanee

Fishing for trophy kokanee usually means the use of ultralight tackle. In Alaska waters, this fish rarely exceeds 2 pounds, which happens to be the current state record, caught from Lake Lucile in 1977 by James E. Gum, Jr. But don't be deceived into thinking that this fish requires ultralight gear to make it appear to be a tough customer. On the contrary, kokanee will often double a light-action rod in battles lasting up to several minutes! In my book, those are fishin' words!

I find the best time to try for kokanee is immediately after ice out. Shoreline shallows sometimes literally boil with the feeding activity of young kokanee. However, larger fish are usually not found in shallow waters; they cruise under the surface of bays and at the mouths of freshwater inlets. Often they are suspended below the thermocline during the heat of summer, where they are extremely difficult to catch unless an angler is equipped with a downrigger and sonar unit. Since the summer has a wide variety of more desirable sportfishing opportunities, I confine my fishing time for kokanee to the spring.

Longlining is probably the most effective method of catching early season kokanee. The fish are constantly moving at this time, and a lure buzzed directly under the surface seems to be the ticket to catching a mess of these delectable gamefish.

Hidden Lake is one of the best kokanee fisheries within driving distance of Anchorage. You'll need a boat to fish the kokanee hotspots effectively, and don't forget to pack a lunch. If you find the kokanee in a feeding mood, you won't want to head back home until after dark.

However, ol' silversides are particular about lure offerings. They refuse spinners and plugs any normal salmonid would smash with reckless abandon. To cope with this disinterest, you'd better attend to both technique and lure choices in order to put fish in the boat.

One May, conditions encountered on Hidden Lake with my friends Lin and Lee Dohaniuk indicated that kokanee fishing would be a disaster. The sun was shining brightly at 5 a.m., and the water was as smooth as plate glass. We motored to several isolated bays with extensive weed beds, that attracted—in turn—plankton, crustaceans, and hungry kokanee. We anchored and proceeded to watch the

Lee Dohaniuk prepares to fillet a string of kokanee. They have bright orange flesh and are excellent eating.

shoreline activity. We saw not so much as a mayfly rippling the water. We even tried trolling deepwater structure with 6-ounce Bait Walkers and small plugs without success. I was ready to switch our gear over for laker fishing when the surface formed a slight chop. Soon this transformed into foot-high waves. As I began retrieving my spoon, I felt a sharp strike. Immediately there was a crazed kokanee flipping across the waves. I was using four-pound line, and although the fish weighed less than a pound, I needed several minutes to bring the spunky battler to net. I honestly didn't know what I did: Lin and Lee were using the same lure, but without success. Finally Lin opened my 72-tray tackle box and picked out a flame and black No. 4 Rooster Tail with a black and white feather dressing. She longlined the lure about 75 yards behind the boat as I trolled in a zig-zag pattern parallel to shore. Suddenly the boat rocked wildly as Lin set the hook into a tail-dancing kokanee. Lee tried to calm her: She was so excited about the fish's acrobatic performance that she was jumping up and down in her seat. She handled the fish like a pro, and continued to catch five more kokanee that hour. Lee and I caught 3 apiece. The trick was a troll slow enough to keep the Rooster Tail buzzing from 3- to 4-feet

A nice catch of Hidden Lake kokanee. They struck a fluorescent red Rooster Tail buzzed under the surface. The best time to catch large kokanee is immediately after ice-out.

beneath the surface. A small twitch every now and then seemed to draw the most aggressive strikes. Since, I've learned that trolling glossy, red-colored lures within several feet of the surface, in isolated bays as well as along dropoffs, is what puts spring kokanee in the boat.

Another point to remember while trolling is to work the boat in wide figure S patterns along structure points such as weedbeds, dropoffs, and in wide-open bays. When making S turns, it's important to allow the lure on the inside of the curve to sink, as this often triggers the kokanee following your lure into striking. As the boat begins to move out of the curve, the lure will pick up speed, then an added jigging action has proved quite effective. Kokanee usually strike as the lure is being jigged forward.

If I'm into a big school of kokanee, it would take dollar bills falling from heaven to pull me away from the action. On many occasions, I've stayed with a school for hours by using an ol' crappie fishing trick. Tie a small fluorescent float on a 20-foot section of nylon sewing thread and attach this to the mouth or directly beneath the dorsal fin of a fresh-caught kokanee. On one occasion, I was able to stay with the fish for an entire afternoon, even after they migrated out into 32 feet of water. But then again, kokanee fishing is always full of surprises.

Kokanee are great sportfish. And except for their larger sockeye cousins, there's not a better eating salmon. The kokanee flesh is ruby-red and delectable. And because of its superb aerial performances, I wouldn't be surprised if anglers began requesting that Alaska lakes be stocked with kokanee rather than with rainbow trout!

Where to go for Sockeye Salmon

Southeast

Auke River	Chilkoot River	Situk River

Southcentral

The Kenai River offers excellent sockeye fishing. Flippin' and drift fishing lures are most effective.

The Russian River is located at Mile 55 of the Sterling Highway on the Kenai Peninsula. The river hosts two runs of sockeyes: The first run usually arrives by June 10 and averages 19,000 fish. These salmon spend two years rearing in upper Russian Lake and three years at sea before returning to spawn in mid-August. These fish weigh from 6 to 10 pounds.

The second or late run arrives in mid-July. It is the largest of the two runs and averages 45,000-plus fish. These salmon return to the Russian in their fifth year of life after spending two years in freshwater and two in salt. The average size of these fish is somewhat smaller because of one less year of ocean growth. Fishing is best at the confluence of the Russian and Kenai rivers, and at Mile 55 where a privately operated ferry transports anglers to the south bank of the Kenai. Records indicate that over 50 percent of the anglers fish here. However, once the fish have entered the Russian, they can be readily caught anywhere along its course. Check current Alaska sportfish regulations for closed areas.

Additional restrictions require fishing with an unweighted, single-hook fly with a gap between point and shank not to exceed 3/8 inch. Any weights used must be attached at least 18 inches above the fly.

The Copper River is excellent fishing for salmon up to 10 pounds in late June and July.

Cook Inlet
English Bay
Kenai River
Russian River

Copper River
Gulkana River
Klutina River

Southwest

The Bristol Bay region is termed "The Sockeye Capital of the World." During the months of July through September, almost any watershed will have from several hundred to several hundred thousand sockeyes. The Kvichak, Nushagak, Alagnak, King Salmon River, Ugashik River, Naknek River, and Togiak River and tributaries are all excellent waters from which to catch a trophy sockeye.

Afognak Island
Afognak River

Kodiak
Buskin River
Karluk River
Saltery River
Uganik River

Northwest

Grand Central River

Identifying
Alaska's
Sportfish

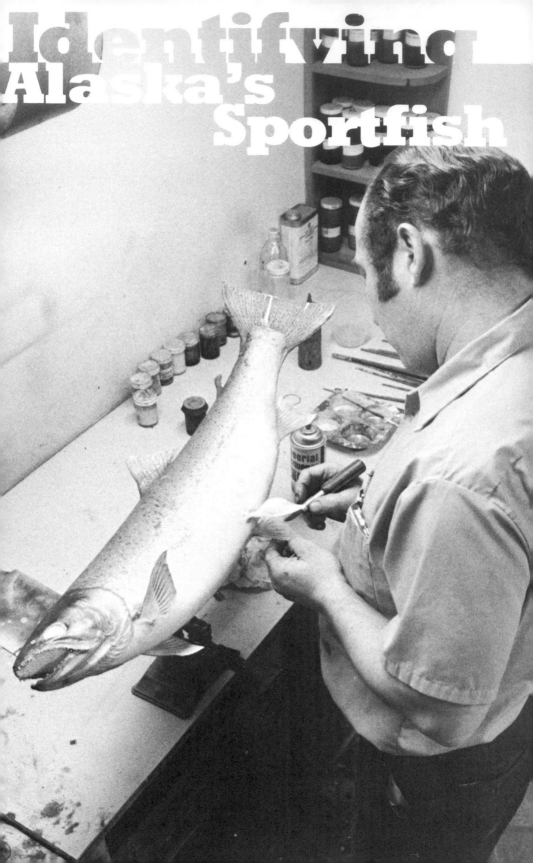

Identifying Alaska's Sportfish

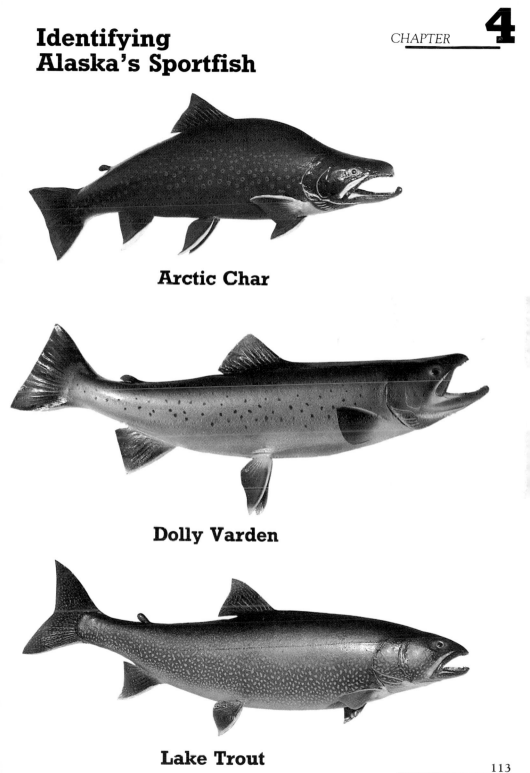

CHAPTER 4

Arctic Char

Dolly Varden

Lake Trout

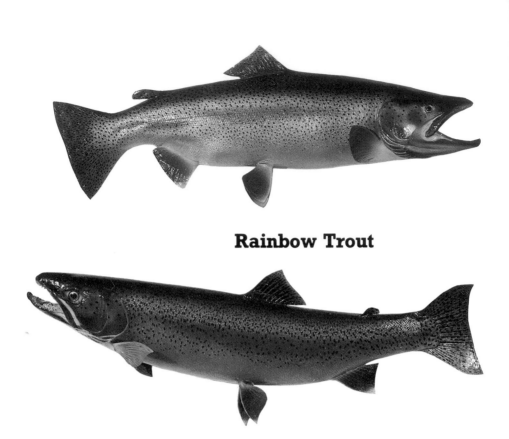

Rainbow Trout

Rainbow Trout

(Body configuration, coloration, and spotting in
rainbow trout, as well as other freshwater species,
may vary considerably between watersheds.)

Steelhead Trout

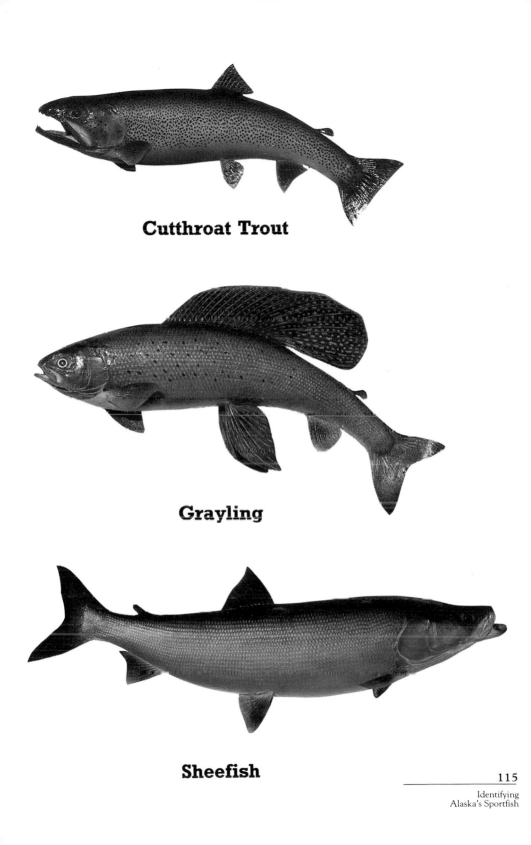

Cutthroat Trout

Grayling

Sheefish

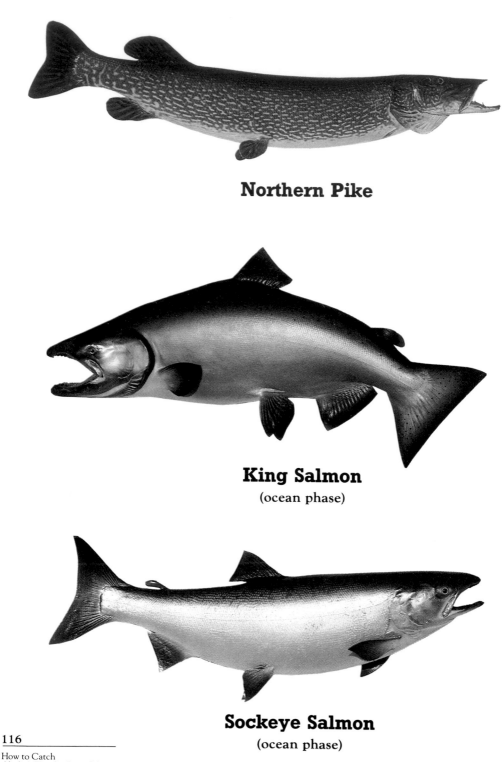

Northern Pike

King Salmon
(ocean phase)

Sockeye Salmon
(ocean phase)

Halibut

King Salmon
(spawning phase)

Sockeye Salmon
(spawning phase)

Identifying
Alaska's Sportfish

Pink Salmon
(ocean phase)

Silver Salmon
(ocean phase)

Chum Salmon
(ocean phase)

Pink Salmon
(spawning phase)

Silver Salmon
(spawning phase)

Chum Salmon
(spawning phase)

Field Care for Trophy Fish

You've caught a trophy fish, and you want to have it mounted. What do you do? Here are a few tips to help ensure the best-looking mount possible.

• Remove the fish from the net immediately after landing. The net will destroy the tail if the fish is allowed to thrash in it long enough. Do not use gaffs.

• Dispatch the fish quickly. Either stick a fillet knife blade into its brain or give the fish a good rap on the head. This prevents the fish from damaging or losing scales.

• After the fish is dispatched, take several, full-length color photos of the fish to help the taxidermist match the original color and pattern. Afterwards, wrap the fish immediately. A damp diaper or burlap bag will keep the skin moist and create a uniform pattern on the fish. If the fish is laid unwrapped on a bank or the bottom of a boat, the fish will discolor from any object it touches. These discolorations can detract from your mount.

• On an extended float trip, refrigeration is impossible. Catch and release is the general policy. However, there are two options. You can release the fish and order a fiberglass mount from the taxidermist. Or if you prefer to have a skin mount, fish taxidermist Ken Guffey recommends equal parts of salt, borax, and powdered milk mixed into a paste. After the fish is dispatched, apply the mixture around the gills and anus. Brush the remainder on the fish. If the fish is kept moist and covered, it will keep in a semi-preserved state for a few days. Be sure to wrap the tails and fin with cardboard or stiffeners to prevent damage. Never gut the fish.

• One last tip. Do not wrap your fish in plastic in the field. This will spoil the fish and make it unsuitable for mounting. Upon returning from your trip, drop the fish off at a local taxidermist as soon as possible.

This 51-pound, spinner-caught king is still full of fight after a 40-minute battle. Small streams and rivers offer plenty of opportunities to catch a large king on light tackle.

Fish mounts courtesy of Ken and Carol Guffey of Ken's Taxidermy, Anchorage.

Pink Salmon

CHAPTER 5

Pink Salmon

There's nothing in Alaska that can compare with trophy pink salmon fishing. It's not the size of this fish that prompts me to hang the "Gone Fishin'" sign on my desk when they migrate en masse along coastal waters in mid-July. Nor is it their non-finicky attitude toward striking lures that makes an afternoon of pursuing these saltwater scrappers a real workout. What makes trophy pink fishing so enticing is that they require a journey to the coastal environment of tidewater glaciers, snow-capped mountains and rolling, whitecapped seas. Complement this with surf casting to schooling pinks in 70-degree temperatures that burn the refreshing tang of the salt air into your nostrils, and you have the basis for a salmon fishing experience that is as unique as the coastal wilderness country that provides it.

While the pink holds the distinction of being the smallest of the Pacific salmon, this should in no way imply the fish is unworthy of sportfishing pursuit. Pinks may be small, but their numbers compensate for their size. They are the most numerous of all Pacific salmon, and provide the most opportunities for sportfishermen. And while a pink may not exhibit the aerial displays of a coho or sockeye, it has a fighting heart that is sure to please the most discriminating angler.

The pink salmon (Oncorhynchus gorbuscha) is also known as humpback, humpy, and fall or autumn salmon. It's called "pink" because its red-orange flesh turns pink in the canning process. The name humpback describes the grotesquely shaped hump the males grow after entering freshwater. Because "Humpback Salmon of Alaska"

Surf casting is a popular method of taking trophy pink salmon. These pinks and a bonus coho were caught from Resurrection Bay in Southcentral Alaska.

sounds more like a horror sequel to "Jaws III" than a tasty food item, marketing specialists insist on using "pink" rather than "humpback" on salmon cans.

In Alaska, the pink salmon ranges from Southeastern coastal areas to the Bering Sea. It is also native to the Aleutian and Kodiak Islands.

Pinks vary from 3- to 5-pounds, with genetically superior stocks under ideal conditions sometimes reaching 14 pounds. The current Alaska state record is a 12-pound, 9-ounce pink taken at the confluence of the Moose and Kenai Rivers in 1974 by Steve Alan Lee. I caught a 10-pound, 14-ounce pink from the same watershed in 1976.

While it's possible to catch large pinks from small, inland streams and rivers, trophy strains of pinks are more commonly found in coastal Southeastern waters north of Ketchikan, Kodiak Island, and several Southcentral watersheds such as Kachemak Bay and Prince William Sound.

The trophy pink angler should realize that pinks mature and return to spawn at two years of age. Because of their strict adherence to this two-year cycle, pink salmon from consecutive years do not interbreed. This results in two genetically distinct stocks. Odd-year-cycle adults in Southeast waters are generally larger than even-year cycle adults in Southcentral waters, even though substantially more pinks return to spawn in even-numbered years.

Saltwater specimens from both cycles can be identified by their silvery sides and large, black oval spots on both the top and bottom halves of the tail. The back is steely blue to blue-green with predominant black spots. The belly is pearly white.

Pink spawning migrations, which in Alaska can occur anytime from late June through September, cause three changes in males: a severely humped back, sharp teeth, and a drab green coloration with brown blotches. While the pink prefers to spawn in the lower sections of a watershed and intertidal areas, the Kuskokwim strain of pinks have been known to travel as much as 100 miles to their spawning beds.

Spawning is like that of other salmon. The female digs the nest or redd and deposits anywhere from 800 to 2,000 eggs, which are immediately fertilized by the male. Another redd is dug upstream from the first, and the gravel is used to fill in the first redd. This is done several

times, until both fish are spent. Adults die several days after spawning.

Depending upon water temperature, egg development takes anywhere from 60 to 130 days. Excess eggs that do not hatch and decay can reduce the quality of the spawning bed for up to a year. Their decomposition fills the water with free carbon dioxide and ammoniacal nitrogen, robbing oxygen from the juvenile salmon and the aquatic life they feed upon. Parr salmon that survive begin their outmigration to sea in the spring. Once at sea, young pinks feed on crustaceans and plankton forms, later switching to a diet of small fish.

Pinks are often called "humpies" because of the large hump males grow prior to spawning (top). Females (bottom) are more streamlined.

Techniques

Saltwater

Many pinks never totally enter a freshwater body, preferring to spawn in an intertidal area. This is that portion of stream inundated by periodic tidal and freshwater flows. Such areas, often located at the tidal breakline, are known for attracting large numbers of trophy pinks. Also,

Pink salmon are excellent fighters when hooked on light tackle. Intertidal areas on an incoming tide provide the most action.

the many waterfalls and steep stream gradients of Southeast Alaska's intertidal areas often prevent upstream spawners from accessing potential spawning gravels. Thus, I always make it a point to fish intertidal areas first before searching elsewhere for large pinks.

Other factors influence distribution of pink salmon throughout a watershed. Pinks' homing instinct is less acute than that exhibited by other salmon species and results in a certain degree of saltwater wandering. Researchers have found pinks in spawning streams up to 400 miles from their natal waters. Timing is another variable. If pinks start their spawning migration too late, they may not make it to their natal stream, and will spawn wherever they can. Thus, what may be a great pink producing area in 1992 may be lousy in 1994. Freshwater runoffs also act as short-term, aqueous magnets that attract migrating pinks. Such a place exists just outside the city limits of Seward on the shores of Resurrection Bay.

It was early July, and Glenn Clawson and I had a charter reservation to catch some large rockfish out near Rugged Island. However, gale warnings outside the bay forced the operator to cancel the trip. Because we had to at least wet

126

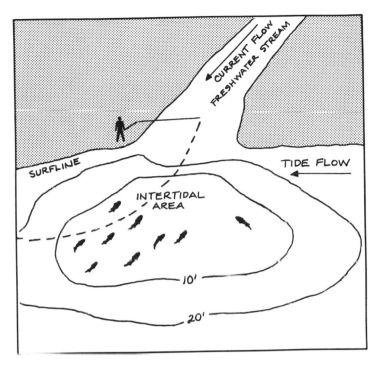

CURRENT FLOW
FRESHWATER STREAM

SURFLINE

TIDE FLOW

INTERTIDAL AREA

10'

20'

Pink salmon preparing to spawn in an intertidal area will hold on or near shallow water gravel bars and along the edge of a fresh/salt-water breakline. Small spinners, spoons, or flies worked down with the current will catch them.

a line before heading back to Anchorage, we drove to the edge of town, parked on the beach, and walked down the coast for several miles. We finally came across a trickle of a creek that bubbled out of the mountainside and emptied into the surf. Glenn tied on a Pixee spoon while I chose a No. 4 chartreuse Rooster Tail.

As I stood on a submerged gravel bar, ready to make my first cast, I was surprised to feel a quick slap of a tail on my waders. I quickly flipped down my polarized sunglasses in time to view a 5-pound pink fin quickly away. A further search through the foam-flecked water revealed small groups of pinks scattered along the sloping edge of the gravel bar. As if on cue, both our rods bucked simultaneously and commanded our full attention as two silvery forms thrashed across the swells. Ten yards downshore, Glenn's fish exploded again in a heart-stopping display of salmon and spray. Glenn was into a rampaging silver, while I had my hands full with a headstrong pink that favored deep water. Glenn attempted to put the reins to the fish, but found it easier to chase the enraged silver down 200 yards of boulder-strewn shoreline. Five minutes later, he came strolling back with a

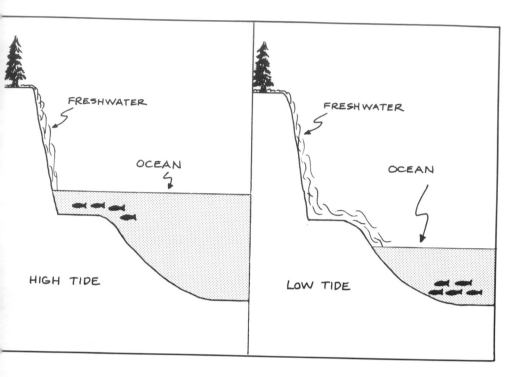

FRESHWATER

OCEAN

HIGH TIDE

FRESHWATER

OCEAN

LOW TIDE

In intertidal areas with extreme tidal fluctuations, fish shallow on a high tide and deep on a low or minus tide.

12-pound silver draped over his shoulder.

I was embarrassed that I was still battling the pink on my ultralight rod. However, my pink soon succumbed to the light but steady pressure of the 4-pound test and turned belly up in the whitecaps. I carefully released what I judged to be a 7-pound, dime-bright pink, and took a breather on a nearby rock.

"Now this is what I call fishing," Glenn said as he emptied his waders. "Despite the 200-yard chase, I had to keep the pressure on, even after I tore a hole in my boots and wrestled him into shallow water. Rather than risk losing the fish, I fell on it, right in the surf."

I grabbed a handkerchief and wiped the tears of laughter out of my eyes. It takes some pink salmon novices longer for the "green" to wear off, or in Glenn's case, wash off. But despite the dunking we both received from the crashing waves, we stayed by that small trickle of water which yielded over 20 pinks as well as Dolly Varden during the next several hours. Since then, I've made it a point never to pass up any freshwater streams or runoffs emptying into the salt without first fishing the area. More times than not, I catch pinks.

In addition to freshwater inlets, pinks prefer holding structure such as gravel bars running horizontally to shore, old pilings, and large rock formations. Locating such structure calls for walking along the beach at minus tide. And don't ignore any spits, sandy beaches and gravel bars, entrances to bays (especially those with feeder creeks) and shoreline channels. All these structures tend to break the tidal current, allowing the salmon to rest for an indefinite period of time before continuing their migration.

I usually start fishing for pinks an hour after low tide, and hang in there until high tide forces me off the gravel bars. Incoming tides bring in fish, but salmon can be caught throughout the day when the run is going strong. My records also show the evening tide seems to be better than the morning tide for catching large pinks.

Two fishing methods are popular. Anglers fishing off the docks at Seward and other coastal cities do extremely well with cut herring impaled on a No. 4 Siwash hook on an adjustable leader and a float. The bait is cast into the tide, and allowed to float through migration channels, which are often right at dockside. Depth should vary from 6 inches to rarely more than 18 inches. The old adage, "large

Bill Batin, the author's brother, admires a pink caught off Resurrection Bay's Lowell Point. A small skiff or inflatable with a graph recorder is invaluable when searching for schools of migrating salmon. This salmon struck a No. 4 chartreuse spinner worked slowly along a sloping dropoff.

Glenn Clawson unhooks a big saltwater pink. Ocean caught pinks are larger and spunkier than pinks hooked in the upper stretches of freshwater.

bait for large fish" holds true here. I've yet to see a runt pink attack one of these rigs. The only disadvantage of this method is that it also tempts such bottomfish species as tomcod, flounder, and Irish Lords.

I prefer to use the other method for pinks: ultralight and light-action tackle and lures. Not only are they important in duping the larger fish into striking, but they also contribute to the arm ache that at day's end brings an ear-to-ear grin.

Without question, long, slim-bodied lures are my best producers for trophy saltwater pinks. I favor spinners because they best telegraph both the soft and hard strikers. When I feel that spinner blade stop, I set the hook instantly. More times than not, I'm into a good pink. Rooster Tails in sizes 4 and 5 in chartreuse, red, yellow, or green work extremely well, with chartreuse and green patterns my favorites. I always carry a good supply because saltwater pinks are rough on tackle, often twisting the wire shafts into a variety of angles.

Spoons are also effective, and 1/4-ounce Pixees with a red, chartreuse or orange insert, 1/8-ounce Fjord spoons in blue/chrome, 1/2-ounce chrome HotRods and ham-

How to Catch
Alaska's Trophy Sportfish

mered chrome Dardevles in 1/4- to 1/2-ounce work best.

Trophy pinks are generally lazy and will seldom chase a lure far. Therefore it's important to fish either type of lure across the pink's direction of travel. Lures retrieved from directly behind or toward the fish will usually be ignored or grabbed at half-heartedly. I find pinks will strike readily and aggressively a lure that is cast no less than 45 degrees opposite to shore.

I hook most of my large pinks by retrieving the lure about six inches above bottom. A slow, steady retrieve is best, but an occasional variance in speed is often productive.

Fly fishing for saltwater pinks is premier sport. A 6-weight rod and small No. 4 or 6 herring patterns, Black Nose Daces, and virtually any flashy, but not gaudy, fly exhibiting either green and/or blue will take pinks regularly. A 6-foot sink tip will handle shallow water pinks quite readily. However, it's wise to have a heavier outfit on hand when those Gulf of Alaska gale winds crumple your best double haul at your feet.

Freshwater

Freshwater fishing for trophy pinks can be as productive as saltwater fishing, if done in watersheds near the ocean. Pinks found at the headwaters of many rivers and streams are usually in poor condition and are rarely trophy specimens.

One of my favorite freshwater fishing hotspots for trophy pinks is Alexander Creek. Lee Langbehn and I overindulged on pink salmon in 1976 at the mouth of the Alexander, where it empties into the Susitna River. Within three days we caught over 400 pink salmon, all on ultralight tackle. But we had done our homework: We knew where the pinks congregated, and carried at least 10 pounds of ultralight lures with us, much to the pleasure of many bank anglers who weren't as successful with their oversize spoons and spinners.

The first thing to remember when fishing for freshwater pinks is that males are usually larger than females and tend to enter freshwater systems first. So whenever you hear reports of commercial set netters taking pinks, start planning to intercept those same schools at the mouth of clearwater streams within the next few days.

Also, research has shown that an upstream run seems to

be triggered by high water. There's something about a brief summer rainstorm that gets pinks to migrate upstream by the thousands. However, an abundance of rain and subsequent flooding forces the fish to stay out of the strong current. They will wait in backeddies for the water level and speed to drop to levels suitable for upstream migration.

Freshwater pinks can be aggressive. While they won't charge a lure with the power of a rampant grizzly, they will chase a lure across a stream, especially if other pinks are nearby. The tendency to strike in low water and high fish concentrations is known as species pressure. Fish are forced to compete for the best migration routes upstream, spawning beds, and resting areas. Competition is fierce, and aggressiveness high. Even a mild-mannered species such as the pink can turn into an underwater warlord when several thousand of its kind are funneled into the narrow confines of a stream or small river.

If species pressure is in force, practically anything in your tackle box will take pinks. However, the larger fish tend to stay somewhat deeper than the smaller, porpoising males that frequent the upper currents, especially in slow flowing waterways like the Alexander and lower Deshka. I prefer to use either a No. 5 Rooster Tail, 1/4-ounce HotRod, or chartreuse Krocodile, allow it to sink through the surface activity, and begin my retrieve slowly along the bottom. Both pinks and chums grow large teeth for defending the nests against other males, and there always seems to be a large brawler that chomps on anything within a 6-inch radius of its kype. A slow, steady retrieve along bottom, with an occasional twitch of the rod tip, is the "red flag" that triggers these bullish pinks to strike.

Fly Fishing

In fast current, pinks often jet up chutes of water that are usually too fast for anglers to stand in safely. In such a situation, hardware is generally ineffective. A small, fluorescent fly is the best way to catch fish at this time.

A popular example of this is the Bird Creek Fishery at low tide. This stream, located 29 miles south of Anchorage, has a fairly steep gradient at low tide, and pinks don't waste any time scrambling up to the safety of deep-water pools. Weighted flies, fished with either a drop sinker rig or weight added to the fly line, work most effec-

tively in water 2- to 5-feet deep. Chartreuse is unquestionably the most effective color. The brighter and more iridescent, the better. I've found fly patterns with additional colors such as black and purple—contrasting with the chartreuse—are even more productive than solid colors. Keep the flies small, on a number 4 short shank hook, and needle-sharp. It's not uncommon for a pink to grab your fly, and if the water is swift enough, the drag on the line will often set the hook for you. Nevertheless, this is not cause for the angler to be lax in setting the hook.

Technique is a simple matter of tossing the fly upstream, and drifting it down and across the kype of the fish. The flippin' technique detailed in the sockeye salmon chapter is excellent here, especially when pinks are quickly moving upstream with the tide. It may be necessary for fly anglers to use a small weight to take the fly down in swift water. Rubbercore sinkers work well in most cases.

Trophy pink fishing is not without its dangers, however. Many years ago, out in Resurrection Bay, I fished an elevated gravel bar separated by several channels. The fishing was spectacular—large pinks migrating all around me, bumping into my legs and porpoising everywhere, like a popcorn popper out of control. I was so intent on catching and releasing salmon, many exceeding 7 pounds, that I failed to notice the slowly rising tide. When I did glance

Sculpin or herring patterns are excellent for saltwater pinks. In lower freshwater or intertidal areas, chartreuse or fluorescent green Glo-Bugs or jigs work well. Notice sea lice above the anal fin.

around, I discovered that the driftwood marker pointing the way back across the channel was underwater!

I had no choice but to tighten the belt around my chest waders and slowly inch across the slippery gravel to shore. My legs wobbled in the current as the swells of the waves broke just below my wader tops. I desperately tried to remember the number of steps to the dropoff. After several minutes of "toe-touching" I let out a big sigh of relief when the water began retreating down from my wader tops, and I was able to take larger steps. If I fish isolated gravel bars nowadays, I always bring my two-man inflatable. More than once has this craft allowed me to set the steel into trophy pinks out of range of shoreline anglers at high tide, and to make it safely back to shore afterwards.

Excitement, scenic beauty, and sheer enjoyment is what trophy pink fishing is all about. I think the quantity of fish and the quality of the fishing combine to make an unbeatable sport. Try it soon. You won't be disappointed.

Where to go for Pink Salmon

Southeast

Southeast pink salmon are some of the largest found in the state. Pinks up to 8 pounds have been caught, however, 5 to 7 pounds is the average catch. Some of my favorites are the Chilkat River, Situk River, the Breadline beaches, Lynn Canal, Pybus Bay, Starrigavan Bay, Kah Sheets, and Kadake Creek.

Admiralty Island
Doty's Cove
Point Retreat
Pybus Bay

Haines
Chilkat River
Chilkoot River
Lynn Canal

Juneau
Aaron Island
Auke Bay
Auke Creek
Breadline beaches
Cowee Creek
Fish Creek
Lena Cove
Lena Point

Middle Point
Montana Creek
North Pass
Point Louisa
Shelter Island

Ketchikan
Bell Arm
Karta River
Naha River
Unuk River
Yes Bay

Petersburg
Castle River
Kadake Creek
Kah Sheets Creek
Petersburg Creek

Sitka
Katlian River
Starrigavin Bay

Wrangell
Anan Creek
Stikine River

Yakutat
Situk River

Southcentral

My recommendations for large pinks in this area are: Homer Spit, Resurrection Bay, Alexander Creek, and Bird Creek. The mouth of the Kenai River also offers an excellent fishery for pink salmon.

Freshwater streams emptying into Prince William Sound are often packed bank-to-bank with pink salmon. While not the size often caught from Kodiak or Southeast watersheds, pinks are nevertheless available in large numbers. Mineral Creek and Valdez Harbor are noted for 5- to 6-pound pinks.

Cook Inlet/Kenai Peninsula
Alexander Creek
Bird Creek
Deshka Creek
Homer Spit
Lake Creek
Lower Kenai River
Resurrection Bay
Talachulitna River
Tutka Bay

Copper River
Mineral Creek
Seven-Mouth Creek
Valdez Harbor
Whittier Harbor

Southwest

Pinks can be found throughout these systems. Largest pinks are found in the lower sections of these watersheds.

The pink salmon found in Kodiak watersheds are trophy fish weighing up to 9 pounds. Excellent trophies can be caught from the many saltwater beaches accessible by road. July and August are the best times.

Egegik System
Mulchatna Sytem
Naknek System
Nushagak System
Tikchik System
Togiak System
Ugashik System
Wood River System

Kodiak
Afognak River
(Afognak Island)
American River
Anton Larsen Bay
Buskin River
Kalsin Bay
Karluk River
Middle Bay
Monashka Bay
Olds River
Pasagshak River
Red River
Saltery River
Women's Bay

Northwest

Fox River
Kuzitrin River
Niukluk River
Nome River
Pilgrim River

Safety Lagoon
Sinuk River
Snake River
Solomon River
Unalakleet River

Chum
Salmon

CHAPTER 6

Chum Salmon

Chum salmon are the Rodney Dangerfields of the salmon realm. They are a fish overflowing at the gills with spunk and stamina, yet due to their reluctance to strike lures, they fail to command the respect they deserve from anglers. Anglers also scorn chums for having a merely palatable pink flesh, rather than meat as ruby-red and delicious as that of sockeyes and kings. It's rare when anglers toss chums the second glance given smaller catches of coho or trout. And making the chum's reputation even humbler is its nickname "dog salmon", a result of its past and present use as dog food by many Interior Alaska Indians and trappers.

But when a chum does strike—and they often do if the proper techniques are employed—the fish has no reason to apologize for its place on the fisherman's scale of values. Chums will bruise knuckles, smoke drags, and just downright stage an airborne and underwater ruckus that equals, pound for pound, any that their Pacific cousins can dish out. In fact, I'm thankful chums are smaller than king salmon. Otherwise the battle between angler and fish would truly be a one-sided sport, with the laurels of victory going to the chum!

For such an "underdog," chum salmon attain respectable size. Commercial netters have reported chums weighing up to 40 pounds, although this is rare. Most chums caught in Southcentral Alaska weigh from 7- to 10-pounds, and 12- to 14-pounders are common in Yukon, Kodiak, and Southeastern waters. The current Alaska state record is held by Robert Jahnke for a 27-pound, 3-ounce chum taken in Behm Canal in 1977.

An angler eases a fresh-from-the-sea chum into shallow water. The fish struck an Alaska Mary Ann on a dead drift.

Life History

The chum salmon (Oncorhynchus keta) is also known as calico, keta (Russian), fall or autumn salmon. In Alaska, it is found from Panhandle waters to the northwest Bering Sea, giving the chum the distinction of being the northernmost spawner of all the Pacific salmon. The nickname "dog salmon" has another source besides the chum's use as dog food: The fierce, dog-like teeth this fish grows before spawning. At sea, the chum exhibits a minted, silver dollar coloration, unmarked, save for an occasional black speckling of its sides and upper back. But upon entering freshwater, males display intense spawning coloration, with red, pink, or purplish vertical markings etched on their olive-green sides. The females are similar in appearance, but less vivid in color.

The chum is generally considered a late summer, early fall spawner, yet arrival times into Alaska's streams and rivers can vary greatly. I have caught fresh chums in the upper Susitna drainage as early as July 5th, and biologists have discovered ripe males in a Fairbanks stream in February. However, it is the Yukon strain of chum salmon that takes the prize of "Marathon Salmon." These fish enter the lower Yukon the first of June for a 2,000 mile, 4-month or longer journey to Teslin Lake, Canada. They and other chums that make long distance migrations exhibit a red, oily flesh that sustains them through spawning. However, most chums travel less than 100 miles to their spawning areas, and subsequently exhibit a lighter-hued flesh that is less oily.

Chum spawning grounds vary, ranging from intertidal areas to coarse gravel beds, boulder-covered bedrock, and shallow waters where spring seepage prevents their redds from freezing. After the female digs the redd with her tail, her drifting into the pit apparently stimulates the attending males. The dominant male joins the hen and as they hover over the redd, they expel eggs and milt. The female then covers the eggs with gravel, and along with the male, dies several days later.

Depending upon water temperature, the eggs hatch between December and February, with smolt outmigrating to sea 60 to 90 days later. Young chum remain close to shoreline structure, and grow fairly rapidly, attaining weights of 8- to 12-pounds in 3 to 4 years. Then they return to spawn in their fourth or fifth year of life.

Author with a nice catch of large chum and pink salmon. These fish struck a No. 4 chartreuse Mepps spinner fished along the edges of fast current. The vertical markings are why this fish is often called calico salmon.

139

Chum Salmon

Techniques

Saltwater

Saltwater fishing for chums is less elaborate than trolling for kings and cohos. This is because chums move fairly rapidly through straits, narrows, and inlets to reach their spawning grounds, generally stopping for what may be several hours to several days at the mouth of their natal stream. These stopping times are without question the best opportunities to try for saltwater chums. My first encounter with "salty dogs" was with Gehr Englund on the south side of the Alaska Peninsula near Wide Bay.

It was late August and we were flying the Cessna 180 along the beachfront, looking for schools of silvers. Flying low over the mouth of an unnamed stream, I practically strained my neck trying to keep my eyes on a long, black ribbon of salmon that extended down the coast from the mouth for nearly a half-mile. Gehr quickly landed the aircraft on the beach. We half-ran, half-walked to the mouth, fitting rods and tying on lures as we went. Gehr's spinning rod assembled faster than my fly rod, and his first cast into the black ribbon of fish resulted in a dynamite strike. The hooked salmon thrashed the surface, exploded several times head over tail into the ocean air, and tore at Gehr's reel with its surging runs. This reaction sent the entire school into a frenzy that boiled the surface of the slightly rolling surf. My No. 2 blue/green herring pattern wasn't in the water long enough to get wet before an enraged salmon sucked in the fly and headed for the tail of the school a half-mile away!

Fifteen minutes later, I carefully led the fish in on its side through the surf. Expecting it to be a coho, I was surprised to see the faint tint of vertical markings on its chromed flanks. After reviving the fish and releasing it, I checked with Gehr who was busy cleaning his catch in the surf. The meat was red, yet the dark-green back and faint vertical markings were present. Not until we caught 8 more salmon did Gehr finally believe they were actually chums and not silvers.

I've found that when schooled at river mouths, chums prefer a large lure or fly. Short, squatty spoons such as the Dardevlet, Steel-ee, Johnson Sprite, and Kastmasters in blue/chrome, hammered metallic blue, chartreuse, blue-green and bronze/red have worked the best for me. Char-

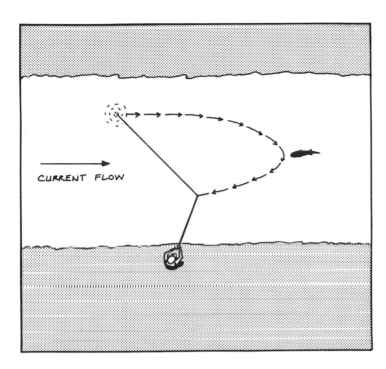

The "crowbar" technique is an effective method for taking chums. Stand a few yards upstream from the fish, and make a cast up and across current. Regulate the drift and speed of retrieve so that the lure makes a U-turn within 6 to 8 inches of the chum's mouth.

treuse Mepps Aglias in sizes 3 to 5 have been the most effective spinners. And herring patterns, tri-colored bucktails, and blue/white smolt patterns with silver mylar the most popular flies.

On an outgoing tide, or under heavy fishing pressure, chums often become skitterish. Under these conditions, try a No. 4 black Woolly Worm or Teeny nymph fished with a sink-tip line on a dead drift. Spin anglers should try a No. 10 Lil Corky or Aqua Cone with fluorescent red or chartreuse yarn trailer tied to a standard drift rig. Use only enough weight to keep the rig drifting above bottom.

Freshwater

Over the years, I learned that there are two places to find chum salmon. The first is in shallow, clearwater streams. Here, chum are unquestionably more difficult to catch. My first ever freshwater chum took 54 casts with a No. 4 Mepps Aglia before striking. Little did I realize at the time that this was a chum with quick reflexes! Catching chums visible in the shallows is best termed as an exercise in futility. But they can be caught, and I will tell you how later is this chapter.

141

Chum Salmon

The second place chums are found is in deep pools or sections of river. You know the chums are there, but you can't see them because of turbidity, glare, or other factors. These deepwater fish seem easier to catch, mainly because such pools hold more than one chum. Remember, the more chums in a pool, the better your chances of catching one or more. This principle holds true with other salmon species also.

A deep pool or section of river likely to hold chums should be fished systematically and precisely. It is imperative that the lure travel across the kype of the fish, at the same latitude as the corner of the mouth. A few inches up or off to one side invariably results in an ignored lure. I usually like to make my first cast to the head of a pool, and fish the lure barely fast enough to keep the spoon wobbling or blade spinning. Remember, all stream factors being equal, retrieve speed, rod angle, and countdown of lure sinking to bottom must be the same with each cast. If the lure hits bottom at the count of seven on the first cast, I'll start my retrieve a fraction before the count of seven each time after. Repeated casting is the key.

If after approximately 10 casts I haven't had a strike, I'll initiate my next 10 casts 6- to 12-inches below the first and finish working out the pool.

A chum strike under these conditions is similar to that of a steelhead strike: soft, and barely noticeable. Thus it's important to:
- Keep casts as short as possible to detect soft strikes.
- Keep hooks needle sharp.
- Avoid belly in the line.
- Keep rod pointed at lure, ready to strike.
- Set the hook at the slightest hesitation.

Remember that a favorite chum hangout is the tail end of pools. A lure or fly that has ended its swing, and is starting to lift up and cross the current, is a prime invitation for a strike.

However, shallow streams are a different ballgame. While sunny skies and low, clearwater conditions make it extremely easy to spot the darkened forms of migrating chums, fishing at this time can be very exasperating. Shallow water angling strategy is basically the same as fishing for deepwater chums except that it's necessary to employ what I call "crowbar techniques" due to the

Fred Hardin nets a Sheep Creek chum for the author. The fish struck a spinner worked along the edge of a deep channel. Be careful when handling chums, as their teeth can inflict painful wounds.

143

Chum Salmon

The best way to catch chum salmon is to cast to individual fish, working the lure as close to the kype as possible. Repeated casting is often necessary to provoke a strike.

chum's unwillingness to open its mouth. I vividly remember that Kobuk River chums take the largest "crowbar" and the most patience.

David Ketscher of Sourdough Outfitters had just dropped off Mark, Fred and Maurice Ketscher, and me via floatplane to start a float trip for grayling and sheefish. While we were inflating the rafts, Mark noticed a large school of chums holding across the river at the mouth of a feeder stream. We soon found ourselves paddling a half-inflated boat across the swift current for a bit of "hook settin' " practice.

For nearly two hours we cast to chums less than five feet

away without so much as a strike. Maurice was becoming
increasingly frustrated, and seriously eyed the landing net
as a means of catching these uncooperative salmonids in
one easy scoop. I switched over to single hooks, as my
ultralight, treble-hooked flies would occasionally snag on a
dorsal fin or tail. This also indicated that my weighted
tube flies weren't sinking deep enough, and that they
didn't have the action necessary to induce a strike. I
switched over to a No 2 Mepps Black Fury with a small,
rubbercore sinker attached 14 inches above the lure. I
flipped down my polaroids, picked out a particularly large
fish, and worked it for 12 casts. On lucky 13, the chum was

Trophy chum salmon are powerful fish, and require medium- to heavy-duty tackle to bring to net.

obviously fed up with the spinner blade knocking skin off his nose. In the soft-striking manner often exhibited by clearwater chums, the greenish, hook-jawed male opened its mouth as the lure drifted by and chewed on my lure with those canine-like teeth. As I set the hook, the spine of my ultralight rod creaked, and it continued to complain for the next 20 minutes as I tried to reel down the much-aggravated chum. When the fish zipped past for the fifth time, I caught a glimpse of what appeared to be devilment in its eye. My interpretation wasn't unfounded. Finally beaching the spunky salmon in about 4 inches of water, I got a thorough and most unwelcome dousing of icy Kobuk water from the chum's incessantly flapping tail. I swear that as I released that chum, it was laughing, and rightly so. I was totally drenched.

I quickly dried off and explained to Maurice, who was wielding a landing net rather than a fishing rod, that these chums required a dead-slow retrieve. It was necessary for the lure to drift within 24 inches of a particular chum before starting the spinner with a quick twitch of the rod tip. And the lure had to be exactly at mouth level. I later learned that most strikes occur only when the spinner enters the chum's strike zone—a 180-degree, 5-inch arc that originates at the kype. After the lure exits the strike zone, you have to reel in quickly and repeat the procedure. Sloppy casts do nothing but spook salmon.

Maurice soon learned that this "crowbar technique" not only caught fish, but opened the lid to some exciting fishing. By the time we finished hooking and releasing chums late that afternoon, we were too bushed to even think about fishing for grayling or sheefish. My "crowbar" method has since proven itself on clearwater chums from Montana Creek to the tributaries of the Noatak River.

The basic fly patterns mentioned earlier for saltwater chums are equally effective once they enter freshwater. However, I prefer to fish clearwater chums with a lead-core line rather than with a sink-tip, as the lead-core allows me to strip the fly across the mouth of the chum with greater precision. And it's important to use a large fly, tied on at least a No. 2 hook. A spawning chum sports a mouthful of teeth and bone that can create hook-setting problems with smaller hooks. And don't forget to use a short leader of 15 to 18 inches, which keeps the fly from bellying in the current. For chums in swift water, I'll often add a strip of lead to the line or a small split shot directly to the leader for greater depth control.

Fly fishing gear should include a 7- or 8-weight rod and matching reel filled with at least 200 yards of 15-pound Dacron backing. Spinning and level-wind anglers prefer 6- to 7-foot, medium-action rods with plenty of backbone. Reels should be rated medium freshwater, and hold at least 200 yards of 12-pound monofilament. I prefer to fish chums on ultralight tackle. But if you go this route, be prepared to lose lots of fish and lures.

Additional gear should include needlenose pliers, a must for removing lures. Chums' dog-like teeth can inflict a nas-

The chum, as well as all Pacific salmon, are born orphans and die childless. A chum carcass will decompose, adding nutrients to the water which enhance zooplankton and crustacean life. Several months later, newly hatched chums feed on these invertebrate organisms.

ty wound that can become easily infected. I always carry a small tube of antibiotic cream in my vest, along with a couple Band-Aids. And most important, don't forget the polarized sunglasses! Not only are they vital in locating fish, but they also provide a spectacular opportunity to watch an angered chum smash your lure.

Chums are excellent smoked, and make good fishcakes. I smoked up a batch of Dolly Varden and chum salmon for a group of fishing buddies once, and no one could differentiate between the two. My wife prepares fresh-from-the-sea chums the same as any other salmon. Seasoned with lemon and garlic, they are scrumptious! Keep one for the larder next time and try it yourself.

While the chum may not be in the same class as the coho or chinook, it certainly ranks No. 1 in my book for showmanship, tenacity, and spunk. Chums are without question one of the most challenging of all Pacific salmon: They require precision casting and fishing technique, along with continual experimentation to determine exactly what lure they will hit. And despite popular belief, chums will strike. It's just a matter of choosing the right "crowbar."

How to Catch
Alaska's Trophy Sportfish

Where to go for Chum Salmon

Southeast

Admiralty Island
Pybus Bay

Haines
Chilkat River

Juneau
Auke Creek
Cowee Creek
Echo Cove
Favorite Reef
Fish Creek
Montana Creek
Peterson Creek
Pybus Bay

Ketchikan
Bell Island
Karta River
Naha River
Salt Lagoon Creek
Unuk River

Petersburg
Castle River
Falls Creek
Kadake Creek
Kah Sheets Creek
Petersburg Creek

Sitka
Katlian River

Wrangell
Stikine River

Southcentral

Cook Inlet/Kenai Peninsula
Alexander Creek
Clear Creek
Montana Creek
Susitna Drainage
Willow Creek

Southwest

Alagnak System
Egegik System
Igushik System
Kvichak System
Mulchatna System
Naknek System
Nushagak System
Painter Creek Watershed
Togiak System
Ugashik System
Wood River System

Kodiak
American River
Anton Larsen Bay
Middle Bay
Russian River
Women's Bay

Interior

Chatanika River

Salcha River

Yukon River System

Northwest

Fox River
Kobuk River
Kuzitrin River
Niukluk River

Noatak River
Nome River
Pilgrim River

Sinuk River
Snake River
Unalakleet River

Lures

CHAPTER 7

Lures

Over the years, I've tested hundreds of lures in all types of water throughout the state. The lures listed in this section are the basic colors, shapes, and sizes that have worked best for me in catching Alaska's trophy sportfish. These lures, fished with the specific techniques listed in each chapter, will put you that much closer toward catching your trophy.

	King Salmon	Silver Salmon	Sockeye Salmon	Pink Salmon	Chum Salmon	Dolly Varden	Arctic Char	Lake Trout	Rainbow Trout	Steelhead Trout	Cutthroat Trout	Grayling	Northern Pike	Sheefish	Whitefish	Halibut	Rockfish
Attractor Lures and Jigs																	
1. Sonar	•	•	•						•	•	•		•		•	•	•
2. Vibro-Tail (small)						•	•		•		•	•			•		
3. Beetle Jig									•	•		•	•		•		
4. Vibro-Tail (large)						•	•	•						•	•		•
5. ½ oz. Ducktail Jig						•	•	•						•			•
6. Super Spin-N-Glo	•	•															
7. Cherry Drifter	•	•				•	•		•	•							
8. Size 2 Peach Spin-N-Glo	•	•															
9. Size 2 Metallic Blue Spin-N-Glo	•	•															
10. Size 8 Fluorescent Red Spin-N-Glo				•	•	•	•		•	•	•	•			•		
11. Size 0 Clown Spin-N-Glo	•	•															
Spinners																	
1. 1 oz. Little George									•	•				•	•		•
2. ½ oz. Little George						•	•	•	•								
3. No. 2 Black Rooster Tail											•		•	•			
4. No. 3 Metallic Blue Rooster Tail			•		•	•	•		•	•	•	•	•	•			
5. No. 4 Flame Coach Dog Rooster Tail	•	•		•	•	•	•		•	•	•						
6. No. 5 Chartreuse Coach Dog Rooster Tail	•	•	•	•	•	•	•	•	•	•	•				•		
7. Sonic Rooster Tail		•			•												
8. Black Vibrax									•	•	•	•					
9. No. 1 Red Dot Mepps Black Fury						•			•	•	•	•			•		
10. No. 3 Fluorescent Red Mepps Aglia Long	•	•				•											
11. No. 3 Copper Mepps Aglia								•	•	•	•		•	•			
12. No. 3 Red Dot Black Fury		•			•	•	•		•								
13. No. 2 Rainbo Scale Mepps Aglia Long						•					•	•	•				
14. No. 4 Chartreuse Mepps Aglia	•	•	•	•	•	•	•	•	•	•	•				•		
15. No. 3 Fluorescent Red Mepps Aglia	•	•	•	•	•	•	•			•	•	•	•				
16. No. 4 Rainbo Scale Mepps Aglia Long	•	•						•	•	•			•	•			
17. No. 4 Rainbo Scale Mepps Aglia Long Minno	•	•							•				•	•			
18. No. 5 Tee Spoon	•	•							•				•	•			

Angler Bill Coffey ponders over the right lure to use for Dolly Varden on a small wilderness stream.

Spoons

	King Salmon	Silver Salmon	Sockeye Salmon	Pink Salmon	Chum Salmon	Dolly Varden	Arctic Char	Lake Trout	Rainbow Trout	Steelhead Trout	Cutthroat Trout	Grayling	Northern Pike	Sheefish	Whitefish	Halibut	Rockfish
1. Chrome Mann-O-Lure						•	•	•					•	•			•
2. Gold Mann-O-Lure							•	•					•	•			•
3. Chartreuse Mann-O-Lure	•	•		•													
4. Fluorescent Red Aqua Spoon	•	•	•	•		•	•		•	•							
5. Red and White Dardevle	•	•		•		•	•	•	•			•	•	•			•
6. Silver Mepps Spoon	•	•					•	•				•	•	•			
7. 1/64 oz. Blue/Silver Fjord Spoon												•	•			•	
8. HotRod	•	•							•	•			•	•			•
9. 7/8 oz. Green Pixee	•	•		•	•				•				•	•			•
10. 7/8 oz. Chartreuse Pixee	•	•	•	•	•				•	•			•	•			•
11. 1/2 oz. Fluorescent Red Pixee	•	•		•	•	•	•	•	•	•	•	•	•	•			
12. Rainbo Scale Mepps Spoon	•	•							•	•	•		•	•			
13. Fjord Spoon		•		•		•	•	•	•			•	•		•		
14. Swedish Pimple				•		•			•			•	•				
15. Johnson Silver Minnow													•				
16. Gold Fjord Spoon									•	•			•	•			
17. Chartreuse/Red Krocodile	•												•				•
18. Fluorescent Red/Black Dardevle	•	•	•				•	•	•		•	•	•				

Plugs

	King Salmon	Silver Salmon	Sockeye Salmon	Pink Salmon	Chum Salmon	Dolly Varden	Arctic Char	Lake Trout	Rainbow Trout	Steelhead Trout	Cutthroat Trout	Grayling	Northern Pike	Sheefish	Whitefish	Halibut	Rockfish
1. Magnum Glo-Tadpolly	•								•								
2. Magnum Clown Tadpolly	•																
3. Magnum Chrome/Fluorescent Red Herringbone Tadpolly	•	•							•				•				
4. Fluorescent Red Hot Shot	•	•							•		•						
5. Chrome/Fluorescent Red Hot Shot	•	•															
6. Chrome J-Plug	•																
7. Gold Flatfish								•	•	•	•		•				
8. Fluorescent Red Flatfish				•			•	•			•	•	•				
9. Torpedo													•				
10. Bill Norman Minnow							•	•	•	•		•	•	•			
11. Nickel/Blue Tadpolly							•	•	•	•			•				
12. Floating Rapala							•	•	•			•	•				
13. Nickel/Blue Flatfish	•	•							•								
14. Shad Plug (Kokanee imitator)									•								
15. Fluorescent Red/Black Devil Diver		•															
16. Nickel/Blue Devil Diver		•							•								

Saltwater Jigs

	King Salmon	Silver Salmon	Sockeye Salmon	Pink Salmon	Chum Salmon	Dolly Varden	Arctic Char	Lake Trout	Rainbow Trout	Steelhead Trout	Cutthroat Trout	Grayling	Northern Pike	Sheefish	Whitefish	Halibut	Rockfish
1. 14 oz. Krocodile																•	•
2. Sebastes Jig																•	•
3. Wild Willie																	•
4. Flowering Floreo																	•
5. Bucktail Jig																	•

Saltwater Trolling

	King Salmon	Silver Salmon	Sockeye Salmon	Pink Salmon	Chum Salmon	Dolly Varden	Arctic Char	Lake Trout	Rainbow Trout	Steelhead Trout	Cutthroat Trout	Grayling	Northern Pike	Sheefish	Whitefish	Halibut	Rockfish
1. Dodger	•	•															
2. 1 oz. HotRod	•	•													•		•
3. Hootchie	•	•															
4. Hootchie	•	•															
5. Hootchie/Herring Harness	•	•															
6. Flasher/Dodger	•	•															
7. Herring Aid	•	•															
8. Poor Man's Downrigger	•	•															•

Attractor Lures
and Jigs

1. Sonar

2. Vibro-Tail (small)

3. Beetle Jig

4. Vibro-Tail (large)

5. ⅛ oz. Bucktail Jig

6. Super Spin-N-Glo

7. Cherry Drifter

8. Size 2 Peach Spin-N-Glo

9. Size 2 Metallic
Blue Spin-N-Glo

10. Size 8
Fluorescent Red
Spin-N-Glo

11. Size 0 Clown
Spin-N-Glo

Spinners

1. 1 oz. Little George

2. ½ oz. Little George

3. No. 2 Black Rooster Tail

4. No. 3 Metallic Blue Rooster Tail

5. No. 4 Flame Coach Dog Rooster Tail

6. No. 5 Char CD Rooster Tail

7. Sonic Rooster Tail

8. Black Vibrax

9. No. 1 Red Dot Mepps Blk. Fury

10. No. 3 Fluorescent Red Mepps Aglia Long

11. No. 3 Copper Mepps Aglia

12. No. 3 Red Dot Blk. Fury

13. No. 2 Rainbo Scale Mepps Aglia Long

14. No. 4 Chartreuse Mepps Aglia

15. No. 3 Fl. Red Mepps Aglia

16. No. 4 Rainbo Scale Mepps Aglia Long

17. No. 4 Rainbo Scale Mepps Aglia Long Minnow

18. No. 5 Tee Spoon

Spoons

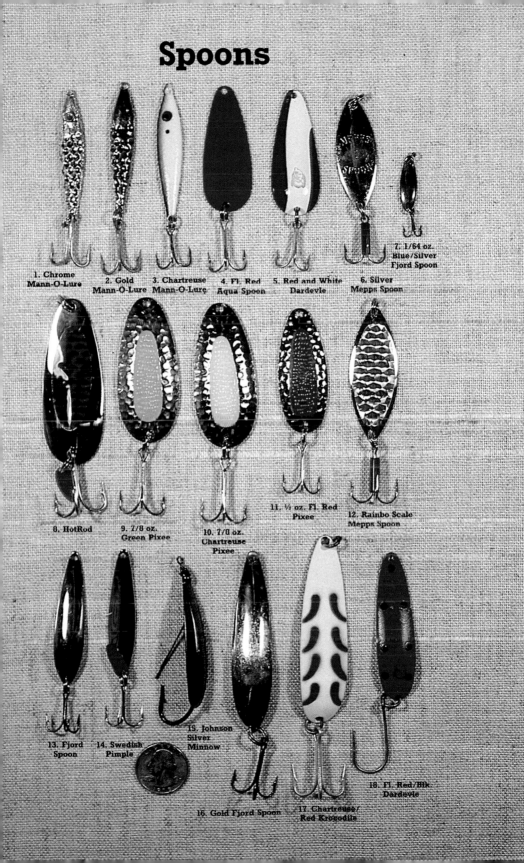

1. Chrome Mann-O-Lure
2. Gold Mann-O-Lure
3. Chartreuse Mann-O-Lure
4. Fl. Red Aqua Spoon
5. Red and White Dardevle
6. Silver Mepps Spoon
7. 1/64 oz. Blue/Silver Fjord Spoon
8. HotRod
9. 7/8 oz. Green Pixee
10. 7/8 oz. Chartreuse Pixee
11. ½ oz. Fl. Red Pixee
12. Rainbo Scale Mepps Spoon
13. Fjord Spoon
14. Swedish Pimple
15. Johnson Silver Minnow
16. Gold Fjord Spoon
17. Chartreuse/Red Krogodile
18. Fl. Red/Blk. Dardevle

Plugs

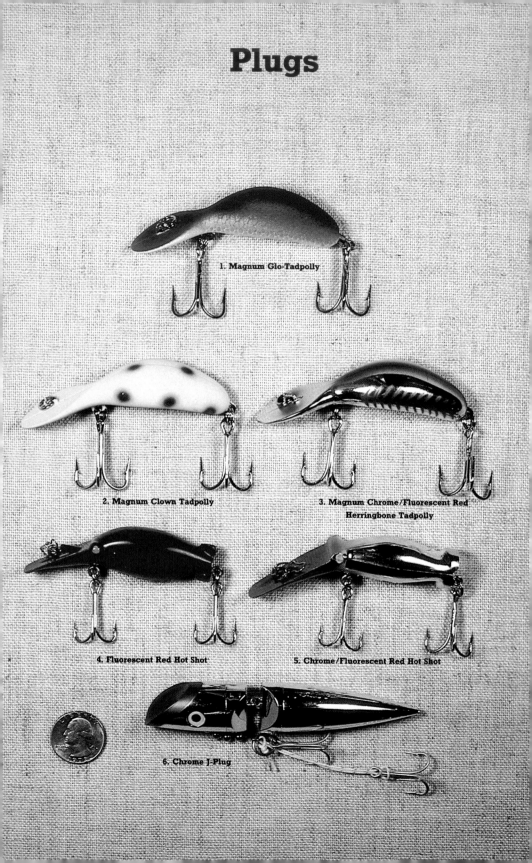

1. Magnum Glo-Tadpolly

2. Magnum Clown Tadpolly

3. Magnum Chrome/Fluorescent Red Herringbone Tadpolly

4. Fluorescent Red Hot Shot

5. Chrome/Fluorescent Red Hot Shot

6. Chrome J-Plug

Plugs

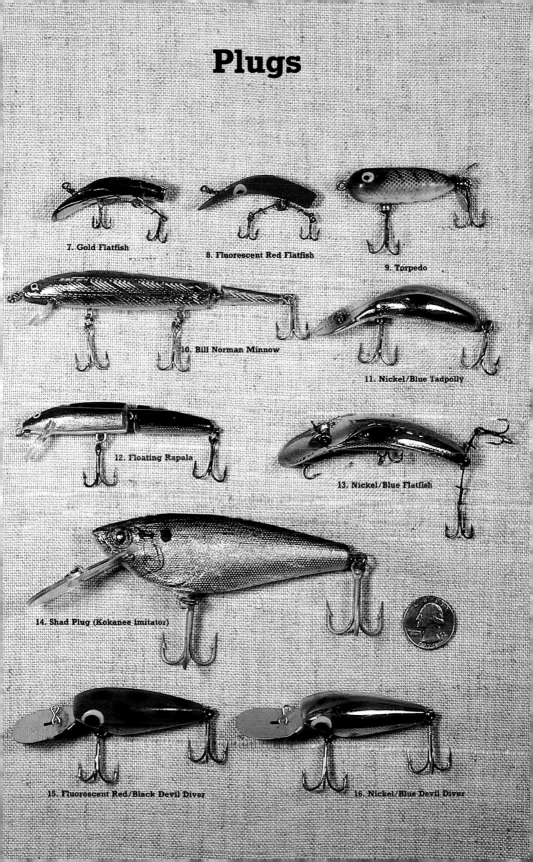

7. Gold Flatfish

8. Fluorescent Red Flatfish

9. Torpedo

10. Bill Norman Minnow

11. Nickel/Blue Tadpolly

12. Floating Rapala

13. Nickel/Blue Flatfish

14. Shad Plug (Kokanee imitator)

15. Fluorescent Red/Black Devil Diver

16. Nickel/Blue Devil Diver

Saltwater Jigs

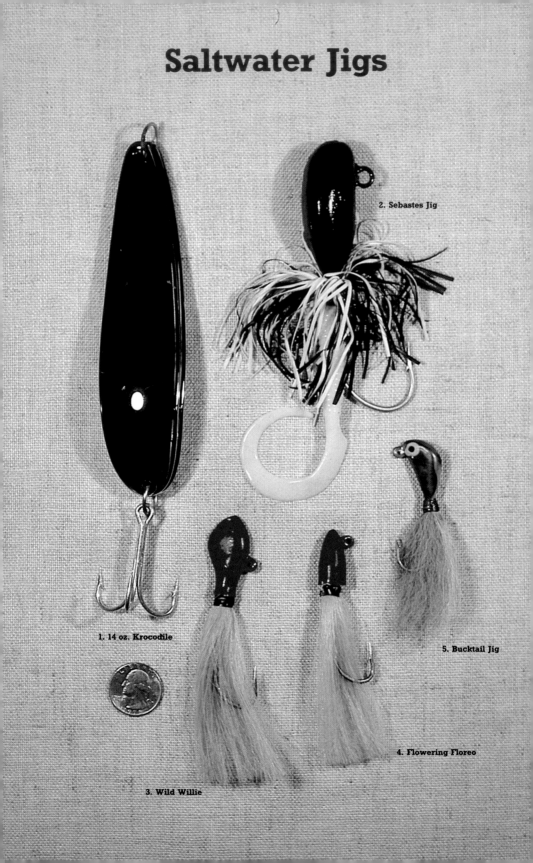

1. 14 oz. Krocodile

2. Sebastes Jig

3. Wild Willie

4. Flowering Floreo

5. Bucktail Jig

Flies

	King Salmon	Silver Salmon	Sockeye Salmon	Pink Salmon	Chum Salmon	Dolly Varden	Arctic Char	Lake Trout	Rainbow Trout	Steelhead Trout	Cutthroat Trout	Grayling	Northern Pike	Whitefish	Sheefish	Halibut	Rockfish
1. Boss		•						•	•		•	•	•				
2. Yellow Stone Fly									•		•	•	•		•		
3. Dark Caddis									•		•	•	•		•		
4. Stone Fly Nymph								•	•	•	•	•	•		•		
5. Comet	•	•	•	•	•	•	•	•	•	•	•	•	•	•	•		
6. Silver Hilton		•	•			•		•	•	•	•	•	•				
7. Yellow Woolly Worm								•	•		•	•	•		•		
8. Black Woolly Worm											•	•	•		•		
9. Two-Egg Marabou	•	•	•	•	•	•	•	•	•	•	•	•	•		•		
10. Steelie Stopper	•	•	•	•	•	•	•	•	•		•	•	•		•		
11. Glo-Bug	•	•	•	•	•	•	•		•	•	•	•	•				
12. Fin-Chilla											•		•	•			
13. Juicy Bug Double Header	•	•	•	•	•	•	•	•		•	•	•	•	•			
14. Thor	•	•	•	•	•	•	•		•	•	•	•	•				
15. Mickey Finn	•	•	•	•	•	•	•	•	•	•	•	•	•	•	•		
16. Umpqua Special	•	•	•	•	•	•	•	•	•	•	•	•	•	•	•		
17. Hot Shot Pink	•	•	•	•	•	•	•	•	•	•	•	•	•	•	•		
18. Skykomish Sunrise	•	•	•	•	•	•	•	•	•	•	•	•	•	•	•		
19. Alaska Mary Ann (variation)	•	•	•	•	•	•	•	•	•	•	•	•	•	•	•		
20. Polar Shrimp	•	•	•	•	•	•	•	•	•	•	•	•	•	•			
21. King Killer (variation)	•	•															
22. Shrimp								•	•	•	•		•		•		•
23. Bucktail Streamer	•	•	•	•		•		•	•	•	•	•	•	•	•		•
24. Spuddler (Sculpin variation)								•	•	•	•		•		•	•	•
25. Black Marabou Muddler										•	•	•		•	•		•
26. Sculpin								•	•	•	•		•		•		•

Dolly Varden

CHAPTER 8

Dolly Varden

Very few anglers are ambivalent about the Dolly Varden. They either love the fish for its numbers and sporty nature, or look upon it with the disdain given a bass caught in a blue-ribbon trout stream. This disdain may be based on having caught the Dolly on heavy-duty salmon gear. Or it may be a carried-over effect from Alaska's pre-territorial days when the Dolly was labeled a "salmon egg glutton." But biological research has vindicated this maligned species, while the Dolly's tail dancing acrobatics and fighting heart has established it as the trout par excellence of the angling realm.

The Dolly Varden trout is not really a trout at all, but a member of the char family. Its scientific genus classification, Salvelinus malma, means "small salmon." Its species name, malma, is a Russian name first used to describe the fish on Kamchatka. The Dolly is also referred to as Western brook trout due to its striking similarities to its cousin, the Eastern brook trout. In Alaska, the fish is known as the Dolly Varden, a name given to it by a group of fish taxonomists on California's McLeod River in 1919. They thought the fish's color pattern resembled a popular dress fabric by that name. Lesser landlocked Dolly populations have been nicknamed "golden trout" or "golden-finned trout" because of their bright, yellow and brown flanks and fins. These Dollies do not grow large. They are native to alpine lakes and streams of Southeast and a few lakes of the Kenai Peninsula and Interior.

As with all char, Alaska Dollies exhibit color patterns that vary considerably according to locale, size, and sexual

Author with a September Dolly Varden. The fish was holding behind a school of sockeye salmon and struck a No. 4 fluorescent red Mepps Aglia tumbled down in the current.

maturity of the fish. Ocean Dollies, or those caught immediately after they enter freshwater, are full-bodied with a silver to bluish-gray dorsal area and silvery sides peppered with pink or pale red spots.

Spawning colors are spectacular. The males turn a vivid emerald green to black on the upper sides, with a bright orange or reddish splash of color on the lower sides and belly. Pectoral, anal and pelvic fins are outlined with white or creamy leading edges followed by a black or red line. Brilliant red or orange spots are randomly distributed along the flanks, and are usually smaller than the pupil of the fish's eye. Sexually mature males also develop an extended lower jaw which hooks upward, fitting into a groove in the upper jaw. Mature females are similarly marked, but are less brightly colored. Also, a female's hooked jaw is not as pronounced.

Range and Habits

The Dolly Varden is the most widely distributed fish species in Alaska. According to biologists, this population is composed of two groups: The southern variety is commonly found in coastal and inland waters south of Bristol Bay, down the Aleutian Chain, and into Southeast Alaska. The northern version, often mistaken as an Arctic char, is common in the waters of the Alaska Peninsula north of Bristol Bay to the Arctic coast. Nearly all streams in both regions contain Dolly Varden throughout at least part of the year, and Dollies can be found in saltwater every month of the year. Throughout the state it is from May through November that they are most abundant and accessible to sport anglers in both fresh and saltwater.

This species can also be divided into anadromous and non-migratory Dolly Varden. Little is known of the habits of the non-migratory types, especially those of Interior Alaska. Populations there are small and of little interest to the trophy Dolly Varden angler. Fishermen who concentrate on anadromous populations of big Dollies experience excellent results. However, this success is greatly dependent upon the angler's knowledge of the fish's life history and migratory habits.

The life history of the Dolly Varden is quite complex. Spawning takes place in freshwater from late August through November, with a breeding ritual similar to that of other chars. The male courts the female by swimming around and alongside her, occasionally pressing against her and quivering. The female then selects a nest site consisting of clean gravel in a moderate current flow and digs a redd with her tail. The male takes no part in the nest-building activities. He spends most of his time fighting and chasing off other males, in addition to courting the female further. When the redd is finished, both fish drop into the shallow depression. While quivering and pressing against each other with arched backs, they simultaneously release milt and anywhere from 700 to 6,000 eggs. The act lasts several seconds, and may be repeated several times before the female begins to cover the fertilized eggs with gravel. Unlike the Pacific salmon, Dollies survive after spawning. The female's swollen and extended ovipositor soon retracts after spawning, while the male's pronounced kype returns to normal sometime in November.

Development and hatching takes anywhere from 4 to 7 months, depending upon location. Young fry are somewhat lethargic in their feeding habits, possibly influencing their slow growth rate at this time. However, 2 to 4 months after hatching, the fish begin to feed actively, their growth varying significantly from area to area and population to population. The young Dollies spend from 3 to 4 years in freshwater before outmigrating to sea. During this migration, which usually occurs in May or June, the smolts are generally 5 inches long. Some populations outmigrate as late as September and October.

After their first seaward migration, Dolly Varden that were hatched and reared in a lake system establish an annual migration to a freshwater lake to overwinter. However, Dollies originating from non-lake watersheds must seek out a system with a lake in which to overwinter. Research indicates that these fish search out various streams and creeks until they find one with a suitable lake. Both types usually conduct annual seaward migrations in the spring.

Somewhere between the ages of 4 to 9 years, Dollies reach sexual maturity and return to spawn in their natal stream. Fish on their first spawning migration will range from 12 to 16 inches and weigh up to a pound. A "chemical memory" of their birthplace allows the fish to "home in" on their natal stream while at sea. This memory also prevents them from repeating the random scouting done in their original search for a wintering lake.

Dolly Varden experience a high mortality. Males suffer the most casualties, due to the fighting and subsequent damage inflicted upon each other during spawning. Once at Ptarmigan Creek, I saw two fish splash themselves out onto the bank, one with a bulldog grip on the other's tail. They stayed like that until I gently toed each back into the creek. After viewing such behavior, it's not hard to believe research figures that say less than 50 percent of the Dolly Varden population live to spawn a second time, while a small number do live to spawn more than twice. The Dollies of Southeast Alaska have been known to reach 10 to 12 years of age, although most fish average 5 years or less. Studies also indicate that mortality is less severe in Arctic waters, where the majority of the spawners range from 8 to 9 years old.

Most Dollies vary from 1 to 3 pounds, with fish of 6 to 20 pounds reported caught from the larger watersheds such as the Kenai River, Bristol Bay, Alaska Peninsula and Southeastern waters. Any Dolly over 10 pounds is technically considered a trophy, and 20-pounders are exceedingly rare. I personally classify any Dolly over 6 pounds a trophy, and I wouldn't be ashamed of keeping such a fish for the wall.

The Dolly Varden closely resembles the Arctic char. Some biologists consider Dolly Varden a subspecies of the Arctic char, while others consider each a distinct species. For all practical purposes, the physical characteristics of both fish are so similar that even trained fishery biologists often have difficulty identifying variations of either species.

In most Alaska watersheds, Dollies can be distinguished from Arctic char by counting gill rakers on the first left gill arch. Arctic char have 23 to 32; Northern Dollies 21 to 23, and Southern Dollies 17 to 19. Also char have more pyloric caeca (35 to 75) than the Dolly, whose caeca count ranges from 13 to 35, and only rarely as high as 39. However, it's not uncommon to find either fish with both more or less of these counts. Other identifying features are the spots on the flank of the fish. A Dolly's are usually smaller than the pupil of its eye, while on the Arctic char, they are larger than the pupil.

Because it is so difficult to identify the two species, the State of Alaska has made the Dolly Varden/Arctic char one classification for trophy award certification. The cur-

Adela Batin with a Kenai River Dolly. Big Dollies are almost entirely piscivorous, but will also feed on salmon eggs and invertebrate species when available.

rent Alaska state record for this species is a 17-pound, 8-ounce char taken in 1968 by the late Peter Winslow. However, the International Game Fish Association considers the Dolly and Arctic char to be separate species. So fish must be properly identified before they can be considered for world record purposes.

History

However, early commercial salmon fishermen could have cared less about distinguishing between the two species. To them, the Dolly was without question a "trash fish" and "eater of salmon eggs." According to their way of thinking, Dolly Varden often returned in numbers rivaling certain salmon runs. Furthermore, the Dolly followed the schools of salmon upriver to the spawning grounds. So it's easy to see why commercial fishermen erroneously assumed that the Dolly was perpetuating (along with gorging) itself at the expense of the salmon and supposedly jeopardizing the commercial fishing industry.

As the result of heavy lobbying in 1921 by Alaska Commercial Fisheries members, the United States Bureau of Fisheries initiated a predator control program to eradicate the Dolly Varden. The Alaska Territorial Legislature established a bounty on the Dolly, requiring that tails from the fish be cut off, salted, and strung 40 to a makeshift wire ring. "Bounty anglers" were paid 2½ cents per tail and these rings were often legal tender in many trading posts throughout Alaska. It wasn't uncommon to see Gold Rush card players use the tails as "chips" in their poker games.

Estimates indicate that over 6 million of these sportfish were harvested for bounty before the legislature abolished the system in 1940 when it was discovered that the tails of young salmon, steelhead, cutthroat and rainbow trout were also being harvested. Bob Armstrong, Alaska Department of Fish and Game fisheries biologist and world renowned expert on the Dolly Varden, revealed that in one instance, out of 20,000 tails collected for Dolly bounty, 3,760 were rainbow trout, 14,200 were coho salmon and only 2,040 were Dolly Varden!

Armstrong has also conducted studies on the food habits of Dolly Varden. Evidence strongly indicates that Dollies don't consume any more eggs or salmon fry than cutthroats or rainbow trout. In fact, many of the eggs that

How to Catch
Alaska's Trophy Sportfish

are consumed are those that have washed out of the redd and wouldn't have hatched anyway. And Armstrong's analysis of thousands of Dolly stomachs has shown a very small percentage of salmon fry or smolts. However, once Dollies enter saltwater and fatten up a bit in the spring, there's not a marine baitfish, crustacean, or lure that's safe. In fact, my first experience with big Dollies proved to be a valuable lesson in angling the spring feed.

Techniques

Saltwater

It was early June and friend Steve Harrison, his wife Jackie, and I were just informed that our rockfish charter was cancelled. Rough seas had closed the entrance to Resurrection Bay out of Seward. However, along with returning our deposit, the skipper gave us some advice. He had heard that several people had been catching a few Dollies about a mile past Lowell Point. The tide would be coming in within the hour, and the Point was a short drive and walk from a gravel road that led out of town. We purchased a few recommended spoons and spinners, and figuring we had nothing to lose, headed out for the hotspot with a zest temporarily dampened by the charter cancellation.

An hour later, we were walking down the sandy beach to the windswept point. Rolling, gray-blue swells had replaced the ragged-tipped whitecaps. Sea gulls lined the water's edge, squawking angrily when a large swell doused them unexpectedly. Not a soul was in sight, despite the sun that was beginning to peek through the clouds and brighten up what was pegged to be a dark day. Steve walked down the beach, casting from shore while I waded out to thigh level, preferring to cast horizontally to shore.

Steve had the first strike. I saw a flash of silver rocket out of the waves, flip across three swells and re-enter with a splash that made me wince. The fish continued a surging run beneath the waves for 20 yards before the line went slack. Steve yelled something indistinguishable, shook his head, and quickly reeled the lure in for another cast. My eyes widened as I watched the following scenario take place. His lure skittered across two waves. When it hit the third, the rounded peak of the swell exploded into a flurry

Surf fishing for Dolly Varden is best done on an incoming tide. Look for concentrations of fish near stream or river mouths, points, gravel bars, and sandy spits.

of spray. Steve's rod bucked sporadically as the fish zipped through the waves, its grayish dorsal frequently breaking the surface. Just as I was about to walk down to the action, I noticed a flash. Then another. Then the entire area was glittering like a tinseled Christmas tree.

I fired my lure past what I had guessed to be a large school of sand lances and right into the mouth of a hungry Dolly Varden. The fish was strong, unusually strong, and for the next five minutes gave my 4-pound-test line and ultralight rod a healthy workout. The Dolly rolled, twisted and careened through the silvery needlefish, an action that sent them skittering through the waves and on to safer pastures. It wasn't until 10 minutes later that I managed to work this powerhouse of a fish into the landing net. It was a beautiful 5-pound male, with an orange-tipped kype and pink dots decorating its meaty, silvery flanks. I opened my hand and the fish finned quickly back into the waves.

It was then we realized Jackie wasn't getting any strikes. Upon checking her lure, we quickly pieced together the

How to Catch
Alaska's Trophy Sportfish

puzzle. She was using a gold and bronze spinner, while Steve and I were both using narrow chrome spoons. She was fishing a steady retrieve while Steve and I were buzzing the lures under the surface.

While Jackie and Steve looked through their tackle box for a chrome spoon, I went searching for the sand lances. I found a few of them buried in the soft sand, a sure indication that Dollies were cruising offshore in deeper water. I motioned Jackie to come down and fish the area. It wasn't long before she was struggling to keep her rod tip up against the powerful surges of a saltwater Dolly.

The action remained hot until two hours after high tide. Our three largest tipped the scale at 6, 5, and 3 3/4 pounds, with numerous fish that pegged the needle between 1 and 3 pounds. I've had similar experiences with Dollies in waters from Southeastern to Bristol Bay, and have concluded that saltwater angling for Dollies during late May, June and early July not only offers large, sassy fish, but also provides action seldom matched by other salmonids. And all that's required to cash in on this excitement is to know the type of structure that attracts these fish, and how and when to fish for them.

Since that initial spring outing, casting spoons while wading the shoreline in late spring is one of my favorite ways to fish for large Dollies. But there's more to it than just making a few casts off the neighborhood beach.

Large Dollies and structure are synonomous. My records indicate that I've had best success for Dollies over 4 pounds at the mouths of freshwater inlets (especially those with gravel or sandbars near their mouths), the tip of spits and jetties, old pilings and boat docks (especially those near fish and crab processing plants), saltchucks, and gravel or sandy beaches with steep dropoffs within casting distance from shore. However, gravel shoals near the mouth of freshwater streams or creeks account for most of my fish. These areas produce not only in the late spring, but also in the early fall when Dollies, fat from a summer of feeding, migrate back to their freshwater wintering homes.

Another important factor is tide. While it is possible to catch Dollies at any time in saltwater, the larger fish tend to cruise shoreline structure immediately after low tide to feed on sand lances, needlefish and small crustaceans. This feeding frenzy picks up momentum approximately two hours before high tide, and continues until both baitfish and predator move back out with the tide.

Stealth is extremely important when fishing this feeding frenzy. Dollies will be in water depths ranging from 1 to 5 feet and will spook at any quick movement or unnatural noise, such as dragging your feet through the gravel or slipping on a seaweed-covered rock. I prefer chest waders at this time: They allow me to concentrate on the fish and my movements rather than worrying if the next swell will be higher than my hip-boot tops. Waders also allow coverage of a broader range of areas, and keep you in business if you slip on a washed-up jellyfish.

When Dollies are cruising islands or distant points inaccessible by foot, I experience good fishing by boating out to a hotspot and quietly poling along any dropoffs. My graph recorder has indicated that Dollies will often hold in these areas at low tide, waiting for an incoming supply of baitfish on the high tide. I like to anchor the boat and fish as much structure as possible. Two of my favorite methods of fishing at this time are to jig bright spoons along the dropoff breakline or to bounce a sinking plug from shallow to deep.

When high tide inundates the shallows, a pair of polarized sunglasses cuts surface glare and enables you to see the Dollies finning offshore and darting after baitfish. Always investigate any large gray "rocks" that you might find at the bottom of a depression or in intertidal channels. More often than not, these "rocks" will be a school of Dollies resting in the current. Such fish are easy to catch *if* you're quiet and avoid unnecessary movements.

I've found presentation makes a big difference in the number of trophy Dollies I put in the creel. The way not to fish for Dollies is best exemplified by the crowds and tourists fishing off the Homer Spit in July and August. They walk down to the beach, cast straight out, and retrieve their lures faster than a sea gull can swallow a skein of fish eggs. Granted, you can catch some fish this way. However, fishing your lure to best imitate the behavior of the sand lance will almost always result in more and larger fish. Sand lance schools swim parallel to shoreline, darting and flashing sunlight off their silvery sides—a perfect temptation to hungry Dollies that also cruise parallel to shore, following the baitfish. This feeding corridor may be several feet to 25 or more yards wide.

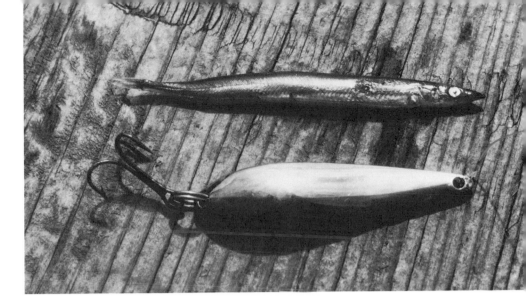

Thus the longer you keep your lure in this corridor, the better. The best way to accomplish this is to wade out into the corridor and cast parallel to shore. If water depth or tides prevent this, fish the lure at an angle no greater than 45 degrees to shore. Retrieve it diagonally into the current. On many occasions, I've watched Dollies attack with reckless abandon a lure fished in this manner. It is effective year 'round.

Sand lance or needlefish, a favorite saltwater Dolly food, are best imitated by long, narrow lures like this Fjord spoon. For best results, work this type of lure slowly through shoreline structure on an incoming tide.

My top three lures for saltwater Dollies are spoons, spinners, and flies. After 10 years of testing various patterns and techniques, I consider them most effective in Alaska waters.

• **Spoons:** Long, narrow spoons in a blue/chrome pattern outfish the wide, stocky variety by a 3 to 1 margin. My favorites are a variety of 1/8- to 1/2-ounce Fjord, Krocodile, Swedish Pimple or similar spoons. These lures are the closest imitations to needlefish and sand lance on the market, and big Dollies strike them savagely. A white feathered dressing seems to increase the effectiveness of the smaller lures.

I like to cast the lure out, allow it to sink to the bottom, and after several seconds, jump it with a twitch of my rod tip. I'll continue to keep the lure wobbling over bottom and into the tidal flow, while occasionally twitching it ever so slightly. At mid-retrieve I speed up the lure, working it through mid depth. About 10 feet out, I'll raise the rod tip while continuing to reel slowly. This forces the lure to the surface and usually triggers a Dolly that hasn't struck by

Dolly Varden

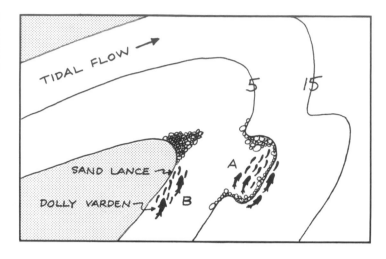

now into doing so with a solid punch. Of course, variations of the above technique are often necessary with changes in weather and locale. I've encountered Southeastern Dollies that have ignored all lures and techniques, except for a 1/32-ounce spoon fished so slowly a passerby swore I was bait fishing on the bottom. But overall, when using spoons, a slow, steady retrieve with a constant break in the rhythmic wobbling action has been my best producer of large fish.

• **Spinners** are most effective when spoons fail to work properly in slow tidal currents or at slack tide. Here again, it's the narrow-bodied spinners with oblong or willow leaf blades that seem to be the most successful. Size 3 to 5 Rooster Tails, ABU Reflexes and similar spinners in chartreuse, red, white, yellow/black, and silver induce the most strikes. The undulations—in the current, at the slowest retrieves—account for the extra productivity of the feathered treble. Silver blades outfish gold blades, except in early morning and late evening, when color doesn't seem to make much difference.

The key word to remember when fishing spinners for saltwater Dollies is slow! The slower the better. As long as the spinner blade is rotating at a steady clip and the lure is fished within 2 to 6 inches above bottom, you'll hook Dollies. But the strike can come more as a mouthing or grabbing of the lure than with the viciousness often experienced when fishing spoons. No matter what lure you use, hooks should always be needle sharp.

Fly fishing for saltwater Dollies can offer some of the most exciting angling experiences you'll ever encounter. Here are a few tips to get you started.

• **Flies** should be No. 4 to 6 streamers and bucktails tied with plenty of mylar and natural baitfish colors of blue, green, and purple. Herring patterns, salmon smolt imitations, marabou muddlers, and sculpin imitations also produce here. More important than size is color, so stock a variety of patterns.

A rod capable of handling a 7-weight line offers the most fun. However, when the wind is blowing, and that is 75 percent of the time in Alaska's coastal areas, you may need a No. 8 or 9 line to do the same job. I prefer a saltwater taper as it allows me to make a fast presentation to a feeding Dolly at short to moderate distances. And I like 12-pound-test leaders no longer than 36 inches with this type of line.

Once you have a structure or fish target, cast the fly line several feet beyond and to the side of it. You will spook fish if you cast directly over them. Work the fly back in as natural a manner as possible, with an occasional twitch or pause to allow it to drift freely with the tide. Use unweighted flies on the flats and weighted versions near dropoffs. And if fish are being stubborn, add a touch of herring oil to the fly, and watch your luck change.

Freshwater

While saltwater fishing offers an excellent opportunity to catch a trophy Dolly, more of them are incidentally caught by freshwater salmon anglers. Dollies are aggressive feeders in freshwater, and will often strike edible and non-edible objects that resemble baitfish and drifting salmon eggs.

Palmisano's study of the freshwater food habits of Dolly Varden on Amchitka Island, Alaska revealed some interesting facts. Out of 3,672 Dolly stomachs examined, 3,100 had food in them. Aquatic insects were the predominant food item of stream fish, while terrestrials and crustaceans were most common in the diet of lake fish. Landlocked Dollies fed primarily on aquatic insects, fish, and fish eggs. In lakes with access to the sea, the major food items in waters with firm bottom adjacent to shore were first, crustaceans, followed by aquatic insects. Crustaceans were the dominant food item in those waters with a muck bottom adjacent to shore. However, as Dolly size in-

Spoons are excellent lures to use for freshwater Dolly Varden. Chartreuse/red dot patterns are highly visible in glacial or murky waters. Bronze spoons imitate sculpins, and work best in rocky, clearwater streams and rivers.

creased, feeding activity decreased, and aquatic insects became less important while crustaceans, fish, and fish eggs became more abundant. Fish over 17 inches fed almost exclusively on fish and salmon eggs. Lures that best imitate these two items are preferred by trophy Dolly anglers.

Anglers wishing to catch a trophy Dolly in freshwater should plan on fishing creeks, rivers, and streams from mid-summer until ice-up. There are several reasons for this. Angling for wintering Dollies is fun, but generally doesn't produce large fish. Armstrong speculates that little if any feeding occurs in mid-winter, and the spring out-migrants are snakelike from having used up their body fats and nutrients. It also takes a while for the Dollies to start feeding actively, as research figures from one study show: May, with 59 percent, had the lowest percentage of feeding fish, while September had the highest at 94 percent. And since Dollies can spend anywhere from 52 to 116 days at sea, the huskiest fish usually start returning with the latter salmon runs in August through October.

It is indeed possible to fish for non-migratory Dollies and still come out with a trophy fish. These fish feed year 'round in the deepest rivers, and are about as easy to catch as a mossbacked, pot-bellied river rainbow. Dollies are particular about type of lure, size, appearance, and most of all,

How to Catch
Alaska's Trophy Sportfish

presentation. In fact, studies indicate that the percentage of Dolly Varden with empty stomachs increased with fish size.

With this in mind, large non-migratory fish can best be caught by imitating the chief forage fish species common to the watershed. In Alaska, this is usually the sculpin or stickleback. Sculpin usually exhibit a bronze, copper or gold coloration, while sticklebacks are black with silvery flanks. I favor 2- to 4-inch hammered bronze and copper Dardevles in mid-river holes, pockets, and undercut banks, and 1½- to 3-inch silver or chrome spoons at inlets and outlets. Both types should be fished slowly through holes and down channels, and close to gravel bars, especially right before or after a sockeye smolt or hooligan migration. I've found that fishing for Dollies during these migrations is often futile during late evening and early morning hours when the smolts are actively moving downstream. However, fishing activity does pick up during the daytime after the Dollies have had a chance to digest their evening meal.

Summer and fall fishing for either anadromous or non-migratory Dollies is a different scene. Fish are often available in such large numbers that they literally blacken the bottom of a stream. Salmon anglers get burned-out setting the hook into rambunctious Dollies attempting to devour Tadpollies half their size. And fishing for pot-bellied trophies couldn't be better.

Dollies are usually concentrated in certain areas. On smaller streams and creeks, look for them at the confluence of a clearwater stream emptying into a silty or glacial river. Upstream pools—especially those beneath fallen logs near shore, and at the head and tail of riffles—also attract large Dollies. Favorite lures are fluorescent bladed Mepps Aglia in sizes 1 through 3; small to medium Dardevles; Fjord spoons; Spin-N-Glos in sizes 4, 6, and 8; Lil Corkies in sizes 10, 12, and 14, and Aqua Cones and Fenton Flies in all sizes. Best colors have proven to be flame, red, orange, peach, clown (in murky water), pink, and on occasions metallic blue and gold.

In murky or glacially silted water, it's hard to beat a size 6 chartreuse Spin-N-Glo and a standard drift-rig combination. I learned the effectiveness of this rig at the outlet of Lower Trail Lake several years back with Mike Ticonni. It was late August, and the sockeyes were already in the neighborhood lakes preparing to spawn. We were just returning from a successful sockeye venture on the Russian River (we took a total of 10 minutes to catch our 3-fish-each limit) when Mike, still desiring a fishing experience away from the crowds, insisted on wetting a line in untried waters. Lower Trail Lake Outlet was the closest choice.

Mike rigged up with a small spoon and I tied on a size 6 Spin-N-Glo with a pencil lead drift rig. Ten minutes later, we understood why we had never observed many people fishing this stretch. The bottom was a mass of boulders and strong currents which gobbled up our offerings. After I lost my initial rig, I tied on a chartreuse drift lure, while Mike chose a fluorescent Glo. Losing spoons on the rocky bottom was costing him too much folding money.

I waited patiently as the lure drifted down the chute and swirled through the currents behind a rock. However, my patience soon turned into frustration as my lure hung on bottom. As I walked upstream to get a better angle to work my lure free, my rod tip throbbed with that familiar sensation of a "head shaker"—a mannerism exhibited by large fish when they realize something's not quite right.

I buried the steel and hung on as the enraged fish cut across the heavy current and down to the next boulder some 50 yards away. The fish continued to hug the bottom, a trait typical of a large king or sockeye. I prayed for deliverance from this fate, especially in the fast current. The Fish Gods must have been listening. The fish rocketed off again downstream and came to rest in a pool no larger than a desktop. I busted through alders and willows trying to keep up, and as I cleared the bend, I was pleased to see Mike into a fish that was giving his rod a spinal hernia. Then, like something glimpsed in a fog, a silvery slab with red dots materialized on the sun-splattered water. While the markings identified it as a Dolly, I couldn't believe the 25-inch spread between head and tail! The fish disap-

peared as quickly as it had appeared, along with my lure. The rocky bottom had done an excellent job of abrading my line. The first two feet of line felt like coarse sandpaper. I fell back, and in my mind's eye replayed the image of the fish before Mike's yelling broke the trance.

I looked up in time to see him hoist a nice 4-pound Dolly out of the water. After he dispatched the fish, he whooped and hollered his way back upstream. He had every right to be proud. His fish was a burnished gray with light red dots

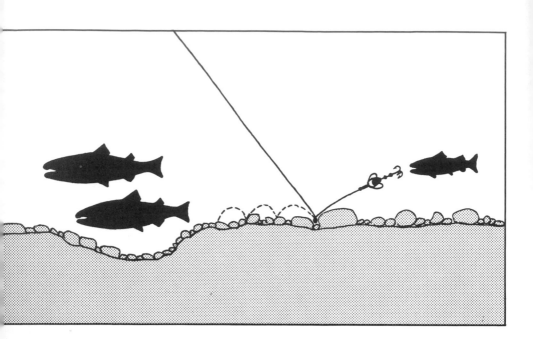

A very effective way to take large Dollies is to bottom bounce a Spin-N-Glo behind spawning salmon. In deep holes, fish the lure stationary for best results.

and a yellow-tipped kype. A beautiful trophy. We packed the Dolly in ice and beelined it to the city of Seward, purchased more Spin-N-Glos, and made it back in time to catch and release 3 more fish totaling 12 pounds. Since, I've learned that glacial or large rivers are excellent choices for trophy Dollies and catching them is easy if you:

1. Keep the lure on bottom. Bottom bouncing is good along the boulder-free stretches, but many trophy Dollies prefer mid-river sanctuaries. Drop your lure into pools, behind large rocks, at the tail of islands and gravel bars—and keep it there!

2. Use enough lead to keep your lure in one spot. It's not uncommon for me to use 3 ounces in fast sections of river.

3. Use a slip-sinker rig. I've found this to be far more effective in sensing strikes than the standard pencil lead or rubbercore sinkers, especially when several ounces of lead are required. I prefer the snagless variety found in most sporting good stores.

4. Use Spin-N-Glos. This lure has an action that seems to outfish any other lure in glacial waters. While the fluorescent colors work best, to find an effective combination it may be necessary to experiment with colors under various light conditions. Also, a small piece of salmon egg skein attached to the hook often adds a "smell factor" which helps big Dollies home in on the lure in milky water.

When fishing from a boat on a large river such as the Kenai or Mulchatna, large spoons, spinners, and drift lures may not stay in the strike zone. Here, knowledgeable anglers tie on a floating/diving plug such as a Tadpolly, Hot Shot, or Flatfish. Keep these points in mind when choosing the right plug:

1. Lure size is critical for big Dollies. Their voracious appetites will trigger them to strike lures half their size, yet many of the large Dollies will smash lures and immediately let go because the lure is too large. You'll hook more fish by using the smaller 2- to 3-inch plugs rather than the larger 4-inchers commonly used for both Dollies and salmon.

2. Metallic finishes in silver, blue, and gold work extremely well, with the metallic/solid color finishes equally effective. Try chartreuse/silver, fluorescent red/silver, and a fluorescent red with black side markings. In the spring, the smaller gold and silver plugs seem to outperform the larger combination types.

However, there is a time when it is necessary to fish large plugs for Dollies. Some watersheds in late September and early October will see thousands of Dollies move into freshwater streams and rivers. Most of these fish will be in the 12- to 14-inch range, and will strike anything they can get into their mouths. There are plenty of old timers in the group, but the younger, more agile Dollies often beat them to the lure. You can reduce the number of small fish hookups by switching to larger, single-hook lures, and casting to various sections of stream. However, at times the action is so spectacular for both large and small fish that you'll take whatever comes along, which can also include coho salmon and steelhead. So be prepared!

If you can locate a school of spawning salmon, you can almost bet that several or more Dollies will be nearby, usually hiding in the deepest part of a pool, under root tangles, or at the head of the next riffle downstream. Dollies lurk in such areas for several reasons. The salmon are very territorial and dislike other fish near their redds. It's not uncommon to catch a Dolly with its sides raked by the sharp teeth of a sockeye or chum. So the Dollies remain out of the way, but not too far. They want to be on hand to snap up any salmon eggs floating free from the redd. And they often do with reckless abandon. I've caught Dollies that have regurgitated a handful of eggs when I merely touched their sides. However, both large and small Dollies may strike nothing but salmon eggs at spawning time.

Flies seem to produce the largest fish under these conditions, and Two-Egg Marabou, Skykomish Sunrise, Thor, Polar Shrimp, Glo-Bug, and yarn-fly patterns are the most effective. Fish them on a dead drift directly above bottom structure.

Small Aqua Cones and soft, plastic salmon egg imitations threaded on a single egg hook will also dupe a gorged-to-the-gills Dolly into inhaling your lure.

Equipment

Most any rod used for small- to medium-sized trout will work well for Dollies. In saltwater, I prefer ultralight tackle and 6-pound-test, low-visibility line. It should be abrasion resistant, as barnacles and rocks can cut through light line like a razor blade. In areas with seaweed or a very rocky bottom, I'll switch to a 12-pound spool of line on a light-action spinning or casting rod. In freshwater, I use a medium-action rod only if I intend to use plugs. I need the extra backbone in this type of rod to effectively sink the hooks into big Dollies that are holding in heavy currents.

Any spinning reel with a smooth drag and a large spool capacity will suffice. When fishing drift lures, I prefer a level-wind reel and casting rod. I always carry extra spools of line for changing conditions.

When wading for Dollies, take along a small landing net in order to release carefully the fish you'll catch in the surf. Even a played-out Dolly can be a squirmy customer. And for those you don't release, a small burlap bag that keeps the fish moist and cool will aid in preserving the delicate flavor the Dolly is noted for. Here is one more tip. Immediately after dispatching a trophy Dolly you intend to have mounted, take several color photos of it. A Dolly quickly loses its colors, which are often too vibrant to describe to a fish taxidermist, especially if the fish's colorations are unusual.

Fishing for Dollies means year 'round sport for most anglers. But with a bag limit of 10 per day in most areas, as sportsmen we should learn a lesson from our ancestors and treat the Dolly as a limited resource, despite its seemingly

endless numbers. Catch and release is definitely not too high a price to pay for a species that has suffered greatly from man's ignorance and greed. Now that the Dolly is holding its own, I hope it will continue to prosper. And with the growing interest given to it by anglers, I have no doubt it will attain the respect and recognition it truly deserves as a premier trophy sportfish.

Dollies are noted for their aggressive aerial acrobatics, especially when hooked on light tackle. Therefore, always use single-hook lures to minimize injury to released fish.

Where to go for Dolly Varden

Since Dolly Varden and Arctic char are two closely related species, the where to go for these fish is found at the end of the Arctic char chapter.

Arctic Char

CHAPTER 9

Arctic Char

A rugged expanse of snow-capped mountain peaks, sculpted by the icy blasts of storms and glaciers, stretches far out of sight in the brisk Arctic air. Blue ribbons of virgin rivers and streams nourish hundreds of lush green valleys that have yet to know the footprints of man. Myriad wildflowers, most no more than several inches high, emblazon the rolling tundra with a spectrum of color, while their fragrance sedates the angler into the low-keyed pace necessary to fully appreciate this region. This land is the exception to the phrase, "Beauty is only skin deep." For beneath the sapphire-blue surface of gurgling pools and glacially carved lakes is beauty in the form of emerald greens, garnet reds, golden yellows, and brilliant oranges. Indeed, no amount of treasure in the Far North can match the beauty of an Arctic char.

Arctic char fishing invigorates the soul like no other. The combination of a pristine wilderness environment this fish requires for survival and the incredible beauty of the char itself, along with its equally impressive fighting ability, makes memories of a trophy angling experience that will last for a lifetime.

The Arctic char, (Salvelinus alpinus) is also known as blueback char or blueback trout. Char itself means beautiful, elegant, or graceful, a most appropriate word for describing this species. Like its cousin the Dolly Varden, a char's coloration varies greatly depending upon sexual maturity, time of year, and locale.

In areas where both char and Dollies are found, coloration is not a dependable identification aid. Fish returning

An angler battling a sleek Arctic char in "No Man's Land" south of Katmai National Monument on the Alaska Peninsula. In addition to producing big char, the area is also prime brown bear habitat.

185
Arctic Char

from the sea or lake fish are often silvery with faint spots, while body size, shape and color varies considerably among spawners in both species. In other words, Dollies and char in the same watershed can look either identically the same, or totally different. One thing is for certain. Many variations exist throughout the state, and in the look-alike cases, only a trained fisheries biologist can distinguish between the two species.

Generally speaking, however, the dorsal area of the char ranges from emerald green to almost black. Its sides can range from silver to a sapphire blue, with faint pink to ruby-red dots. The largest spots along the lateral line are usually larger than the pupil of the eye. The size of these dots help serve as an identification aid in distinguishing the char from the Dolly Varden, whose spots are often smaller than the pupil of its eye. The char's ventral sides, along with the pectoral, anal, and pelvic fins, turn a brilliant orange-red in mature male spawners, and are off-set by a white to creamy leading edge.

The Arctic char is the most northerly of all salmonids, and is circumpolar in distribution. In Alaska, the species can be found from the Aleutian Islands north into Bristol Bay, and up around the coast into Canadian waters. Isolated populations can also be found in the cold, deeper lakes of the Interior and Kenai Peninsula.

Both anadromous and resident races of char exist. The largest are the non-anadromous char of Bristol Bay, where individual fish commonly exceed 10 pounds. Yet, according to biological reports, a 20-inch, 3-pound char taken from lower Alaska Peninsula and the Aleutians would be considered a large fish.

Biologists are still uncertain as to whether true Arctic char are either anadromous or strictly a freshwater species. According to research on the char in Alaska (Morrow, unpublished) all Arctic char in the state are technically freshwater lake and river dwellers. While the species has been reported as being anadromous from Bristol Bay to Barter Island, numerous reports and research investigations have indicated these fish to be the northern form of the Dolly Varden. Some biologists will argue that Alaska char are definitely anadromous, as there are anadromous char populations in Canada, Europe, and Siberia. Yet again, opinion varies greatly as to the extent of this saltwater lifestyle: Some say char stay in the freshwater

A pot-bellied char taken near an underground spring. Nickel or bronze spinners and spoons are excellent choices for stream char. Tumble them slowly downstream along the inside breakline of fast water.

How to Catch
Alaska's Trophy Sportfish

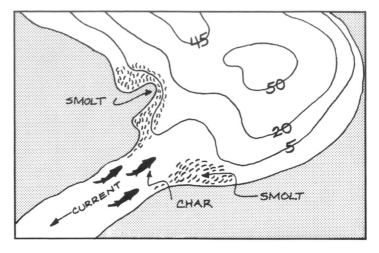

In spring, char gorge on migrating salmon smolts at the outlets of lakes. Early morning and late evening hours are best for large char, as smolt migrations are highest during these times.

regions of intertidal areas and never fully enter a saline environment, while others believe char travel great distances along shoreline routes. Until more research is done on Alaska char, this subject will definitely remain a gray area in fisheries biology.

The anadromous issue aside, Arctic char in Alaska do migrate between freshwater lakes and interconnecting rivers for feeding and spawning purposes. In Brooks Range watersheds, spawning takes place from late August to early September, and September through November in·Bristol Bay and Alaska Peninsula waters. Gravel shoals in lakes or quiet pools at the outlets of lakes are typical spawning locations in both regions.

Spawning habits are similar to that of the Dolly Varden. The male becomes very territorial, guarding its established area and fighting with other males to maintain territorial hierarchy. However, as soon as an egg-swollen female exhibits spawning behavior, she will invade the male's territory, oftentimes being attacked by him. However, the female persists and the male quickly loses interest in territory and devotes his attention to the spawning ritual. The female will scout the area, with head and tail bent downwards and eyes scrutinizing bottom cover until she finds a suitable spot. She begins digging a redd in typical salmonid fashion. The male continues courting by swimming around the female and quivering at her side. The female will test the depth of the redd with her erect anal fin, and if suitable, she will eject her eggs into the nest, which are immediately fertilized by the male. The redd is filled in. The female may repeat the procedure, which may take up to several days, until she has exhausted all her eggs. Males often mate with more than one female, while larger females may mate with two or more males.

Eggs develop during the winter and hatch sometime during the spring. Exact incubation times are unknown for Alaska waters, yet obviously vary from region to region. Fry grow quite slowly in freshwater lakes and streams, generally feeding on whatever is available. A 17-inch char caught from waters in the Brooks Range can be as much as 10 years old.

Techniques

Char move seasonally from the lakes to rivers and back, wintering in the lakes. In the spring, during salmon smolt outmigrations, anglers will find char concentrated near the mouth of rivers, especially in the Bristol Bay region. A trip to the Wood River drainage late one spring for trophy char was an eye opener for me in terms of fishing action and the feeding habits of these fish.

The smolt migration was just about over. Friend Michael Johnson and I had set up camp in an alder-protected embankment that overlooked several streams emptying into Nushagak River. Except for the occasional squawk of fighting seagulls over a salmon smolt, the scene couldn't have been more peaceful. Peace ended after I made the first cast.

The ¼-ounce chrome Krocodile wobbled twice in the current before my rod tip snapped down and flexed the spine of the medium-action rod into a darn healthy U. The line quickly cut across the main current for 50 yards before the fish exited the water near the far bank in a series of tail dances that left me stunned. My reel screeched in protest as the char rocketed downstream, forcing me to sprint after it. Before I caught up with it, I was treated to two more head-over-tail cartwheels. I was sure the fish was going to break loose when, without warning, it beached itself. I quickly ran over to the fish and touched it, proving to my overworked lungs and tired legs that this 8-pound fish was responsible for a workout that a coho salmon twice the size would be hard pressed to duplicate. Releas-

Schools of char can often be pinpointed by watching bird activity, such as gulls feeding on smolts.

ing the fish, I walked back upstream, where I almost collided with Mike. He was half-running, half-falling down the rocky bank, trying to put the reins to a char with similar spunk.

For the next two days, we experienced char fishing that was virtually a fish a cast. Twenty hours of daylight had us fishing until our arms couldn't take anymore, at which time we'd take a break, grab a bite to eat, and head back out to the mouth for more action. Fishing was best from 50 yards up any of the streams to about 100 yards downriver. Casts elsewhere seldom produced the quantity or quality of fish. On numerous occasions, the char would spit out several silvery salmon fry, proving the effectiveness of our chrome spoons. A slow retrieve was all that was necessary. In fact, we experimented with other colors when we wanted a break in the action. But fish over 6 pounds were almost always taken on a silver spoon, with bronze a close runner-up.

Char fishing hotspots can vary from year to year. When examining char habitat, it's important to remember that

190

natural phenomena such as high or low water and stream channelization may extend or decrease the char's range from year to year. In times of low water, it's possible to find entire populations in the deepest part of a lake, especially after spring turnover. When confronted with these conditions, it's a waste of time to use anything but ultralight gear, with 4- to 6-pound, clear monofilament.

Lure choice is critical at this time. Deepwater jigging with flutter spoons at the edges of thermoclines, over gravel bottom, and at freshwater inlets have produced lake char for me when all else has failed. I especially favor Red Eye spoons, size 2 and 3 Mepps spoons, and Worden's Sculpins dressed with prism tape. To be most effective, these lures must be used on relatively windless days or at anchor to allow maximum utilization of an "up and down" fluttering effect. Remember, the slower and more enticingly the spoon flutters in or above bottom structure, the more strikes. I almost always add a 2-inch strip of white pork rind to the spoon. This effectively slows the rate of descent of the lure.

If fishing from shore or deepwater jigging in the wind, I'll replace the flutter spoon with a ¾-ounce, prism-taped HotRod, Devle Dog, or similar spoon. The added weight is needed to reach deepwater dropoffs and to keep the lure deep when retrieving in a slow, tantalizing manner.

If a thorough workout through the depths to bottom fails to draw a strike, I'll attach a floating Rapala or Flatfish to a ½- to 1-ounce trolling sinker, cast it parallel to a dropoff, and inch it across the bottom. I've also caught some nice, "hermit" char by twitching the rig along bottom, causing the lure to kick up clouds of mud or debris. This technique proves most effective when fished at the mouth of inlets or during July and August Dog Days.

Deepwater lake char often require persistence and patience. I remember fishing a particular lake in Alaska's Lake Clark region with Homer Circle and Glen Van Valin, owner of Van Valin's Island Lodge. The lake was inaccessible by any means other than float plane. Two rugged mountain peaks jutted up on both sides of the lake, dropping their rocky faces into the dark-blue water at shoreline. Glen lined the Cessna up between the two peaks and touched us down at the far end of the lake, where a sizable freshwater stream created perfect holding structure for lunker char. But while fishing for five-pound-

A landlocked char caught from King Lake on the Kenai Peninsula. This fish struck a flutter spoon jigged in an erratic manner in 40 feet of water.

plus char had been excellent for previous groups of anglers, we now couldn't interest a single fish in any of our lure offerings. Glen's father-in-law finally did manage to hook and land an orange and pink 6-pounder, which he quickly released. It had been no surprise that the fish was hooked at 60 feet on a prism spoon, but try as we might, we couldn't duplicate that success. We left the area several hours later, having learned that to fish successfully for deepwater Arctic char requires time and mobility. These particular trophies don't come easy, but the rewards are worth every ounce of patience you can muster.

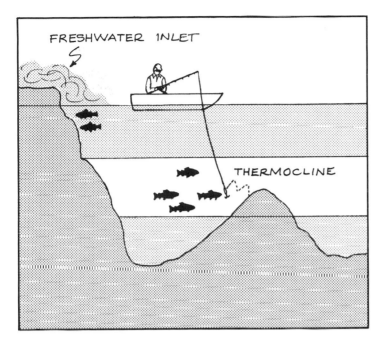

FRESHWATER INLET

THERMOCLINE

In summer, lake char are deepwater fish. They are often found holding in a thermocline near freshwater inlets. Jigging with a lightweight trolling spoon is effective, especially during periods of low light. During noon or bright-light conditions, troll deep for fish.

Summer and Fall

During the summer and fall months, trophy char anglers again devote their attention to freshwater rivers and streams, where big char are usually close to spawning salmon. As a rule, larger fish are easier to catch from the shallower salmon spawning streams than the major rivers. This is because the salmon have slowed their upstream migration considerably and are digging redds. In the Bristol Bay watersheds, where thousands of fish vie for the same spawning areas, it's not uncommon for salmon to dig up recently made nests and consequently dislodge fertilized eggs. Nearby char greedily consume quantities of these tidbits. However, on a week-long char fishing trip on the Alaska Peninsula, I learned that despite a char's almost exclusive diet of salmon eggs, the larger lure takes the largest char.

I was fishing Painter Creek with J.W. Smith, a top-notch fly fisherman and manager of Painter Creek Lodge. The creek was packed with char and spawning salmon, presenting a perfect opportunity to set several International Game Fish Association line-class records. I tied on a salmon egg jig I had created several years earlier for catching big rainbows and grayling, while J.W. tied on a No. 4 Pink-Butted

During a salmon run, fluorescent red or orange salmon egg or attractor patterns fished through deep pools and along undercut banks will usually take large char.

Baboon. Half an hour later, we had caught a dozen char, but none exceeded 3 pounds. I switched to a heavier spinner while J.W. switched to spinning gear and a 1-ounce, fluorescent orange spoon. His first cast soon resulted in a rod bent by what was clearly an 8-pound-plus char. Minutes later, I too, struggled with an uncooperative, 7-pound male that was snapping mad. We quickly released both fish into the current and proceeded to catch three more char, all over 8 pounds. As long as we used large lures, the fishing remained hot for big char. Smaller lures, despite the fact that they more closely resembled the salmon eggs the char were feeding on, seldom produced large fish.

Fly Fishing

When fishing small, spring-fed watersheds for char, it's best to cast up and across stream, landing the lure as close as possible to the opposite bank. I've had several large char strike the lure while it was sinking. But most strikes will come as the lure is slowly worked across bottom and across current, especially at the end of the drift where the lure swings and begins to straighten out in the current. Therefore, it pays to fish out each drift as if trophy char were following it, as they oftentimes do.

Flyrodding for char is a totally different sport altogether. The angler should be prepared with plenty of backing, flies, and a healthy dose of endurance. It's not uncommon to change flies every three fish, as char are notorious for chewing a fly to bits.

I favor the large, attractor patterns for char, especially those tied with plenty of marabou, hackle, or bucktail. I usually carry an assortment of Baker Busters, Thors, Hot Pink Sparklers, Polar Shrimps, Bosses, and Spruce patterns. In low water conditions, fish will often shun the bright colors, and will only take the darker patterns such as a black Woolly Worm with a red tail, Black Matukas, and non-descript nymphs. I always carry several weighted flies in all patterns for large char in deep pools or river channels.

Fishing technique varies with the time of year and water conditions. A sink-tip line is normally used in low water, while a sinking line is often necessary when fishing deep channels and undercut banks. Keep leaders short. I've found 14- to 17-inch leaders work best. Cast slightly upstream and allow the fly to drift as close to bottom as possible. Strikes will usually occur when the fly is twitched slightly during the drift or as it swings across the current at the end of a drift. When fishing for char positioned below salmon schools, I've found that stripping the fly across current at the base of riffles will often induce savage strikes. I've had char literally come out of the water attacking a fly retrieved in such a manner, obviously thinking it's a salmon egg that is about to escape them. As char are not noted for sharing, the strikes this technique provokes will convert you if you crave action.

In my book, it isn't an Alaska fishing trip unless you include a fly-out for Arctic char. If you're planning to fish Alaska, inquire with the lodge as to the possibilities of pursuing this superb gamefish. And please, keep one trophy for mounting and return the rest unharmed. The char is a universal symbol of virgin waters fed by snow fields that crown wilderness mountains, and beauty that is often prevalent in wild things. I hope this fish stays around for generations to come.

Where to go for
Dolly Varden/Arctic Char

Southeast

The Katlian River is considered one of the best Dolly Varden fisheries in the region.

Haines
Chilkat Peninsula
Chilkat River
Chilkoot River
Lower Taku
Lutak Inlet

Juneau
Auke Creek
Cowee Creek
Dupont Creek
Eagle River
Echo Cove
Fish Creek
Montana Creek
Salmon Creek

Sitka/Petersburg
Petersburg Creek
Blind Slough
Starrigavan Bay
Starrigavan Creek
Katlian Bay
Katlian River

Yakutat
Doame River
East River
Italio River
Situk River

Southcentral

King Lake has a good population of landlocked Arctic char, as do other lakes of the Swanson River Drainage. The Kenai River is noted for producing large Dolly Varden throughout the summer months. The Anchor River is an excellent Dolly fishery in September and October.

Cook Inlet/Kenai Peninsula
Anchor River
Homer Spit
Kenai River
Lake Creek
Resurrection Bay
Susitna Watershed
Swanson River Lakes
Talachulitna River
Talkeetna Watershed

Copper River/Upper Susitna
Gulkana River
Klutina Lake Outlet
Klutina River
Little Tonsina River
Lowe River
Robe River

How to Catch
Alaska's Trophy Sportfish

Southwest

The mouth of the Agulukpak and Agulowak rivers provide excellent char fishing in June and through the first week in July. A char a cast is not uncommon. Excellent fishing for Southern Dolly, Northern Dolly and Arctic char throughout the region.

Kodiak (Dolly Varden only)
Akalura River
Barbara River
Buskin River
Fraser River
Karluk River
Little River
Malina River
Pasagshak River
Portage River
Red River
Saltry River
Uganik River
Upper Station River

Kuskokwim
Agulowak River
Agulukpak River
All Bristol Bay/
    Alaska Peninsula drainages
American River
Becharof Drainage
Brooks River
Copper River
Iliamna River
Kvichak River
Lower Talarik
Nushagak River
Painter Creek
Togiak River
Ugashik Drainage
Wood River Lakes

Northcentral

The Sagavanirktok River is considered to be the top char fishery in this area.

Aichilik River
Canning River
Colville River
Hulahula River
Kobuk River
Kongakut River

Noatak River
Prudhoe Bay
Sagavanirktok River
Upper Kobuk System
Walker Lake

Northwest

The Wulik River is noted for having large populations of trophy char. Considered by many to be the best char fishery in the state.

Cripple Creek
Grand Central River
Kelly River
Kivalana River
Kugururok River
Kuzitrin River
Lower Noatak River
Niukluk River
Nome River

Penny River
Pilgrim River
Safety Lagoon
Salmon Lake
Sinuk River
Snake River
Solomon River
Unalakleet River
Wulik River

Lake Trout

Lake Trout

Pursuing trophy lake trout is not a sport for the faint of heart or the purist who pursues ten-ounce fish with a two-ounce element rod. It's a gutsy type of angling when the fish is given half a chance to show off its stuff. The laker is gifted with the ability to do underwater what a steelhead is capable of doing above water. I've seen lakers twist, roll, and fight with a vigor that would knock the scales off most other sportfish. Lakers' gyrations are like cement mixers, and they have a bull-dog tenacity for staying deep. On many occasions, I've worn out my arms and wrists fishing their spring feeding frenzies. Yet the lake trout can also be elusive, reclusive, and frustrating: They're downright inconsiderate of an angler's time. Maybe those characteristics are why I favor this species so much, finding them the most challenging lake fish in Alaska.

The lake trout (Salvelinus namaycush) is not really a trout at all, but rather, the largest of the North American chars. It is also known as gray trout, togue, laker, and mackinaw. Lake trout have the most impressive display of markings and vermiculations of any freshwater fish. Their coloration can vary according to season, watershed, and food availability. And their small, irregularly-shaped spots can be any color from gray to a brilliant gold on a background ranging from silver to black. Lake trout fins are a transparent orange-red, complemented by a milky white leading edge, a trademark of the char family.

Lake trout in Alaska are native to cold, deep lakes north of the Brooks Range, but not in the watersheds of the North Slope flatlands. Lakers are present in the Kobuk

Maurice Ketscher with a 9-pound, Brooks Range laker. The fish struck a copper spoon fished along the edge of a weedbed bordering deep water.

drainage, but not within 400 miles of the Bering Straits or the lower elevations of the Yukon or Kuskokwim basins. The fish is common in Bristol Bay watersheds, in the Pacific drainages just south of Cook Inlet, and in several lakes on the Kenai Peninsula.

Spawning takes place between early September in the northern sections of the state and late October and November in lakes in the Bristol Bay area. Anglers after a mature, spawn-ripe trophy in late autumn should remember that in smaller lakes, spawning is usually completed within 7 days, while in larger lakes, spawning can take up to a month or longer. In Seneca Lake, New York, trout have been known to spawn at depths of up to 200 feet. But Susitna Lake studies show Alaska lake trout prefer to spawn over a clean, rocky bottom at depths from 4 to 12 feet. The males are the first to reach the spawning beds, and instinctively clean the area of any silt and debris with their fins and snouts. Several days later, the females arrive, and after a brief courtship ritual, lay anywhere from a few hundred to 17,000 eggs. These hatch between mid-February and early March.

Alaska's current lake trout record is a 47-pounder caught in 1970 from Clarence Lake by Daniel Thorsness. Apocryphal reports say that a lake trout weighing 54 pounds was taken with a rod and reel, though there is no substantial evidence to verify this. But huge lake trout do abound in many of the Brooks Range watersheds. Test nettings have revealed numerous specimens that were aged at 24 to 28 years, and some lakers were older than 40. However, capturing these behemoths takes an angler knowledgeable in structure fishing fundamentals, habits of lake trout and bait fish, and a quantity of quality tackle blessed with good luck.

Feeding Habits

It's hard to pinpoint any specific or consistent food preferences of lake trout. Their diet changes with the seasons, so choose lures and fishing techniques accordingly.

In the spring, baitfish and aquatic insects are plentiful in the shallow waters. However, the variety of food items greatly decreases when the lake undergoes thermal stratification. At this time, lake trout are usually found at or immediately below the thermocline. Forage fish may move into the epilimnion. Thus, a thermal barrier separates them from the lake trout. Studies of the stomach contents of a large number of lake trout netted at this time showed many with empty stomachs. So anglers should remember that in many cases it is the availability of food that determines the entire diet of a lake trout, rather than the fish's preference.

For instance, in lakes where lake trout are the only fish present, studies have shown that they will invariably feed on clams or gastropods. Once at Wiener Lake, Denali National Park, I spent an entire day trying with every lure in my box to entice lake trout to strike. Later, I learned there were no forage fish in that lake; the trout fed primarily on snails. I did catch several trout the next day by working a fly dead slow along the bottom, and by fishing with bait. But these fish—and the test-net study specimens mentioned earlier—rarely exceeded 20 inches. Studies show that where the chief forage species is whitefish—such as along the Denali Highway—lake trout 10 pounds and over are not uncommon. Thus my first rule of thumb for catching trophy lakers is to determine what species of baitfish, if any, are present, and to match them as closely as possible.

Another important factor to consider is migration routes. Granted, lake trout are not migratory to the extremes exhibited by salmon, but trophy fish are mostly solitary wanderers, and they travel greater distances than smaller fish. However, exact migration habits depend on the size of the watershed, time of year, and again availability of food.

Large lakes, especially after the spring dispersal of fish into the thermoclines, seem to give anglers the most headaches. Canadian studies have shown such fish are somewhat territorial, usually remaining in their own areas throughout the year. A study by Keleher showed that in Great Slave Lake, N.W.T., 65 percent of 221 recoveries of lake trout occurred within 12 miles of the tagging site, despite a mean time of 471 days between tagging and recapture. Other research supporting this theory dealt with the infestation of lake trout by tapeworms. In one location, where 23 fish were examined, 16 were infested with this parasite. However, in another location 8 miles away, 8 fish were checked and none had tapeworms. I've had similar experiences with lake trout catches in Lake Clark and Skilak and Louise lakes.

Despite the season, I've caught fish consistently in various sections of these lakes. But extensive fishing efforts in other areas of these lakes fail to duplicate the success of the hotspots. However, the lake trout I do catch in these hotspots range from 3 to 9 pounds. Invariably I hook fish larger than 10 pounds while trolling some distant point or new area removed from the hotspots. So if you want large lake trout, stay away from the schools of spunky youngsters and fish the outside perimeters of fish-attracting structure. There's one exception to this: Small lakes, such as those in the south slope country of the Brooks Range, where relatively shallow depths inhibit substantial thermal stratification. I love these little gems, especially for trophy lakers, and I usually fish these waters as hard as I possibly can. Pot-bellied lunkers in those lakes can be anywhere—at any time—and they have a total disregard for the habits of their cousins living in larger impoundments. But bait fishing is the trick to harvesting any laker, wherever it lives.

Techniques

Bait

I cringe at the thought of such a sporting fish as the lake trout inhaling bait off the bottom. But bait is unquestionably a very effective method, the downfall of several 20-pound fish I've seen caught in my 10 years of laker fishing in Alaska.

A lake trout exceeding 15 pounds has about 10 pounds of protruding belly. Such creatures are extremely susceptible to properly fished bait. A lunker like this is generally lazy, preferring to cruise shoreline structure at night. They'll go wherever their sense of smell leads them. These fish are big because they feed on bottom, scavenging up whatever dead fish, salmon carcasses, and miscellaneous aquatic life they can find. And at times, bait will be the only way to catch them, especially in glacially silted lakes.

I learned the art of fishing for lakers in such waters from Archie Wainwright, a guide working out of Tuwalaqua Lake Lodge on the shores of Crescent Lake on the Alaska Peninsula. Early in the summer, laker fishing was hot near the several streams emptying into the lake. However, at the end of July, the trout had gone deep. To further com-

plicate matters, underwater visibility was two feet or less. The water was a dark bluish-green, due to the refraction of light off the suspended microscopic particles of silt. Despite the conditions, and the temptation to experience the fantastic fishing for Dollies and sockeye salmon at the lake's outlet, I opted for lakers

We trolled a variety of lures from noisemakers to spinners, spoons, and plugs at all hours of the day without so much as a solid strike. Later that evening, I agreed to Archie's suggestion that we try bait. We rigged up a standard slip-sinker rig, using a one-ounce bell sinker, a 14-inch leader and a No. 2 hook baited with a piece of salmon belly.

Archie suggested that we fish a steep dropoff directly in front of the lodge, where most of the salmon carcasses from the clients' daily catch were dumped. It wasn't long before we were fighting lake trout from 8 to 12 pounds. We released each fish, and subsequently kept our secret from the guests, who obviously questioned our sanity as we walked off into the darkness each night.

A few points to remember when fishing bait. Use fresh

Sue McLain hefts a 20-pound lake trout caught from Hidden Lake in late May. The trout inhaled a herring fished along a deep-water breakline at night. The fish took over an hour to land.

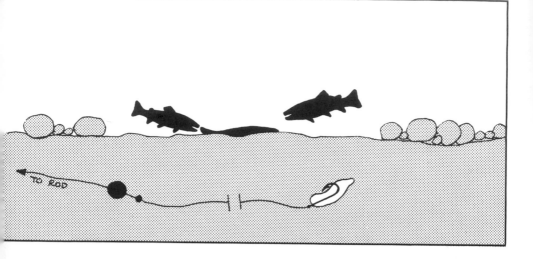

Lake trout in glacial water depend heavily on salmon carcasses for food. Fish deepwater gravel bars or spawning beds at night with a slip-sinker rig baited with chunks of salmon, whitefish, or herring.

salmon, herring, or whitefish sections, preferably belly strips. Salmon eggs also work extremely well. I often add several drops of herring oil to any bait I use, and have been pleased with the results.

Lakers are choosy about how they swallow bait. Expect them to pick it up, thoroughly masticate it, spit it out, chew on it again, and finally move off to deep water with it. Thus, it's important to leave your reel bail open. This allows the fish to pick up the bait without feeling any resistance. Do not touch your rod unless the line is moving out at a steady pace, otherwise the laker will drop the bait and spook. Slowly pick up the rod, close the bail by hand, and reach out with the rod tip before striking. I've seldom had my patience rewarded with anything less than a solid hookup.

Lures

I've found most lake trout can't resist a properly fished lure at spring breakup. At this time, it seems they are feeding on any and everything. For instance, a study of lake trout in Chandler Lake pointed out that all the lakers examined—including a 43-pounder—were virtually gorged with whitefish, ciscoes, and zooplankton. The major food item present in their stomachs, however, was mosquito larvae. The marshy areas surrounding the lake served as a large breeding ground for mosquitoes. Thus, the larvae was undoubtedly abundant and easily accessible in the

How to Catch
Alaska's Trophy Sportfish

shoreline shallows. However, don't rush out and purchase a handful of mosquito larvae patterns. Even if larvae is abundant, lakers prefer a large meal over a small one, especially if a substantial forage fish population exists in the watershed.

One of my favorite lake trout lures is a silvery-scaled shad plug commonly used for largemouth bass in the Lower 48. As there are no shad in Alaska, this plug best imitates a kokanee, which is a young or landlocked red salmon. Early in the season, large schools of kokanee of all sizes are found in the warmest water of the lake. This is usually at the head of bays, at river inlets and outlets, and along shallow stretches of bank. Kokanee can also be found under the surface in mid-lake. All these areas are also excellent prospects for lake trout.

It's not uncommon to see kokanee—that were once sucking nymphs from under the water's surface—jump frightfully out of the water when a school of lake trout move into an area. A plug fished through the outer edge of this feeding frenzy will usually result in a solid hookup. Schools of unalarmed kokanee also serve as a guide for big lakers holding off in deeper water. Lake trout often wait for kokanee to move out into the lake before attacking. This is when I like to slowly troll a shad plug along the length of a dropoff nearest the kokanee. Twitch the lure in an erratic manner while fishing it at various depths. This method is a prime, big fish getter when kokanee are on the menu.

However, there are times when lake trout can be under the surface in the middle of a lake, removed from any visible structure or baitfish activity. The best lake trout fishing I've ever experienced involved these conditions.

I was fishing out of Tanada Lake Lodge, located in the heart of the Wrangell Mountains. It was the last of June, and I was excited about experiencing the "always good fishing" that lodge manager Vince Guzzardi kept hinting at throughout the winter months. I soon realized that "good" was an understatement.

I was trolling a section of mud-bottom shoreline at the south end of the lake without success. Wanting to try another area, I power-reeled the lure up from the alcohol-clear depths of the lake. Just as I flipped the lure out of the water, I was shocked to see a stocky, hungry-eyed lake trout suddenly appear beneath the ripples left by my fast-

Lake Trout

Lake trout, like this 12-pounder held by Jim Pister of Anchorage, are found in areas with gradually sloping shorelines in the spring, and suspended in thermoclines and deepwater haunts with water temperatures ranging from 48 to 52 degrees in the summer.

exiting lure. I sat there stunned, and watched the fish quickly lose interest and swim off.

It didn't take long to figure out that a large school of fat lake trout was within seven feet of the surface. However, the heavy spoon brought only an occasional tap, which I'd miss. After a bit of experimentation with leadhead jigs, I knotted on a specially-tied creation meant to imitate a young grayling. I longlined the lure—with an occasional twitch—within 4 feet of the surface. After 50 minutes of battling the spunkiest lakers I've ever encountered, I returned to the lodge with two fish over 9 pounds. Soon lodge partner Lee Conrad "volunteered" to accompany me and check out my story.

In five hours we caught over 70 lake trout. Later, the only way I was able to escape the lodge was to give Vince all my grayling jigs and to promise I'd send more.

Another good method for spring lakers is to anchor and

then work the area with twister-tail type lures such as ¼-ounce Bass Buster Beetle Twists in yellow, chartreuse, and black. The undulating action of the tails during a dead-slow retrieve is what elicits sledgehammer-like strikes. That's because the lure resembles a leech, a favorite and abundant trout food in many Alaska lakes. But always carry extra bodies, for the laker's needle-like teeth quickly take their toll.

Big lake trout also have a sweet tooth for hardware—including spoons, vibrating lures, and spinners. My favorites are chrome, gold, and chartreuse Heddon Sonars. This lure has an extremely fast vibrating action; casting or deepwater jigging with it has produced several hundred lake trout for me. Other standbys are ¼-ounce FSTs in silver/gold, ½-ounce HotRods dressed with prism tape, ¾-ounce Pixees in gold and bronze, and Mepps Minnow lures in all sizes.

When casting these lures to hungry lake trout, use ultra light to light-action rods with matching reels filled with 4- or 6-pound test that will allow the lure to work most effectively. This especially holds true in deep, cold lakes which receive substantial fishing pressure.

If action is slow near the shoreline, search out weedbeds in 20 to 50 feet of water. Weeds are natural cover for sticklebacks and other forage fish hiding from stalking lakers looking for an easy meal. If the wind is blowing, I prefer to drift over the weedbed or anchor to one side and jig a lure in an erratic up-and-down manner. Often this results in exciting action, especially between daybreak and 10 a.m. and from 5 p.m. to about 10 p.m.

However, there are times when casting won't produce fish; for example, when fish are concentrated in tight groups in deep water, or when holding your boat's position is difficult, such as where a river empties into a lake. Alan Swensen and I found both of these conditions while fishing for lake trout out of Lake Clark Wilderness Lodge several years ago. It was late June, and we were trolling the shoreline, hoping to find the fish feeding in the shallows or under the surface. I was using a Gapen's Bait Walker and a Bill Norman jointed minnow in chrome with a reflex-blue back. Alan was longlining a number 5 spinner. Our guide zig-zagged us along the rocky shoreline, where the bottom was consistent at about 47 feet. We had just entered the strong current of a stream emptying into the lake when my

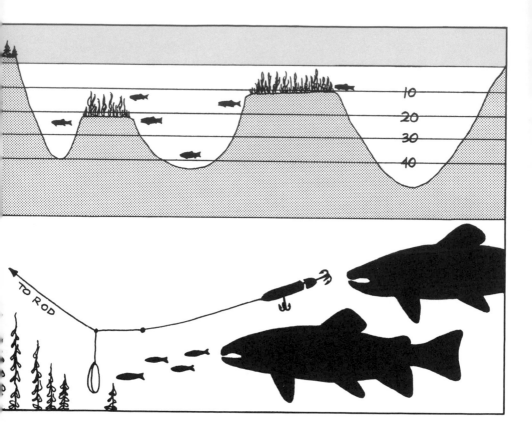

Deepwater islands with weedbeds attract schools of stickleback and kokanee, which in turn attract hungry lake trout. It's common for lake trout to cruise these weedbeds during early morning and late evening. A Gapen Bait Walker and floating minnow plug trolled along the weedbed edge is a good rig to use for trophy lakers at this time.

rod tip hesitated and dipped sharply. I reared back and was immediately treated to the cement-mixer gyrations of an enraged laker. The spunky fish slugged it out with dives, flips, and runs all the way to the surface. Grabbing the plug, I carefully unhooked a 12-pound fish. We tried anchoring over the school of fish but had trouble holding in the current. And jigging lures off the bottom while drifting failed to produce. We cranked up the outboard and in four more passes, I caught four more equally impressive fish. Alan immediately began rummaging through my tackle box for a duplicate rig. Sometime after midnight, with our plugs worn out and our guide falling asleep at the motor, we decided to call it quits. But we learned that certain rigs and trolling methods will catch lakers when other tactics fail to produce.

The Bait Walker or Poor Man's Downrigger/floating-plug combo is the next best thing to a downrigger set-up for fish holding in deep water. The sinker is designed to "walk over" logs, boulders, and debris commonly found in Alaska's lakes. Three-, 6-, and 12-ounce models cover most fishing situations. Natural-finish floating Rapalas, gold, chrome, and blue/chrome U-55 Flatfish, and red/white Lazy Ikes all work well with this trolling device.

An important tip to remember when fishing this combo: Give the rod a short jerk every so often, along with varying trolling speed. This gives the plug the appearance of a crippled baitfish. Strikes usually occur when the plug starts to rise from dropping the rod back or when there's a sudden burst of speed. A lure trolled at a set speed without any additional action will seldom entice large lake trout.

Downriggers and Graph Recorders

Locating and putting lake trout in the boat during Alaska's 23-plus hours of summer daylight is a challenge unsurpassed by any other type of angling. After years of experimentation—with a variety of tackle, trolling techniques, and depth-finding equipment—I've settled on a Scotty downrigger and Lowrance X-15 graph recorder. I've modified both pieces of equipment so that they are portable and adaptable to either my 10-foot inflatable or the boats found at most wilderness lodges I visit. It's exciting to be the first person to "read" the bottom contour of a wilderness lake never before recorded, not to mention the thrill of locating schools of trophy fish.

One of the secrets of summertime lakers unlocked by my graph recorder is that lakers are generally confined within a narrow band of thermocline that varies according to the depth of the thermocline. My recorder has graphed lakers in thermoclines from as little as three feet to as much as twenty feet deep. The average pocket, though, seems to be ten feet, and depending on the lake, can occur anywhere from three to any number of feet below the surface. Unless you fish a lure directly through this activity region, the lake trout won't bother to give the lure a second glance. This is why fishing with lead-core line, diving planers, and heavy trolling sinkers can't offer the precise depth control of a quality downrigger with a depth counter guided with the help of a graph recorder.

When I encounter suspended lake trout confined in a thin band near underwater structure such as islands, weedbeds, or flooded timber, I use a Mepps trolling spoon with either a green or standard prism tape dressing 60

inches behind a 4-pound downrigger weight. But different gear is necessary when fish are dispersed throughout a wide barrier of water in early spring, near deepwater weedbeds, along wide stretches of underwater gravel bars, or in glacial lakes where visibility is poor. Then I use a 3-by 8-inch flasher with a prism-scale face followed by either a herring bait rig resembling what saltwater salmon anglers use, or a "loud" lure like a No. 4 Vibrax, orange/chrome Heddon Sculpin, or a 5-inch cobalt blue Worden's King Fish trolling spoon. When trolling at dead-slow speeds, a lightweight spoon is imperative; heavier spoons tend to sink below the effective strike zone.

Here are three final tips for using a downrigger/graph recorder combo to fish for trophy lakers:

1. First look for surface clues indicating potential holding areas. (For instance, on Hidden Lake, before graphing for suspended fish in the middle of the lake, I usually fish the islands, steep rock walls, and the outside perimeter of bays first.) When scouting such areas, troll ac-

cording to the graph recorder. This is like flying IFR in bad weather: Always watch the instruments for detail and info, no matter how insignificant they may seem at the time. And most of all, believe your instruments!

2. After you've located a school of suspended fish, throw out several marker buoys. They will help guide you back through the school on the next pass.

3. If, after several passes through the school, the fish seem afflicted with lockjaw, motor away from the school and drop anchor. Then either row or drift, paying out anchor line, till you're directly above the fish. That's the moment when I unpack my "crowbar," an ultralight spinning outfit with a 1/8-ounce metal or leadhead jig sweetened with a 2-inch, white pork rind strip. I work the lure in a barely detectable twitch, just enough to make the pork rind flutter. I never have to resort to anything else to put lakers in the boat. But the most important thing to remember when fishing for Alaska's deepwater lakers is patience, patience, patience.

A three-man limit of lakers caught from Tanada Lake, located near Nabesna in the Wrangell Mountains. The fish were caught in mid-June by jigging and longlining spoons and bucktail jigs along sloping dropoffs.

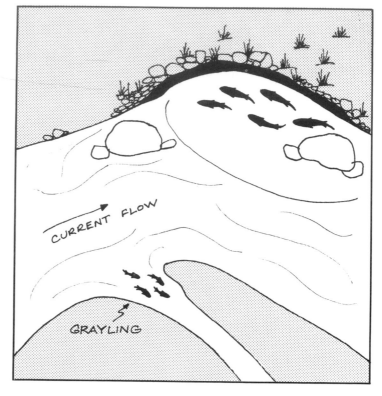

Rivers

It's possible to take lake trout in many rivers during the spring, summer, and fall months. However, these fish are usually small, rarely reaching the 20-pound trophy minimum set by the state.

I once caught a 5- and an 8-pound lake trout from the Alagnak River in June. There the fish were crammed full of salmon smolt outmigrating to the sea. I had similar experiences with lakers on the Kenai River at the outlet of Skilak Lake in early May many years ago. Bright chrome spoons or mylar-dressed flies were the lures that caught most of the fish at this time.

However, lake trout are at home in places other than large rivers. I remember fishing a small grayling stream in the Talkeetna Mountains with Jim Bailey of Stephan Lake Lodge. The stream emptied a lake known to have a population of lake trout, but we were more than two miles from the outlet. Thus, only grayling and rainbow trout would be our quarry. We soon found a deep, roily pool

created by a log jam and couldn't help but notice several schools of grayling finning along the edges. We quickly unpacked and assembled our fly rods. The fish were ravenous, and we had some great catch-and-release fishing. Jim noticed that every so often, after he released a grayling, a ghostly shadow of a much larger fish would fin into view. Our curiosity was piqued. We climbed the riverbank so we could identify the mystery fish: A sleek, four-pound laker, the last species we would have guessed to be in such a small watershed for that time of year.

In early September and October, lake trout can also be found migrating up rivers and streams to their wintering-over lakes. At this time, these fish gorge on salmon carcasses and salmon eggs; prime laker food. I've hooked spunky lakers so pot-bellied that a mere touch to their stomachs caused them to spit up a handful of eggs. At times like these, drifting single eggs, Aqua Cones, attractor flies—or almost any red or orange colored lure—seems to work well.

During May and June, lake trout can be taken in shallow water on a variety of tinsel-dressed flies, sculpin, or herring patterns.

Fly Fishing

Fly fishing for lake trout is extremely effective during the spring. I've found large, mylar-dressed flies fished with a sink-tip line extremely productive during early morning and late evening. My favorite creation is a kokanee smolt pattern. I rarely use anything else, and will fish it with a touch of herring oil on the tail. (You need at least a 7-weight rod to cast this or similar flies: the gaudier the better.)

Action is the key word when fishing feathers. Fish secluded bays that have exhibited previous kokanee or whitefish activity. I like to fish such an area in early and late evening, which in Alaska means anytime up until midnight. You should anchor a short distance away from the feeding activity, and cast perpendicular to shore, rather than shallow to deep or deep to shallow. After the fly settles, it's important to twitch it back sporadically with several sweeping strips, thus imitating a crippled and fleeing baitfish.

Better yet, if you can find an underground spring that empties into a lake, or an open area of water during breakup, you could have the best laker fishing possible on a fly rod. I remember one year at Paxson Lake where lake trout, averaging 9 pounds apiece, were jam-packed into an area of the lake freshened by an underground spring. I was all thumbs with excitement as fish literally boiled the surface of the water trying to nail my fly. It was the kind of experience that makes Alaska fishing legends. However, the same location the following week failed to show as much as a ripple. (But then again, Interior lake trout are like that.)

An Alaska lake trout is more than just another trophy fish. It is the main ingredient of a wilderness fishing experience that is seldom forgotten, and always appreciated. The setting is almost always mountainous. Most lakes are the remnants of a long and bitter Ice Age. The quiet tranquility is often shattered by the insane laugh of a loon, rather than the speeding roar of an outboard. Breezes carry down the refreshing briskness of an alpine glacier to kiss the surface of the water rather than the kiss of death from acid rain. And grebes and goldeneyes, rather than trash and pollution, are the only signs that break the often mirror-like surface. These are the real attractions that make fishing for Alaska lakers a truly total experience.

Where to go for Lake Trout

Southcentral

Fishing is best immediately after spring breakup. Skilak Lake rarely produces lakers over 18 inches. Tustemena produces fish up to 20 pounds near its outlet and at feeder streams. Bait is very effective during the summer months. Hidden Lake is another popular fishery. Several 20-pound-plus fish have been taken from there. Mid-May is the best time to fish it. Divers have reported lake trout to 30 pounds in glacially silted Kenai Lake. However, turbidity makes fishing with lures difficult.

The Copper River/Upper Susitna areas are all excellent waters for catching lake trout up to 10 pounds, with fish frequently exceeding this mark. Louise and Tanada lakes are excellent trophy laker fisheries. June and October provide the best chances for lunker fish.

Tokun Lake in Prince William Sound is a fly-in fishery for good catches of lake trout up to 10 pounds.

Cook Inlet
Hidden Lake
Kenai Lake
Skilak Lake
Tustemena Lake

Prince William Sound
Tokun Lake

Copper River/Upper Susitna
Clarence Lake
Crosswind Lake
Fielding Lake
Lake Louise
Paxson Lake
Summit Lake
Tanada Lake

Southwest

There are many good lake trout fisheries scattered throughout this area. However, this fishery is best noted for large populations of average fish rather than consistent producers of trophy lake trout.

Northcentral

Walker, Chandler and Iniakuk are exceptional lake trout waters, with lakers reaching 20-pounds-plus. Lake trout are present in the deep, gravel-bottomed lakes of the Arctic foothills, however, are seldom found in waters of the coastal plains. Access is by float plane only.

Chandalar Lake
Elusive Lake
Fish Lake
Helpmejack Lake
Iniakuk Lake
Itkillik Lake
John Lake

Kurupa Lake
Narvik Lake
Old Man Lake
Peters Lake
Schrader Lake
Selby Lake
Shainin Lake

Squaw Lake
Walker Lake
Wild Lake

Rainbow
& Steelhead
Trout

CHAPTER 11

Rainbow Trout

The rainbow trout is a refined type of sorcerer. No other fish can induce that finger-fumbling behavior by dimpling mayflies off a glass-smooth surface of a lake, or give you goose bumps when the air temperature is 75 degrees. The rainbow is a fish that often bewitches anglers into indulging in activities too bizzare to even mention, and partaking in a sport that represents one of the most satisfying challenges available to mankind.

Yet the only way to enhance the magic of a rainbow is to surround it with snow-melt streams, banks lined with tundra willows, and deep-blue wilderness lakes. Indeed, fishing for rainbows in Alaska is sportfishing that has achieved perfection.

This fish was first identified as a trout in the taxonomic studies of Sir John Richardson of England. Following its discovery by Doctor James Gairdner at Fort Vancouver in 1833, it was classified as Salmo gairdneri. Sea-going rainbows, known as steelhead, received that name as a tribute to their toughness. Metal workers discovered that mixing alloys with iron resulted in steel, a substance harder and stronger than the original iron. Thus, when fishermen first began catching steelhead in nets on the Columbia River and Pacific Northwest streams, a king or silver required only one smack on the head to dispatch it, while a steelhead often required several or more blows.

Alaska rainbows definitely live up to their name, both in hard-headed stubbornness and dazzling displays of color. One of the most fascinating aspects of this species is that each watershed in the state seems to have its own color

Deb Tinnesand is pleased with this 4-pound rainbow she caught in the Talkeetna Mountains. The fish struck a Muddler fished along the edge of a riffle.

variation of the rainbow. Thus fish from each area are potentially separate trophies. For instance, Talachulitna rainbows exhibit a brilliant red coloration and heavy spotting, while Iliamna fish are more silvery with a subdued lateral stripe. Yet even within each watershed, coloration is extremely variable according to size of fish, sexual maturity, and feeding habits. Generally speaking, however, river or stream fish usually display the most intense, pink-to-reddish flank coloration and heaviest spotting, while the appearance of fresh-run steelhead and lake fish is at the other extreme, almost completely silver with little or no coloration.

In Alaska, rainbows can be found in numerous coastal rivers, streams, and lakes from Ketchikan to the Kuskokwim River. The rainbow is not native to Interior Alaska, but it has been planted in a number of lakes and gravel pits in the Fairbanks and Big Delta areas. These plantings, begun in 1952, seven years before Alaska became a state, were made from the eggs of rainbows native to Montana and Idaho. Of the United States, Alaska was the last to practice the planting of rainbow trout.

Life History

Spawning usually takes place from late April through mid-June when water temperatures are on the increase. Sexually mature rainbows, especially those of the Iliamna-Bristol Bay drainages, are large fish. Studies indicate that over 90 percent of the spawners are 7 to 9 years old, and 94 percent are over 20 inches in length.

Rainbows begin their spawning migration into clear-water streams anytime from early April through mid-June. Before spawning, the male spends time courting the female and chasing away other males. The female digs a redd with her tail and releases approximately 3,400 eggs, which are immediately fertilized by the dominant, accompanying male. The female then covers the eggs with gravel. This protects them from predators and helps anchor them during spring flood waters.

After spawning, lake rainbows usually migrate to their summering lake, while stream and river fish tend to migrate to the headwaters of their particular watershed. River fish may often hold in a limited area of stream throughout their entire lives if depth and food conditions

How to Catch
Alaska's Trophy Sportfish

Jerry Romanowski with a hefty, Mat-Su valley rainbow. The fish was caught in 3 feet of water on a Rapala jig. Look for big rainbows in shallow or open water areas during spring breakup.

are adequate for their needs on a year 'round basis.

Depending upon water temperature, the eggs hatch anywhere from 3 weeks to 4 months later, with the alevins requiring up to 2 weeks to absorb the yolk sac. When they emerge, their length can range from one-half inch to a full inch.

Upon emergence, juvenile stream trout generally stay in their natal stream. Lake-resident fish migrate to the nearest lake over a period of weeks. Growth rates and patterns for these two types vary greatly. Both types reach sexual maturity within 3 to 5 years, with males maturing a year before the females.

There are many prime rainbow watersheds throughout Alaska. The Talachulitna River, located within a 45 minute flight from Anchorage, offers an excellent catch-and-release rainbow fishery for fish up to 8 pounds. Southcentral Alaska's Kenai River has produced rainbows in the 14- to 18-pound-plus class. And the current Alaska state record for rainbow/steelhead is a 42-pound, 2-ounce fish taken at Bell Island by David White in 1970. While it's possible to catch a trophy rainbow from any of these areas, the waters best known for growing the largest rainbows have one thing in common: They are where salmon eggs and smolts are nurtured. And there's no other food item in the far north that can put as many pounds on a hungry rainbow.

With this in mind, there's no questioning why the waters of Bristol Bay and Iliamna, which see the return of millions of sockeye salmon each year, contend for the top trophy rainbow hotspot within the state. However, the Iliamna watershed is the most favorite of them all, noted for the largest rainbow populations and the biggest rainbows. You can fly over the Copper, Talarik, Kvichak, or Dream Creek drainages and witness schools of large rainbow mixed right in with spawning sockeyes. If it weren't for the crimson coloration of the 8- to 10-pound salmon, an angler would be hard-pressed to differentiate between the two from 200 feet up. Yes, 8 to 10 pounds is routine for Iliamna rainbows.

These fish, often called October rainbows, appeal to the angler who has a passion strictly for large fish, and the bucks to turn that passion into reality. It's a super fishery, but it is expensive. It occurs during the season when many sportsmen would rather spend their money on a moose or caribou hunt than on bucket-mouthed trout. For those of us who have been blessed to experience a battle with a trophy October rainbow, it's the Grand Finale after a season of fishing for trout in smaller streams and lakes, where a 3- to 4-pound rainbow is a trophy in its own right.

I believe—and so do anglers better than I—that large rainbows are not easy to catch from any watershed, whether in Alaska or the Lower 48. Over the years, I've experimented with what seems to be a million techniques. The ones listed below have worked best for me in catching hundreds of large rainbows within the 49th State, and I'm confident they'll work for you also.

A young angler with an 11-pound rainbow he caught from Green Lake near Anchorage. The trout was taken on a shrimp and float rig fished near a patch of lily pads.

How to Catch
Alaska's Trophy Sportfish

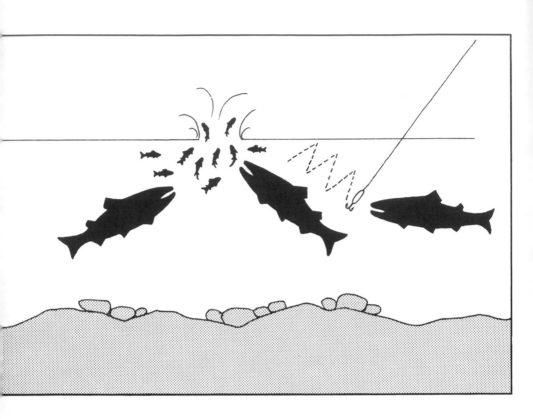

Techniques

Lakes

Immediately after ice-out, jumping or scurrying smolt at a lake's outlet usually indicate large rainbow are nearby. Fish a narrow chrome spoon in an erratic manner along the edge of the activity.

As a general rule, the habits of most lake-dwelling rainbows imitate those of the Iliamna populations. I find that the following techniques are effective on any lake nurturing salmon fry.

Immediately after ice out, salmon smolt of all types begin their outmigration to sea. Depending upon the size of the watershed, this can result in millions of salmon fingerlings crammed into the confines of a lake's outlet, waiting for the hours of darkness to arrive so that they can head for the ocean. This migration may not be readily visible to the angler, but the feeding activity of gulls, mergansers, and furbearers is a good indication that smolts are holding in an area, and that pot-bellied rainbows are also gorging on the smorgasbord of fish.

A boat is indispensible at this time. Its greater mobility allows you to stay with the smolts, and to execute a variety

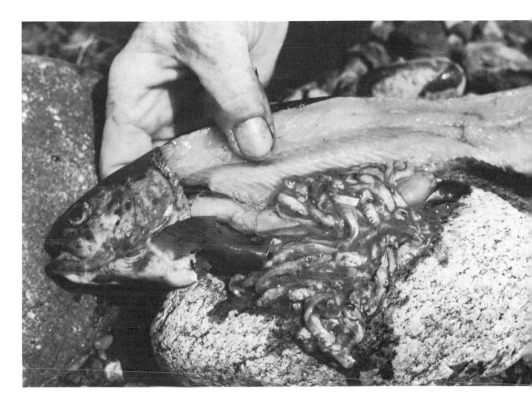

of techniques that can't be done from shore. A boat also removes you from the tactics—often ironically fish-spooking—practiced by some shoreline anglers also intent on big rainbows.

The first order of activity is to study the outlet. It's imperative to find the current flow. How fast is it? Is there a main channel? Are there any backeddies that might serve as resting areas for rainbows or smolts? What type of underwater structure is available? What direction is the wind?

While I'm checking out the area for this data, I also take the temperature of the current at several points around the outlet. I've found that pockets of water below 38 degrees can be an effective barrier, keeping smolts in a lake, or rerouting them down less-than-ideal migration channels. Indeed, water temperature makes a big difference. It's possible to fish what may appear to be perfect-looking structure all day, and not experience a strike. But across the river, where there is no temperature block, rainbows feast on salmon smolts.

This river rainbow was caught on a Coronation pattern during a smolt out-migration. The trout was so gorged with smolts that it regurgitated several prior to landing.

Rainbow Trout

Wind direction also plays a major factor in the migration habits of smolts. When the wind is blowing toward the outlet, the general rule is to fish the shallows or area immediately off shore. But with the wind blowing in the opposite direction, fish deeper water and along dropoffs. It's not uncommon for me to fish near shore one hour, and in the center of the outlet the next. More than once, the small twigs I tossed into the water to test the surface current and wind direction drew comments from shoreline anglers disparaging my sanity. But after they witnessed me catching a few stocky 'bows, I have no doubt that on the next day they were duplicating my wind-testing efforts.

Often smolts in the lower end of a chain of lakes are the first to migrate, sometimes right at ice out. Thus, fishing can be slow until the smolts in the upper lakes of the watershed begin their run. At this time, the lake's inlet, especially during early morning hours, often produces the best fishing of the day. During daylight hours, it's possible to intercept the smolts as they travel down the lake. However, I've found that on cloudy days, smolts tend to group into large schools. Then travel is minimal. Here is a perfect magnet for rainbows, which mill around the schools like a pack of wolves, searching out that solitary straggler or injured smolt.

And that is the key to hooking a large rainbow—imitating a wounded or crippled smolt as closely as possible. This is best done with a narrow, chrome spoon from 2- to 4-inches long. I like to add a white feathered dressing to the single hook, with a touch of red marabou for contrast. Ultralight tackle is a must, whether spinning or level-wind. Reels should be filled with 4- to 6-pound-test, clear monofilament line.

I fish the spoon one of several ways. My favorite is to cast lengthwise along migration routes, and slowly work the spoon through the depths with an occasional twitch. I use a depth finder to pinpoint smolt concentrations, or I watch for smolts jumping in shallow water. I highly recommend fishing a spoon along the outer edges of a smolt concentration, not through the center. It's easier for a large rainbow to see a fluttering lure apart from a baitfish school than in a jumbled mass of fish.

Another favored method is to anchor directly in the mouth of the outlet, and to longline a spoon downstream. Occasionally, I'll open the bail and allow the lure to drop

How to Catch
Alaska's Trophy Sportfish

quickly into a pocket I feel a big rainbow is holding. It's important to snap the bail shut immediately, as strikes can be fast and aggressive. Once I have worked out about 70 yards of line, I'll reel in and repeat the procedure. This technique imitates a smolt that can't hold its own in the current, trying to make it back upriver.

In high and fast current, when I can't fish a spoon effectively, I tie on a silver and metallic blue floating-diving plug such as a Clatter Tad or Rapala. I work it downstream, allowing it to literally rattle the brains of big rainbows. They usually strike the lure with all the power of a torpedo hitting its target.

When I can't find rainbows or smolts, I'm probably between migrations. However, 'bows are usually still holding in the area, waiting for the next exodus of smolts. Under these circumstances, and if the wind is blowing toward the outlet, I'll motor upwind and start a drift along structural breaklines I've noted on my graph recorder. A vibrating lure, such as a Sonar, jigged in an erratic pattern above or through such structure, is usually enough to coax rain-

A 1/32-ounce silver and blue spoon fished along a sudden dropoff produced this rainbow. A graph recorder is invaluable in finding large rainbows, smolt, baitfish, and the structures that attract them.

225

Rainbow Trout

A spunky rainbow takes to the air for this angler. The fish struck a Boss and sinker combo trolled at a snail's pace along bottom.

bows into striking—if they're in a hungry mood. If I fail to entice a strike, I'll come back at another time of day, preferably in the early morning or late evening. Because rainbows often gorge themselves during these smolt migrations, and because of the coldness of spring waters, they may take a half day to several days to digest a meal before feeding again.

Small Lakes

Trophy rainbows are almost entirely piscivorous. Every now and then, an abundance of a certain food item other than fish causes trout to feed on that item alone. For instance, research on Copper River rainbows indicated that from the study period May 21st through October 3rd, the most prevalent food item was Caddis fly larvae, accounting for 34.8 percent of the total diet. But in many Alaska lakes, larvae and terrestrials often take second place when scuds, more commonly known as freshwater shrimp, are present in numbers rivaling the hatches themselves.

I've hooked and released over 70 rainbows from 4- to

For big rainbows in small lakes, the author favors a Fin-Chilla jig. This lure best imitates the freshwater shrimp found in Alaska's waters. The shrimp pictured here were seined from Matanuska Lake near Palmer.

8-pounds in the scud-filled lakes of the Mat-Su valley. The majority were caught on scuds or a scud-imitating lure. These 1-inch (or smaller) crustaceans can be easily caught by netting or seining the shoreline algae and weeds of lakes. More anglers should stop using salmon eggs and take advantage of this natural bait. Then not only would more big fish end up in the ice chest, but also float and ultralight leader sales would skyrocket, since these are two pieces of tackle necessary to fish freshly-caught scuds.

A proper scud-fishing rig calls for a small hook—a thin-wire, number 16 will do nicely. Attach it to a 12- to 16-inch length of clear-nylon sewing thread. Avoid using mono larger than 2-pound test. To the main line attach a small stick bobber, and you're in business.

I like to row around a lake in early spring, and scout the dropoffs. Big rainbows often cruise these structures, and a free-drifting scud will often draw one of these lunker rainbows up from the depths like a filing to a magnet. Lily pads, patches of aquatic weeds, and floating clumps of algae—especially around stands of downed timber—are top areas to fish scuds, especially in early morning and late evening. Keep the scud in the open and above bottom cover. Rainbows usually must work for scuds, prodding weedbeds with their snouts to dislodge them. A scud floating out in the open is a meal that is rarely refused!

Certain spinning lures do imitate scuds effectively. My favorite is a gray or brown, 1/64-ounce jig such as the Fin-Chilla. I've used this lure for years, and have found it to be a most convincing scud imitation, especially when fished with either a fly rod or ultralight spinning rod. Cast it to feeding fish, or twitch it slowly along weedy structure bordering deepwater dropoffs. Of course, standard scud patterns in sizes 10 through 18 will also produce for the fly-rodder. Those tied with light gray hackle seem to be the most effective.

Leeches are another excellent bait to use when fishing for large trout. The black marabou muddlers, devoid of the tinsel dressing and elaborate bodies, best imitate this bloodsucker. I've found this pattern to be extremely effective immediately after ice out in the Wood River Lakes, the Swanson Lake System, and bog-fed streams of Southeastern Alaska. Fish this pattern the same as you would the scud.

It's important to note here that trout can be found anywhere during the late spring and summer months in Alaska lakes. That includes even those oligotrophic lakes: Ones that are deficient in plant nutrients, yet have abundant dissolved oxygen with no marked stratification. Rainbows can be directly under the surface of these lakes or holding at 22 feet in 80 feet of water. While casting and vertical jigging will put fish in the boat, precision trolling, preferably with a graph recorder, is more effective.

Once I find suspended fish, or a section of lake that triggers my "Fish Here!" alarm, I tie on the lure that best imitates the lake's predominant forage fish species. When fish are close to shore or cover, or in small lakes, I like to use a sculpin or stickleback imitation. In larger lakes, or for deep or mid-water fish, a wide, gold or silver spoon that closely resembles a whitefish or pond smelt is my best producer. For years, I thought kokanee was the main food item of Iliamna Lake rainbows. However, a study of the trout's migratory patterns revealed that while kokanee are important, trout over a foot in length also feed heavily on pond smelt. This taught me a lesson. If you don't know the

How to Catch
Alaska's Trophy Sportfish

Fall rainbows are meat-hungry fish, which makes them extremely susceptible to jigs. Here are several patterns the author favors for both lake and stream fish. For added appeal, add a drop or two of salmon egg oil, shrimp, or herring oil.

predominant forage food species in the water you'll be fishing, ask the local fisheries biologist or tackle shop dealer.

While you're at the tackle shop, stock up on a selection of baitfish-matching plugs that work best for those extreme deepwater or suspended fish. Choose those that wobble, wiggle, and dart with the most animation at the slowest retrieving speed. Rapalas, Tadpollies, and Spoonplugs in a variety of sizes are excellent choices.

There is one exception to the "match the baitfish" rule. Fluorescent red Flatfish, from fly-rod size to the U-55, have proven themselves in catching rainbows of all sizes in waters throughout the state. The plug seems to work best in low light conditions and in slightly turbid lakes.

Fishing Flatfish or other plugs is a simple matter: Either longline when rainbows are under the surface or use a Bait Walker trolling rig when trout are deep. In either case, it's important to troll the lure very slowly; the slower the better. Drifting in a slight breeze is ideal.

I always focus my attention on maneuvering the boat rather than imparting additional action to the plug. In following a lure working at a steady pace, trout often tend to go great distances without striking. However, when the lure starts to speed up, slow down, or finally change direction in a turn, be prepared for any trout in the vicinity to smash it. I've found that a zig-zag pattern also imparts an equally enticing action to the lure.

Streams

The autumn weeks, from September 1st through October 15th, are unquestionably the best time to catch a trophy rainbow in Alaska. I like to pursue these fish in Iliamna drainage waters for several reasons.

The rainbows that have outmigrated into the lake after the spring spawn exhibit an enormous rate of growth. Fish 4- to 6-years old tend to show rapid increases in length and weight, a condition which biologists cannot readily explain.

However, once the salmon enter the area's lakes and rivers, these large, healthy rainbows leave Iliamna and follow them to their spawning beds. With such a good food supply in Iliamna, why is it that rainbows venture into relatively shallow stream and river systems? There they subject themselves to predators, injury, and disease.

The answer lies in the availability of large numbers of salmon eggs in the summer and fall. This food enhances the rainbow's chance for overwinter survival, as the fish face a 6- to 8-month period when the lakes and streams are at least partially covered with ice, making for adverse feeding conditions. So it's absolutely necessary that they accumulate adequate energy reserves between May and October. Nutrient-rich salmon eggs are what best provide these reserves.

Therefore, under these conditions, rainbows that once might have been particular about midge and lure offerings resort to scavenging any of the millions of sockeye salmon eggs available. However, competition is great because grayling, char, Dolly Varden, whitefish, and lake trout also indulge in the salmon caviar feast. This competition makes for quick strikes—often as soon as the fly hits the water—and spectacular battles.

So in early autumn, I fish any of the salmon-egg imitations or bright steelhead patterns. Two-Egg Marabou, Polar Shrimp, Thor, Glo-Bugs, Skykomish Sunrise—all take rainbows. An 8-weight system is necessary to handle these large flies and the fish that greedily take them, especially when used with sinking lines or sink-tip lines with shooting tapers. However, a sinking line may be overkill in some waters, especially in shallow riffles immediately behind spawning sockeyes. Therefore, I prefer a floating line and a slightly weighted egg imitation fished on a dead drift: Not only can it result in an exciting stalk, but

Guide Jim Bailey eases a No. 6 Skykomish from the jaw of this wilderness stream rainbow. In autumn, use bright attractor patterns in waters with runs of salmon.

How to Catch
Alaska's Trophy Sportfish

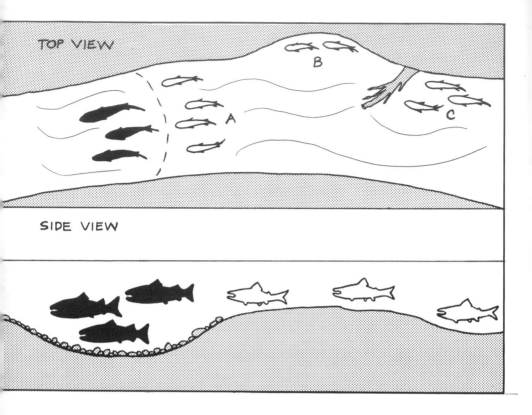

TOP VIEW

B

A

C

SIDE VIEW

In September and October, look for large rainbows behind spawning salmon. They can be identified as grayish forms holding at (a) the tail of a spawning pool, (b) hiding adjacent to undercut banks, and (c) in obstructions such as snags and sweepers. Not only do these structures provide big rainbows with excellent vantage points to intercept free-drifting salmon eggs, but also serve to protect them from aggressive salmon.

it also makes witnessing the take possible.

If there is one thing I've learned over the years fishing for autumn rainbows, it's that they're extremely intolerant of "thievery." If a runt whitefish or stickleback is trying to make off with an egg, a rainbow will frequently ingest two meals with one gulp. In fact, this exhibition of the energy expenditure-mass relationship (the two meals in one gulp) principle is so common that I make it a point of tying the head of my sculpin and smolt patterns with red floss to imitate a baitfish carrying off a salmon egg. Time and time again, this pattern has outfished a standard salmon egg attractor.

However, the type of fly you use doesn't matter if your technique or presentation is wrong. Flies must be cast upstream from feeding rainbows. As the fly drifts down with the current, it's important to keep your line from bellying, either by mending with the rod tip or with a series of wrist rolls. Belly in the line will speed up the drift, rendering the presentation ineffective.

How to Catch
Alaska's Trophy Sportfish

Spin Fishing

The lure angler should use standard salmon egg imitators. Lil Corkies, Spin-N-Glos, Okie Drifters, Aqua Cones, and artificial roe fished with a pencil sinker set-up are the most popular. Equally effective are fluorescent red Mepps in sizes 2 and 3, and orange and fluorescent red or pink spoons smaller than ½-ounce.

It's important to fish these lures with a minimal amount of lead. This keeps them working just above bottom and drifting with the same speed as the current. Any major change in these two points can greatly reduce the effectiveness of the lure.

By the time large schools of rainbow—especially those entering the Talarik Creek and Copper River drainages—have entered freshwater, many sockeyes have already spawned and died. Their fungus-ridden carcasses are strewn along the riverbanks. Thousands of rotted salmon carcasses scattered up and down the river isn't the wilderness image most of us have in our minds. Yet it is important to recognize that the sockeye is a source of food for rainbows—and thus influences the abundance of rainbows—at two different stages.

First, sockeye eggs and flesh are available as food following each year's run. Studies show that big rainbows, especially fish that overwinter in rivers, feed on sockeye salmon remains. This feeding activity continues throughout the winter if other food is in short supply. Second, nutrients released from the decaying carcasses stimulate primary production for next year's invertebrate populations, which both young and mossback 'bows feed upon. If sockeye remains bother you, just hold your nose and remember, they're part of a perpetual and necessary cycle.

According to biological reports, there are Iliamna rainbow populations that do not follow the salmon upstream during the early fall runs. After the salmon are far upstream in late October, these fish will mill around and cruise at the mouth of stream outlets for several days. With a wind or rain storm, the creeks rise and the 'bows immediately migrate upstream. Some go to the headwaters; others remain in the long runs and deeper holes of the stream. Extensive studies indicate these fish are not on a feeding migration, because they arrive after the salmon have spawned. Also, anglers rarely find anything in the stomachs of these fish. This suggests that anglers can expect good rainbow fishing until the icy blasts of winter come blowing down the lake.

I enjoyed catching my largest rainbow in such blustery weather one October at the ol' log marker on Talarik Creek. Sockeyes were still filtering upstream, and the overcast skies made me squint hard to pinpoint the grayish forms of big rainbows among the crimson salmon.

Having found only spawned-out carcasses in the shallows, I made several casts alongside and behind a small school of salmon slowly finning upstream. As I mended the drift of the Polar Shrimp, my fly line snapped outward. Before my rod tip was back over my head from the hookset, a drag-ripper of a rainbow was stripping line and leader off my fly reel at an alarming speed. The rainbow jumped in a series of tail-flips that left me stunned. Even the migrating sockeyes cleared the area as the 'bow proceeded to stir up the stream bottom. The fish fought gallantly, and 15 minutes later, I wrestled it gently into the grassy shallows.

The rainbow was a beautiful sight. Each flank was thick and muscular, sporting heavy black dots and a vivid pink stripe. A silvery scar on the tail hinted of a battle with a territorial sockeye. Each fin was tipped in a pearly white that faded into a translucent olive green. As gills worked the current, the operculum glowed with the brilliance of a saucer-sized ruby. My tape measure stretched and stretched, with the fork of the tail finally stopping it at 28 inches. I was really excited: A 28-inch rainbow is a big fish, no matter where you find it.

Carefully unhooking the fly, I eased the snout of the 'bow into the current, gently feeling the layers of fat surrounding its gorged, pot-belly. With a flick of a tail, it was off, to feed again on helping after helping of salmon egg omelette. That moment was a turning point in my life. I have never killed a wild rainbow after that experience.

At least 10 years are required for rainbows to reach trophy classification in Alaska's cold, subarctic waters. Rainbows that survive the odds against them—predation, disease, natural disasters, and injury—have accomplished a feat worthy of acclaim. Yet don't be fooled into thinking these large schools of big, autumn rainbows are inexhaustible. These schools do not represent large numbers of fish,

Author with an ultralight-caught, Kenai River rainbow. The fish was seen working the flooded weed patch on the far shore for mice and insects. A precision cast with a fluorescent spoon to the edge of the weeds produced the strike.

How to Catch
Alaska's Trophy Sportfish

The rainbow is a fighter par excellence and deserves the utmost in respect. Catch and release of Alaska's wild rainbow stocks will ensure future generations of this fine sportfish.

but rather, they may be the total population of fish from several watersheds aggregated into one area. They exist for one purpose: to feed and to survive.

Alaska's native rainbows are a resource that can't continue unless everyone cooperates. Many lodge owners insist on a catch-and-release policy, and strictly enforce the special state fishing regulations pertaining to the various trophy areas. Please cooperate with them: Abide by the rules, use single hook lures, and properly release each fish. If you're unfamiliar with the proper release technique, don't be afraid to ask. Because losing these wild stocks of rainbow trout means losing an integral part of the wilderness that can never be replaced. And if so, mankind will stand to be judged for a sin that can never be forgiven.

Steelhead

Steelhead are the nomads of the rainbow clan. From their swaggering jaunts in the Pacific Ocean they acquire a wildness that large stream or river rainbow stocks never attain. Steelhead are the sportfish of superlatives. They intrigue and challenge the mind. An angler—muscles strengthened from a summer of fighting large salmon—finds his physique diminished to an exhausted, oftentimes quivering mass of flesh after battle with a steelhead. Such a fish wins either by earning its freedom, or more often than not, by breaking loose with its air-slashing acrobatics and powerhouse runs.

Alaska steelhead make no claim to be the largest. Surely the 20-pound-plus fish of Oregon, Washington and British Columbia take the honors in this regard. But Alaska steelhead have other unique distinctions. First, there's quality of environment—in most cases wilderness areas — and second, quantity of fish. In Alaska, an angler can catch 10, 8- to 10-pound steelhead per day when water and weather conditions are right.

However, steelhead waters are not numerous in Alaska. Southeast Alaska, from Ketchikan to Yakutat, nurtures healthy runs and small to large populations of fish. The streams of the lower Kenai Peninsula are also noted for good runs of steelhead, as are select Kodiak waters.

After two years, sometimes more, of stream life, Alaska steelhead parr begin their outmigration to sea. Increased activity of the thyroid gland make the parr lose their markings and take on a silvery coloration. At this time they technically become smolts. Some young fish readily adapt to the new saline environment. However, the length of their period of adaptation to the ocean chemistry depends on the length of their freshwater life.

Steelhead spend anywhere from several months to 4 years at sea before returning to their natal streams to spawn. Whether a fish returns in the spring or fall seems to be genetically controlled. Biologists attribute the evolution of this response to stream barriers that, over the years, were passable only during periods of high stream flow, which typically occurs during the spring and fall months.

Spring and fall runs predominate in Alaska. Techniques here are virtually the same as those used in other streams throughout the Pacific Northwest. However,

Alaska steelheading is more of a stream or wade fishery rather than a large river fishery requiring the use of drift boats and plugs. Therefore, techniques discussed in this chapter will focus on wading.

Steelhead are cold-blooded creatures. Hence their actions are immediately influenced by fluctuating water levels and plummeting temperatures which are commonplace in both seasonal fisheries.

I remember fishing the Situk River one spring just as a cold front settled over the Yakutat area. The temperature dipped into the teens, and the frosty air rimmed the shore with a narrow band of ice. For two days I nudged a total of two fish. But on the third day, a warm front and subsequent clouds moved in, dropping several inches of rain. During the next two days, I experienced superb steelhead action I've never again encountered with over 20 hookups per day.

Since, I carry my lucky billikin and rub its tummy before starting the day's fishing, wishing and hoping for a freshet. I love 'em. I may get wet, but the action keeps me plenty warm. It's important to fish while the water is rising, yet before it becomes muddied and unfishable. This holds especially true during spring breakup.

In Alaska, however, breakup or fall rains can be long in coming, and such a wait produces low water conditions. At times like these, steelhead hold off the mouth of their natal streams or stick tight to undercut banks, in deep pools, or behind riffles. Many anglers prefer the challenge of ultralight tackle and finesse presentations necessary to hook fish that are spooky and very hesitant to strike. Of course, slightly murky water offers the best fishing conditions for fly fishing and standard spin fishing.

Whatever type of conditions you're faced with, it's important to fish a steelhead waterway first thing in the morning and late in the afternoon, as these are times when big steelies are likely to be moving upstream. During midday hours, especially with a bright sun, it's imperative that you not allow your shadow to fall upon any stretch of water. I often creep through tag alders and willows along a bank, searching for lies where concentrations of fish might be holding.

Finding holding structure on a wilderness stream is similar to reading a highway map. You must first become acquainted with the meaning of various symbols before

you can reach your destination. Some "symbols" that will lead you to steelhead are currents running near undercut banks, the edge of riffles, and the current-free corners of current-filled pools. A small or slight current, and in many instances, the lee behind obstructions in strong currents, will also hold fish.

Underwater snags can gobble lures faster than a Cadillac can guzzle gas, but they are also prime hotspots for both migrating and holding steelies. Alaska steelheaders know how many snags clutter the channels of prime trout streams, especially after breakup. These obstructions cause pools and depressions in the stream bottom, thus producing excellent lies for the fish. Always fish such areas, even at the risk of losing several lures.

While it's usually a good idea to pass up stretches of slack water when scouting for fish, I have found that steelhead often hold right on the edge of quiet water, or at the edge of the main or side current. Get excited when you find such a spot, because it's virtually a sure bet a large metalhead is lurking somewhere along the edge. Cast into

The author battles a steelhead on a Southeast Alaska stream. The fish struck an attractor bait drifted slowly through the pool at the base of the riffle

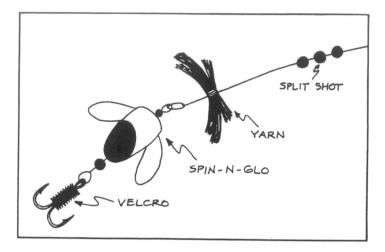

A Spin-N-Glo with yarn leader and Velcro trailer is a top lure for catching soft-striking steelhead.

SPLIT SHOT

YARN

SPIN-N-GLO

VELCRO

a calm area well ahead of the assumed fish lie and work the lure so that it bounces directly down the current's breakline, while moving at a snail's pace across the stream.

One last point on structure. If you hook a steelhead from a particular lie, chances are you'll hook additional fish from that very same spot throughout the season, providing no drastic change takes place in water flow or depth. These spots often prompt veteran steelhead anglers to arise at some ungodly, pre-dawn hour in order to beat other anglers to the jackpot.

Bait

Bait is probably one of the most commonly accepted methods of taking steelhead. However, I don't prefer it for several reasons. First, I'm a lure angler at heart. Changing lures in sub-freezing weather with fingers as pliable as matchsticks is bad enough for me. Even worse is the articulated finger movements required to assemble and fish spawn sacs.

Secondly, I don't want to kill fish. Because spawn is so pliable, steelhead—as well as native rainbows—have a habit of taking it deep into their throats. During a trout's usual display of aerial acrobatics and drag-smokin' runs, a swallowed hook can rip a fish's intestinal tract, sever arteries, and cause shock. You don't need to be a biologist to determine that injuries such as these produce dead fish. And it's my policy to catch and release all wild rainbow/steelhead.

And last, I always seem to catch as many, if not more, steelhead on lures than with eggs, and without the mess. Steelheaders suffer enough from ice-encrusted fingers, noses, and rod guides. The additional headache of keeping gear and tackle free of the corrosive egg milk would make fishing even more difficult.

Lures

Some of the most effective steelhead lures on the market today are the egg imitators. They run under a variety of names such as Spin-N-Glos, Okie Drifters, Glo-Gos, Gooey-Bobs, Lil Corkies, Cherry Drifters, Fenton Flies, and the like. While each has its strengths and weaknesses, the one point to keep in mind is "small." A steelhead can detect, and spit out, a large, hard-plastic drift lure before the angler has a chance to react. But fish often have more difficulty in clamping down on a smaller lure, thus delaying a rejection. This delay is often enough time for the angler to react with a hookset.

Friend and avid steelhead angler Hank Bottemiller of Milwaukie, Oregon, once advised that I should use yarn with these attractors to increase their effectiveness. He has two reasons for tying yarn on the trailing hook and above the lure. One, it keeps the buoyant cork or plastic attractor body from sliding up the line and away from the hooks. Two, the yarn has a Velcro effect on the steelhead's teeth. The yarn snags the teeth of a fish, providing an extra moment for the angler to react to the take. I modified Hank's idea by wrapping the shanks of large flies with Velcro. Now Velcro-accented drift lures and flies have become a staple in my steelhead tackle box because they produce hook-ups when fish are striking softly.

I favor rather stiff yarn under two inches long for tying yarn flies. For an added attractor to drift lures, I favor the same type of yarn in fluorescent red or pink. Chartreuse yarn takes honors in murky water or as the main color in a fly pattern.

Because these lures are meant to imitate roe, the presentation to the fish should follow the care-free drift of a single egg or cluster. The lure must travel with the current and close to bottom. So the sinker—either pencil lead, snagless, or split shot—should be 12- to 16-inches from the lure. Have the leader longer in clear water and shorter in heavy currents. Cast the rig upstream, quartering the lure slowly to the intended target. Make sure the lure is bouncing bottom and working properly before entering the strike zone.

Veteran Alaska steelhead angler Loren Pitchford stresses changing weights to meet the requirements of the stretch of water being fished. For example, if a pencil lead that fished a lure effectively on the previous drift later fails to make contact with the bottom, it's necessary to change the weight immediately. You waste time fishing a lure floating just above a big steelhead.

I've caught my share of steelhead on drift lures, but they can't match the productivity and sensitivity of a spinner. I think a spinner is the best lure an angler can use, provided the proper size is selected and it's fished properly.

For instance, Situk steelies are suckers for No. 3 Mepps Aglias with a fluorescent red or gold blade. In low water, it's necessary to downgrade to a No. 2. Or in turbid water, a certain run of fish may prefer a brass or copper blade. Whatever type you choose, every Aglia blade churns with the power of an Iron Horse. When using a boron or element rod—a definite prerequisite for steelheading—the blade will seem to vibrate any wedding or class rings right off your hand. And when a steelhead mouths the lure—which is usually a feather-like touch—there's no question about it. You know when the blade stops.

If you're interested in the aesthetics of the sport, you'll agree that fly fishing for steelhead is the most challenging and exciting way to catch this fish.

While I haven't had any success enticing steelhead to rise to a floating dry, there are numerous streamer and attractor patterns that Alaska steelhead favor. The Bubble Fly, Two-Egg Sperm fly, Glo-Bug, Polar Shrimp, Meteor, Spruce, Alaska Mary Ann, Skykomish Sunrise, Thor, and Boss are several of the most effective patterns. Anglers should carry both weighted and unweighted versions.

An 8½- to 9½-foot, 8- or 9-weight graphite or boron rod is necessary for fishing most Alaska steelhead waters properly. You also need a sink-tip or sinking line to get the fly down. In shallow water, however, I've concluded that a floating line with a weighted fly is about the only way to take fish consistently without spooking them. On most Southeastern steelhead waters, where snags are commonplace and the rain forest grows right down to the banks, full-sink lines and shooting heads are often

nightmares. Some anglers use a 3-way swivel between leader and fly, with a dropper leader on which several split shot are crimped. For me, a piece of lead-core trolling line between leader and fly line works best.

Fly fishing technique follows the same philosophy as lure fishing: Keep it drifting above bottom. Stay on the bank if at all possible. At least stay directly across or downstream from the fish, as the shuffling of your feet in gravel or sand can easily spook them. Make a quarter cast above the lies or redds and allow the current to sweep the fly to the fish. On certain stretches of the Karluk, a steelheader can go wild with 60-foot casts and textbook-like presentations. However, when using weighted lines in Southeastern waters, you need to lob the fly upstream and drift it from stone to stone. Occasionally, I've triggered a strike response by twitching the fly as it nears a steelhead. Strikes are usually vicious, and hookups secure. But try this only if normal tactics fail to produce, as the unnatural action may spook fish.

Successful steelheading is more than catching fish. It's also living up to the responsibility of perpetuating the species. Anglers fishing the Kenai Peninsula's Anchor River can help biologists' ongoing study of the fishery by

John and Sue Chihuly hold up a nice catch of Deep Creek steelhead. October is an excellent time to fish this and other steelhead watersheds throughout the state. Mark Chihuly photo.

releasing any fish with green disc tags. These fish carry radio transmitters that help biologists understand the wintering habits of steelhead. This information is vital in maintaining this excellent fishery. Anglers who hook a tagged fish that is injured and must be killed should return the tag and transmitter to any ADF&G office, along with information on how, when, and where the fish was caught.

A fly-out excursion for wilderness steelhead is perhaps one of the most challenging forms of Alaska fishing still available to anyone willing to brave the elements. Anglers can usually stay in Forest Service cabins, or rough it in tents in more remote areas.

I remember such a wilderness foray on the Situk River several years ago. Darkness was fast approaching, along with the cold of a lingering Alaska winter. I had been steelhead fishing most of the day and I was dead tired. However, the continuous casting and concentration usually associated with this type of fishing weren't what produced my aching muscles. Rather, I was experiencing the tiring effects of battling steelhead all day long. For this kind of fatigue most fishermen would gladly trade the secret location of their favorite fishing holes. The only thing that prevented me from fishing myself into an unconscious euphoria was the rapidly receding daylight.

Proceeding to drift my line through the dark indigo pool, I felt my line hesitate momentarily. It was a familiar sensation. My tired arms instinctively jerked upwards in a sweeping arc, and though darkness had completely overtaken the area, I could hear an enraged steelhead's response: a series of resounding splashes. Memories of the day's earlier steelhead acrobatics flashed through my mind in lieu of the battle I couldn't witness.

The steelie ran through its maneuvers and eventually submitted itself stubbornly to my constant pressure. I slowly followed the line to the fish's mouth. In the blackness I gently unhooked what I estimated to be an 8-pound fish, still ice-cold from the depths. After releasing my fish, I dragged myself back to the tent camp a few hundred yards downstream. Suddenly, as if someone had lit a match, the eerie glow of the Northern Lights burst into long streamers radiating across the northern sky. It was a fitting and proper way to end a wilderness trip for such a remarkable gamefish.

Where to go for Steelhead

Southeast

east steelhead systems offer excellent fishing throughout
and winter months. The Situk is the most popular, and
often accr   as the "best wild steelheading in the world." A catch of
10 fish per day is not uncommon for the experienced steelheader. Most
fish will range from 5 to 17 pounds, with a 7-pound fish being average.
The river has both a spring and fall run. Prince of Wales streams offer
excellent late fall and late winter steelheading for 10- to 12-pound fish.
Try November, February, and March for the largest fish.

Admiralty Island
Mole River

Juneau
Anan Creek
Black Bear Creek
Martin Creek
Taku River

Ketchikan
Fish Creek
Naha River

Petersburg
Castle River
Kadake Creek
Petersburg Creek
Tunehean Creek

Prince of Wales
Eagle Creek
Harris River
Hydaburg River
Karta River
Klawak River
Miller Creek
Salmon Bay Creek
Staney Creek
Thorne River

Sitka
Plotnikof River
Salmon Creek
Sitkoh River

Wrangell
Olive Cove Creek
Snake Creek
Stikine River
Thoms Creek

Yakutat
Alsek River
Italio River
Situk River

Southcentral

Anchor River is the most popular fishery for fall-run fish. Averaging 7
pounds, with up to 18 pounds possible. Peak of the run occurs in mid-
October. Ninilchik is good for fish ranging from 6 to 11 pounds. The
lower section of the river on an incoming tide is best.

Cook Inlet/Kenai Peninsula
Anchor River   Deep Creek   Ninilchik River

Southwest

The Karluk is considered the best steelhead river on Kodiak Island.
Autumn runs are best, as steelhead are usually in poor condition in the
spring. Fish may be kept elsewhere, but a catch-and-release fishery is in
effect for the road system steelhead fisheries. Steelies range from 4 to 10
pounds, with an occasional trophy reaching the 14-pound mark.

Afognak Island
Afognak River
Portage River

Kodiak
Frazer River
Karluk River

Red River
Saltery River

Where to go for Rainbow Trout

Southeast

Rainbows have been selectively stocked in these lakes. Size varies from pan-size to a maximum of 6 pounds. Also, many excellent rainbow populations exist in the high mountain lakes out of Ketchikan. These fish were first planted in the early 1950s. They can weigh up to 8 pounds.

Baranof Island
Rezanof Lake System

Ketchikan
McDonald Lake
Walker Lake

Petersburg
Swan Lake

Sitka
Blue Lake

Southcentral

The Talachulitna, Deshka, and Alexander are the best rainbow fisheries in the Cook Inlet/Kenai Peninsula region. Fish ranging from 2 to 8 pounds are not uncommon. The best way to fish these rivers is via float trip from their headwaters to any of several pickup points downriver. For Lake Creek rainbows, put in at Chelatna Lake and float to Shovel Lake. The Matanuska Lake and Bradley-Kepler Lake Complex are annually stocked by ADF&G. However, 'bows up to 6 pounds have been taken from both waters. Matanuska was recently chemically treated, and it will be several years before the fish reach trophy size.

The Kenai River has native rainbows to 20 pounds. The mouth of Skilak Lake and upper river are the best areas to fish, especially in early spring and late fall. Six-year-old Kenai rainbows have tipped the scales at 10 pounds, which is a remarkable growth rate for Alaska. In summer, try the first 3 to 5 miles below Skilak Lake.

Upper Russian River and Russian Lakes turn out rainbows up to 24 inches. Both waters can be reached by trail. I recommend a small inflatable for fishing the lake.

Skilak Lake is an excellent spring fishery for rainbows up to 20 pounds, however, most range between 2 and 10 pounds.

Swanson River Lake System offers excellent fishing for wild rainbows up to 4 pounds. Spring and late autumn are the best fisheries. Accessible by air or canoe.

Most rainbows in the Copper River/Upper Susitna area are stocked fish and non-reproductive due to lack of available spawning habitat in most lakes. The Gulkana River offers excellent fishing for wild rainbows up to 6 pounds throughout the spring, summer and fall months. The central section of river is considered best for a trophy.

Cook Inlet/Kenai Peninsula

Alexander Creek	Peters Creek (headwaters)
Bradley-Kepler Lake Complex	Russian Lakes
Deshka River	Skilak Lake
Kenai River	Swanson Lake System
Lake Creek	Talachulitna River
Matanuska Lake	Upper Russian River

How to Catch
Alaska's Trophy Sportfish

Chignik River/Upper Chiaktuak
Blueberry Lake
Crater Lake
Gulkana River
Worthington Lake

Southwest

The waters in the Southwest region offer the best rainbow trout fishing in the state. Fish 10 pounds and larger are not uncommon, and are concentrated behind spawning salmon during the fall months. These same rainbows can be found in area lakes during the summer months.

On the Kodiak Road System most lakes are stocked with rainbows. They are native to specific systems in the Kodiak-Afognak Island group, and support a limited fishery. Rainbows here range from 1 to 4 pounds.

In the Kuskokwim area, the Togiak River is noted for yielding rainbows to 12 pounds; lower 8 miles of river most productive during first half of October. The Goodnews River is an excellent river to float for big rainbows, especially in early to late fall. Logistics may be a slight problem, but worth the effort. Excellent fishing can be had in most of these watersheds throughout the year. However, the largest fish are typically caught in June and late September through mid-October.

Agulowak River
American River
Battle River
Belinda Creek
Branch River System
Brooks River
Copper River
Dream Creek
Gibralter River
Iliamna Lake
Iliamna River
King Salmon River
Kokhanok River
Koktuli River
Moraine Creek
Mulchatna River
Naknek River
Naknek System
Newhalen River
Talarik Creek (Upper and Lower)
Wood River Lakes

Kodiak
Abercrombie Lake
Genevieve Lake
Pasagshak Point Lakes

Kuskokwim
Aniak River
Arolik River
Goodnews River
Kanektok River
Kasigluk River
Kisaralik River
Kisethluk River
Kweethluk River
Nushagak River
Nuyakuk River
Togiak River

Interior

Except for a wild population of rainbow in the Aniak River, all other populations in this area are considered stocked fish. Quartz Lake produces rainbows in the 16- to 22-inch class on a regular basis.

Quartz Lake
Rainbow Lake

Cutthroat
Trout

Cutthroat Trout

Cutthroat trout are fish of beauty. Their crimson-slashed throat, large black specks, pearlescent eyes and fighting qualities are but a few of the many traits anglers admire about this species. Yet it's the cutt's environment that complements this beauty a hundred fold: Rugged, glacial-scarred mountains jutting up 4,000 feet; rolling expanses of emerald green hemlock and spruce forests; isolated alpine lakes where mountain goats are the only inhabitants; and miles of pristine beaches, occasionally split by the whitewater cascades of ice-melt streams. This is cutthroat country, and you'll not find another like it anywhere else in the world.

The cutthroat trout (Salmo clarki) is also known as Clark's trout, red-throated trout, short-tailed trout and harvest trout, a name given to autumn runs of anadromous cutthroat because of their gold, olive, crimson and black coloration. Throughout the remainder of the year, the cutthroat is highly variable in coloration and size. Sea-run fish are usually cadmium-blue to silvery, with inconspicuous black dots and throat slash. Those residing in bog-fed waters commonly take on a dark olive or gold hue with pronounced black markings and a vivid red or orange throat slash.

Other distinguishing cutthroat characteristics are hyoid teeth (located on the back of its tongue between the gills) and spots usually present on the dorsal, anal and caudal fins.

Cutthroat trout in Southeast Alaska benefit from a distribution nearly as universal as that of the Dolly

Fishing for cutthroats on an unnamed stream near Ketchikan. Cutthroat populations in Southeast Alaska benefit from a distribution as nearly universal as that of the Dolly Varden.

This alpine cutthroat fell for a chrome and orange spoon; a lure that best imitates an injured kokanee. Kokanee or juvenile sockeye are prime forage foods that produce trophy-size cutthroats.

Varden. They are native to coastal waters and lakes from Ketchikan northward to Eshamy Lake in Prince William Sound. It's widespread distribution, however, is irregular. The fish may predominate in some watersheds, while only a token population exists in others.

Life History

Spawning takes place in gravel bottom streams with a slight to moderate current. The male courts the female through a series of nudges and prods. The female soon digs a 4- to 6-inch nest in typical salmonid fashion. Two to four hours later, the female will settle into the pit and release approximately 1,000 eggs, which the male quickly fertilizes. The female will then swim a short distance upstream where she will dig another nest, with the debris and gravel material from the second nest being used to cover the eggs laid in the first. Spawning may occur several times, after which anadromous fish eventually outmigrate to sea.

Very few cutthroats survive the rigors of spawning and

How to Catch
Alaska's Trophy Sportfish

predation. Northern Oregon studies indicate that post-spawning mortality rates for anadromous cutthroats averaged 68 percent over a 4-year period. Age-class studies of the upstream migrants indicate that 68 percent had not spawned previously, 26 percent had spawned once, 4.5 percent twice, and only .5 percent had spawned 3 times (Sumner, 1962). While post-spawning mortality has not been studied in Alaska waters, these figures are indicative of the mortality anadromous cutthroats suffer throughout their range.

Cutthroat eggs hatch in 6 to 7 weeks. Growth is quite rapid, with the young reaching 2 to 3 inches by the end of September. Anadromous strains of cutthroats do not out-migrate to sea until they are 2- to 3-years old and 4 to 7 inches in length. Smolt mortality is extremely high at their first outmigration, peaking at 98 percent from the time outmigration begins to their initial return to freshwater. However, some strains may not outmigrate at all, living most of their life in a freshwater lake or stream environment.

About 90 percent of the cutthroat's growth is acquired during the months of April and September. A Southeastern Alaska cutt averages 10 inches at 5 years and 13 inches at 8 years of age. The current Alaska state record for cutthroat trout is an 8-pound, 6-ounce fish taken from Wilson Lake in 1977 by Robert Denison. However, sea-run and lake fish rarely exceed 4 pounds. An angler must catch a 3 pound or larger cutthroat to qualify for a trophy certificate of award given annually by the State of Alaska.

Catching cutthroats is not difficult if the angler will keep in mind the varied environments in which large cutthroat thrive and the techniques best suited for these waters: bog and beaver ponds, lakes, streams and rivers, and intertidal areas.

Techniques

Muskeg Streams-Beaver Ponds

Cutthroats residing in the tea-stained waters of muskeg streams and bogs are the most difficult to catch. These waters are usually small in size, and the fish are extremely alert to predators. There is rarely any cover where the angler can hide easily, and travel is usually near impossible

due to swamp or fallen timber. But for the angler willing to brave these deterrents, the reward is big, colorful cutts that are unlike those found elsewhere in the state.

Muskeg cutthroat feed on whatever is available. Fish eggs, Coleoptera, Chironomids (adults and pupae), and fish such as sticklebacks and sculpins make up the bulk of their diet.

Lures that resemble these forage items must be small, and presentations must be delicate. Muskeg cutts are intolerant of waters thrashed to a froth by the spin angler. I've found a 6-weight fly system using a floating line and tiny, No. 14 or 16 Mosquitoes, Midge, Humpy, Caddis, Black Gnat or Brown Bivisible patterns work well when the surface is glassy smooth and fish are rising to a hatch. With a sink-tip line, my favorites are Sculpin, Woolly Worm, and Black Marabou patterns. I like to fish these flies along stretches of muskeg streams, through deep holes, and along undercut banks. Tunnel-like depressions near beaver houses or the entrances to abandoned dens are also excellent spots to probe for large cutts, especially

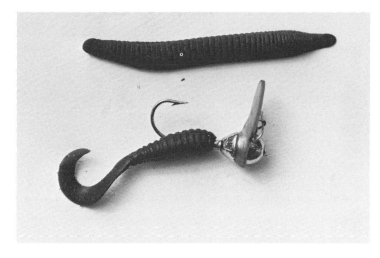

with a Black Marabou.

When ultralight spin fishing, I carry two lures: a black Scrounger or similar lure and a small silver spoon. Cutthroat relish leeches, and they are extremely abundant in many muskeg swamps and beaver ponds. The Scrounger or any twister-tail grub lure—when worked slowly across bottom—exhibits an action that drives big cutthroats into a feeding frenzy. I like the 1/32- to 1/8-ounce sizes, fished with a boron rod and 4-pound-test, clear monofilament line.

During mid-day, it may be necessary to fish the Scrounger directly under the surface. Cutthroat trout are sight feeders and oftentimes can't detect a dark lure against a black, mucky bottom. However, a dark lure against a bright backdrop of sky is extremely effective, especially when trout are feeding under the surface or at mid-depth. I like to give the lure an occasional twitch about every 3 feet, an added action that often triggers an aggressive strike response.

When it's impossible to fish structure, such as heavily timbered water or impassable shorelines, a float and single-egg rig can have deadly results. Concentrate your efforts in and around standing timber, weedy areas, the mouths of trickling feeder creeks, and behind large rocks. Fish the single egg anywhere from 10- to 18-inches below the float. I've had best results when I allowed the egg to fish for at least 15 minutes before slowly reeling in and casting to another location.

Access on large muskeg lakes is often difficult, especially when cutthroats are located near prime structure that is beyond casting range from shore. Under these circumstances, I'll pack-in a small inflatable enabling me to fish structure the shoreline anglers can't touch. Some fishermen prefer to use a truck tire inner-tube with a plastic harness, much like those used in fishing the largemouth bass marshes in the Lower 48. Remember to use either type for greater mobility. It's important to remain close to shore or structure, and at the limits of your casting range. Careless rowing or wading around the lake will do nothing but put the cutts down for hours, if not days.

Lakes

Southeastern cutthroat lakes are absolute jewels of beauty. They are often bordered by cliffs that start at lake shore and rise several hundred to a thousand or more feet. The fish they hold are equally impressive.

My first experience with a lake cutthroat occurred one summer when I was flying over the Misty Fjords area with Tyee Airline's pilot Ned Pleus and his family. We had just returned from completing an afternoon of catching rainbow trout in the high alpine lakes that abound in the area. However, much to my disappointment, we didn't hook into any cutthroats. As we were heading back to Ketchikan, Ned banked the Beaver and dropped us into a smooth glide toward a large, bluish-tinged lake with standing timber at one end.

"You have just 10 minutes to catch that cutthroat," he said as he flipped open the door. "You'll have to stand out on the float and fish, as we don't have time to go ashore."

Not wasting any time, I grabbed my miniature box of lures and ultralight rod and began casting a systematic pattern toward the timbered area about 50 yards distant. Yet, after 3 minutes, the spinner failed to produce a strike. I quickly tied on a small wobbling plug, with equally disappointing results. With 4 minutes left, I tied on a Fjord spoon and let fly. The third cast was stopped short. I set the hook and wobbled precariously on the float as the fish headed for timber. The drag screeched as I applied all the pressure 4-pound line would allow. Ned opened the door and watched in amazement as I carefully stretched out with the net and scooped up a beautiful, 3½-pound cut-

throat. As I squeezed back into the plane with my prize, the engine fired up, flopping me into my seat.

I have since learned that Wilson Lake is a prime example of the many trophy cutthroat lakes scattered throughout Southeast Alaska. These waters consistently produce large cutts due to one common denominator: Kokanee, a juvenile sockeye salmon whose extremely oily flesh makes it a superb forage fish species. Big cutts will feed exclusively on kokanee, which are often the predominant forage species in a lake.

Many of these wilderness cutthroat lakes have Forest Service cabins and rowboats. Thus the angler has both a comfortable base of operations, and also a means of effectively fishing the deepwater dropoffs, freshwater inlets, and sandy shoals big cutts like to frequent.

My favorite rig under these conditions is a lake troll and spoon rig. Depending on conditions, I use a 1- to 3-ounce trolling weight to which I attach a troll with at least 4 chrome or silver blades. Some anglers prefer to tie a snubber between the troll and leader, but I prefer to tie a 14- to 16-inch, 8- to 12-pound-test, clear mono-leader directly to the troll. Most alpine cutthroat lakes are extremely clear, and the less paraphernalia, the better. The lure should be a chrome Needlefish, Rainbo-scaled Mepps spoon, or

Ketchikan pilot Ned Pleus trolls a remote, alpine lake for cutthroat. Boats and Forest Service cabins are available on many prime cutthroat waters throughout Southeast Alaska, and provide for a relaxing, wilderness fishing vacation. Access to the best waters is by float plane only.

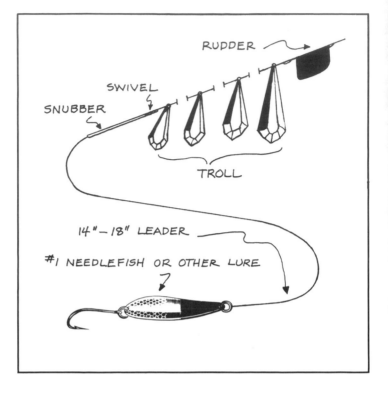

A basic lake troll rig for cutthroats. Fish it slowly along shoreline structure, at stream mouths, and along rock cliffs bordering deep water.

RUDDER

SWIVEL

SNUBBER

TROLL

14" – 18" LEADER

#1 NEEDLEFISH OR OTHER LURE

similar "flutter" spoon. I prefer the lure to be larger than the troll blades, giving the trout a larger target to locate.

When trolled, the blades imitate a school of kokanee, with the fluttering spoon resembling a crippled or injured fish that can't keep up with the school. While cuts will often home-in on this rig from great depths, I prefer to fish the rig within 10 feet of the surface, and as far behind the boat as possible. I prefer rowing because wilderness cuts are often spooked by outboards. Also, it's imperative the troll be fished slowly. The infrequent pauses imparted on the lure by rowing seem to be what has produced as many as 65 cuts for me in an afternoon.

If no boats are available, find a freshwater inlet and use either a ¼-ounce Fjord spoon, HotRod, Krocodile, or my favorite, a leadhead jig. Work the lure in a steady swim along sandbars and dropoffs, occasionally allowing the lure to falter. My catch ratio, and that of anglers whose comments are recorded in the log books in each Forest Service cabin, show that evenings are unquestionably the best time to fish either from boat or shore.

Stream Fishing

Angling for stream cutthroats is chiefly a fall fishery. The fish returning to freshwater at this time are deep and full-bodied, having spent anywhere from 12 to 150 days at sea, gorging on needlefish, herring and other prime baitfish.

The spring fishery consists chiefly of spawned-out fish that are long and snake-like and not usually desirable for a trophy mount. Mature spawners outmigrate earliest, anytime from mid-April to mid-May. A second outmigration of smaller or immature fish usually peaks in mid-June. Studies show that husky-bodied cutts are often found inmigrating during these major outmigrations. However, their numbers are small.

The in-migration for most streams starts in mid-July, and peaks in late September. Sizes vary from 4- to 20-inches, with a 12-inch average length.

The angler after trophy harvest trout pays close attention to water and weather conditions. The largest inmigration usually occurs on moderate to rising stream

Polarized sunglasses and ultralight tackle are necessary when pursuing cutts on small streams. Dark water indicates holes, snags, or obstructions that attract and hold large cutthroat.

This cutthroat fell for a leadhead drifted along the edge of a sandbar bordering deepwater. Bog-fed cutts usually exhibit a dark crimson throat slash, while lake or sea-run fish sport a red or orange slash.

flows. Prolonged high or low water delays migration. Studies show that stream temperature is usually 58 degrees at the start of an in-migration.

It's been my experience that the in-migrants of September and October are fish over 14- to 18-inches. These trophies follow the silver salmon upstream to their spawning beds, gorging on eggs that are oftentimes laid at the head of beaver ponds. Many a big cutthroat has fallen victim to a single egg with yarn attractor, bounced through a hole or along an undercut bank. However, I prefer to leave the real eggs at home and fish an Aqua Cone, Sammy, or any of the soft-imitation, single salmon eggs on the market. I delight in fishing these lures with an ultralight rod and touch of split shot. A slow bounce along bottom through deep pools, behind fallen timber, at the edge of riffles and behind migrating salmon will produce fish when conventional lures fail.

Another excellent lure I frequently use is a white grub or maggot pattern. There is usually an abundance of maggots feeding on spawned-out salmon during this time of year.

How to Catch
Alaska's Trophy Sportfish

High water or rain wash thousands of these larvae into the water, and at times they are the only food big cutts feed upon. At this time, cutts are ripe for picking with a 7-weight fly rod, sink-tip line and 6-foot tapered leader. A white twister-tail or Bass Buster grub will produce the best results for the spin angler.

When faced with high water conditions, an angler may need to tie on hardware to get down to holding cutts. Use small wobbling spoons such as orange and black Krocodiles, red or orange Dardevles, fluorescent pink Pixees, and orange/chrome Fjord spoons. Cast the lure far enough upstream and allow it to reach bottom before entering the structure to be fished. A slow retrieve is all that's necessary. I've found that a piece of red yarn tied to the hook of a lure increases its effectiveness ten-fold.

Intertidal

When cutthroats are at sea, they rarely roam more than 50 miles from their spawning stream. Unlike their salmon cousins, they tend to congregate near shoreline structure throughout their ocean sojourn. Anglers knowing what to look for and when can experience unsurpassed trouting, as cutts at this time will strike most anything thrown at them.

Cutts feed in relatively shallow water. In fact, if you can see bottom or the slope of a dropoff, it's water worth fishing. The edge of a kelp bed is an excellent hotspot, as is the mouth of a freshwater outlet emptying over a gravel or sandbar. I prefer to fish for cutts on an incoming tide. However, avoid the extreme minus and plus tides, which not only put the fish down, but make fishing more work than pleasure, especially when using a fly rod or light spinning tackle.

I prefer to use ultralight gear and lures when fishing for intertidal cutts from shore. Not only is it a lot of fun, but also the larger monos often resemble winch cables in the clear, ocean waters and do nothing but spook fish. Small spoons, plugs, and spinners similar to those used for saltwater Dolly Varden will also catch sea-run cutts.

When fish are cruising beyond casting range, the troll rig used to catch lake cutthroats works equally well for intertidal fish. However, instead of flutter spoons, some anglers favor 4- to 5-inch bait herring threaded onto a light-action

The excitement of fishing wilderness, alpine lakes for cutthroats where few, if any, anglers have fished before is an extremely satisfying experience, especially when an entire family can join in the fun.

mooching rig and experience good success. Another variation is to fish cut herring suspended from a float on an incoming tide. While this method is responsible for many iced trout annually, and the wait for a strike suspenseful, I'm a lure man at heart and prefer casting or precision trolling. However, some ol' timers swear the cut herring/float method is the only way to catch lunker cutthroat.

To reach Alaska's top cutthroat fishing may take hours of climbing near-vertical cliffs, dodging brown bears on kelp-strewn beaches, or fighting mosquitoes as well as dense alders surrounding mucky beaver ponds. But once that red-throated warrior smashes your lure, slices through the water like a rampant salmon, and sparkles like a treasure chest of jewels in the landing net, trophy cutthroating will be a fishing adventure you'll want to relive time and time again.

Where to go for Cutthroat Trout

Southeast

Cutthroats are found as both year-round residents and as a migratory species in many Southeast waters. Wilson Lake is the top producer of trophy cutthroat trout in the state, as is Manzanita, Martin, Hasselborg, Turner, and Chilkat lakes. Best time to fish is early spring or late autumn.

Haines
Chilkat Lake

Juneau
Hasselborg Lake
Jim's Lake
Kathleen Lake
Thayer Lake
Turner Lake
Youngs Lake

Ketchikan
Manzanita Lake
Orchard Lake
Patching Lake
Ward Cove Lake
Wilson Lake

Petersburg
Castle River
Duncan Salt Chuck
Petersburg Lake
Swan Lake
Towers Lake

Sitka
Eva Lake
Goulding Lake
Katlian River
Natwasina River
Salmon Lake
Sitkoh Creek

Wrangell
Kunk Lake
Luck Lake
Martin Lake
Salmon Bay Creek
Thoms Lake
Virginia Lake

Southcentral

These watersheds are the westernmost extension of the cutthroat in North America. Fishing effort is low for both systems. Cutts have been known to reach 4 pounds in Eshamy Lake.

Prince William Sound
Eshamy Lake System
Eyak Lake

Grayling

Grayling

Alaska's wilderness aristocrat is the Arctic grayling. No other species can touch its elegance, grace, and delicate personality that has made it the symbol of the Alaska wilderness. The grayling is intolerant of altered or polluted environments; it requires clear, cold streams and lakes in the most northern latitudes of the world for survival. Its regal behavior—from devouring flies to its spirited fight once hooked—has easily convinced anglers of its worthiness to hold the title "Prince of Alaska Sportfish."

The Arctic grayling (Thymallus arcticus) is a large-scaled, trout-like fish that is also known as "sailfish of the North" due to its unusually large and banner-like dorsal fin. The genus name Thymallus was given to the grayling because fresh-caught fish smell like the herb thyme.

The grayling is a fish of various hues and colors that change with age. Adults vary from a silvery blue to a dark blue, but a few bright yellow individuals have been observed. The grayling's dorsal fin is long and high, its base longer than the depth of the body. Fin color varies from dark gray to black to blue, punctuated with pink and azure spots and deep-blue cross rows, often bordered with red and yellow. On males, the dorsal fin sweeps as far back as the adipose fin, and females exhibit a shorter, more rounded fin. The pelvic fins are crossed by 3 pink stripes, and the belly is white with gray blotches.

In Alaska, the grayling can be found in unsilted rivers which drain into the Bering Sea and Arctic Ocean, as well as in most streams of the Interior, and as far south as the drainages of Cook Inlet. Western distribution is not

The large, colorful dorsal fin is the trademark of the Arctic grayling. In strong current, a hooked grayling will erect this fin, which creates additional drag on the angler's line and often earns the fish its freedom. The male also uses its fin in territorial standoffs with other grayling and in mating.

known, but probably doesn't extend beyond Port Moller
on the Alaska Peninsula. Grayling have been successfully
introduced to selected waters in Southeastern Alaska and
Kodiak Island.

Life History

Grayling begin to congregate at the mouths of clearwater streams and rivers in early spring, just before
breakup. Their spawning urge is oftentimes so great that
they'll head up frozen streams via channels cut in the surface ice by spring runoff. However, most migrations occur
as soon as streams open. Grayling may spawn as far as 100
miles from their wintering waters.

Males quickly establish spawning territory, which they
readily defend against other males. The grayling warning
sign is impressive. The male will erect its large, dorsal fin,
open its mouth, and assume a rigid posture. Grayling defend their territory more through show than by the actual
fighting often exhibited by char and salmon.

A male grayling will follow a female and court her with
an undulating display of his dorsal fin. After he folds his
dorsal fin over her back, both fish arch and release eggs
and milt over a sandy gravel bottom. The eggs—4,700 plus
per female—are adhesive and stick to the substrate and
other bottom structure.

Grayling hatch in 11 days to 3 weeks, depending upon
water temperature. Growth is usually fairly rapid the first
year, with the young averaging about 4 inches long by

September. Growth rate is somewhat faster in the south than the north, but can vary greatly within and amongst various watersheds. Interior Alaska grayling average 12 inches at 5 years, and weigh about half a pound. Grayling in the Ugashik area of the Alaska Peninsula can reach 4 pounds and stretch 21 inches.

The current Alaska state record is a 4-pound, 13 ounce, 23-inch grayling taken in Ugashik Narrows by Paul F. Kanitz of Anchorage, Alaska in 1981. The Ugashik area is tops in the state for consistent catches of trophy grayling. But I've caught large grayling throughout the state, from the Brooks Range to Alaska Peninsula waters, that have stretched the tape at 18 inches. My own all-time record was taken from Lake Clark in 1979: a 4-pound male, 19½-inches long. I used a hand-tied salmon egg jig fished with ultralight tackle.

In most of the waters I've fished throughout the state, I've never had any problems catching grayling from 9- to 14-inches. In fact, fish this size can be overly cooperative when it comes to striking a lure or fly, especially if your intended quarry is a feeding rainbow or larger grayling. However, the larger, pot-bellied trophies are almost always elusive. After years of research and experimentation, I've discovered that big grayling can be caught consistently if the angler takes the time to study the social and feeding habits of this popular sportfish.

Techniques

Habits

Most Alaska grayling spend their lives in two or more waterways. Grayling will leave their summering streams in late fall, usually just before freeze up. They migrate to the large, deeper lakes and rivers, many of which are glacially fed. Normally such waters are heavily laden with silt during the summer melt. However, with the onset of freezing weather, the melting stops and these waters quickly clear up, allowing grayling to overwinter safely there. Just before spring breakup and subsequent river siltation, grayling again migrate up clearwater streams and rivers to their spawning and summering grounds.

However, big grayling are not restricted to clearwater streams and rivers. They can also be found in run off streams, fed by melting snow and ice, and bog-fed streams

Adela Batin plays a Goat Creek grayling. Bog-fed waters, especially those that have a lake at their head, are hotspots for large grayling.

channeling tea-stained waters from muskeg or bog ponds. Some of the best grayling fishing I've ever experienced took place at Goat Creek, an ice-melt, beaver-dammed stream coursing through several bogs in the Wrangell Mountains. With its muck bottom, Goat Creek resembles a duck hunting marsh more than a grayling stream. Yet on one trip there, my wife Adela and I hooked on nearly every cast grayling that averaged 16 inches. The fish were a dark, purplish gray, with iridescent blues, violets, and pinks rimming their elongated dorsal fins. Only the numerous swirls of feeding fish in Goat Creek tempted me to fish it. But, I learned it pays to investigate any and every stream in grayling country with at least a cast or two.

Spring

The grayling's spring migration is a spectacle to behold. I've seen hundreds of them pool up at stream mouths in larger rivers, waiting for the ice to go out. Ice and log jam

barriers also concentrate schools of fish. When grayling are packed together, they are very susceptible to flies and lures. Many such populations accessible by road have been severely depleted within the last 15 years. On small streams, several anglers can deplete a population in less than an hour. Therefore, in road-accessible areas, I strongly urge release of all grayling caught prior to spring spawning. In other areas, a catch should be limited to males only.

Summer

Big grayling go with cold water temperatures. Thus, with the advent of summer, I always make a point of carrying a small stream thermometer to test the waters I'll be fishing. Unlike many of the trout or salmonid species that seek deep, cold thermoclines in the summer heat, grayling escape warm water temperatures by moving to cool inlets and springs rather than deep water. On numerous occa-

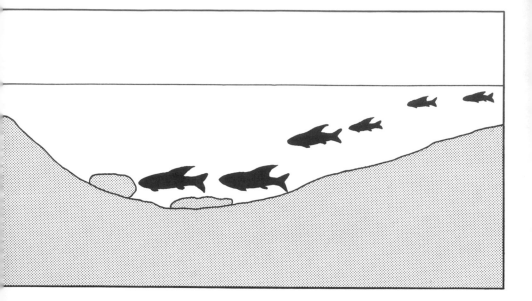

In pools, large grayling are typically found near the bottom and in the most forward positions, while smaller fish trail behind.

sions, especially during mid-summer, I've observed hundreds of grayling packed like sardines at the mouths of ice-melt inlets and at the outlets of underground springs. On more than one occasion these areas offered the only grayling action on the entire lake. They are prime hotspots for lunker fish. In fact, a test net study for deepwater grayling conducted by Alaska research biologists resulted in a catch of only whitefish and lake trout. Oxygen content at all levels was found to be 7 ppm, which is more than adequate for grayling to hold in deep water. Yet grayling were found massed in nearby streams and at the mouths of inlets.

Another study attesting to the grayling's low tolerance of warm water was a July tagging experiment from the inlet of Shallow Tangle Lake in which 85 grayling were captured. The water was 63 degrees and the captured fish, held in shallow-water pens, showed discomfort. Ten of the 85 fish died before tagging could be completed.

I've caught most of my large grayling in water temperatures ranging from 40 to 53 degrees. And, the colder the water, the better the fight. All grayling I've hooked in cold water have been spunky performers. Fish hooked in water warmer than 56 degrees were oftentimes sluggish, especially those caught in lakes. My experience has been that stream grayling offer more fight, and a better chance of catching a trophy.

How to Catch
Alaska's Trophy Sportfish

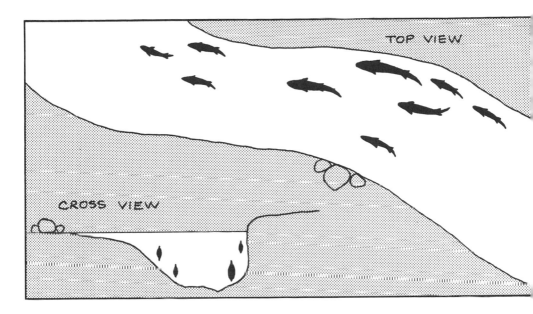

Streams

To consistently catch large grayling in streams requires a working knowledge of the species' social hierarchy. Studies conducted in Alaska streams by Vascotto (1970) show that as a rule, larger grayling occupy positions closer to the bottom while smaller fish are distributed throughout mid-depth. The largest grayling in any given pool are also in the most forward positions in relation to the current. Thus, the social standing of grayling in a stream allows for the largest fish to get most of the free-floating food organisms. Since large grayling usually occupy that position in a pool where water enters in the greatest volume, they have first crack at considerably more drift organisms. The needs of large fish are greater than those of smaller fish, which invariably trail behind.

Upon looking at a cross section of the same pool, Vascotto also found that the largest fish occupy the deepest portion of the pool, often corresponding to the center. The smaller fish to either side become progressively smaller nearer to shore.

In deep, narrow pools, fish hug the far, inside bank. When a grayling was removed from a pool, the remaining fish moved up and occupied different feeding ranges.

I've often observed that once I caught several large grayling from a pool, I would often hook nothing else but

A variation in grayling distribution occurs in narrow streams where trophy grayling are typically found in the deepest part of a pool. Smaller grayling can be found in front, behind, and to the shallow water side of the dominant fish.

smaller ones. According to Vascotto, after a school has been spooked for whatever reason, small grayling are the first to move to the head of the pool in the position formerly held by the largest fish. Larger fish follow about 15 minutes later. In reassuming its territory, each returning grayling displays to get smaller fish to move over. As a fish was displaced, it moved downstream in the pool; and as it did, so did every other small fish behind it. Anglers should note that this hierarchy doesn't hold true during the autumn months when downstream migrations are taking place.

I experienced the grayling hierarchy 5 years ago when fishing the Talachulitna River with Steve Johnson, manager of Tala-View Lodge. It was a sunny afternoon, and the edges of the leaves were just starting to turn a golden amber. Steve was fishing a pool upstream about 15 yards with a Woolly Worm. I was working the tail end of the same pool and the head of another on the opposite, yet deeper side of the river. Steve immediately hooked a beautiful, 16-inch grayling and quickly played and released it. Walking a few yards downstream, he hooked and released two more fish identical to the first.

I was baffled at my lack of success. We both were using the same type tackle and Woolly Worm pattern. Moving downstream to the head of the next pool, I immediately had a heavy strike. I set the hook and was treated to the tail-dancing acrobatics of a 15-inch grayling. The fish surged in the current, diving for the deepest section of river. I had my hands full for a couple of minutes. Then a large, dorsal fin jutted out of the water and I eased the fish to hand. The grayling was very cold to the touch, and glistened a sapphire-blue with violet dots adorning its sail-finned dorsal. I carefully released the fish, and proceeded to hook 7 more, all of similar size. Meanwhile, Steve had suffered a loss in action, with only two hookups in 15 minutes. He quickly moved upriver, and began catching grayling again. I continued to experience good grayling fishing for the next hour in the lower pool. But the action quickly ceased with the arrival of the lodge's skiff. Since, I've made it a point to:

• Fish within inches of the stream bottom.
• Fish the head of pools initially, and when action cools off, move upstream to the tail of the next pool, where I'll cast my fly or lure into the current emptying into the head

How to Catch
Alaska's Trophy Sportfish

of the pool. Rarely do I fish downstream, especially in low water conditions, because large grayling spook very easily.

• In murky water, I'll fish directly over the deepest channel, using a jig-type lure for precise lure control. Otherwise, I'll drift a fly or lure through the deepest channel.

Even if you fish the locations preferred by large grayling, you may catch nothing but small fish. In that case, it might be necessary to trigger the feeding stimulus of the larger fish. In studying the feeding habits of grayling, researchers found some fish need considerable motivation before beginning to feed. Feeding activity increased in intensity only after one fish had reinforced or motivated the other. That is, when one fish began to rise over another, the latter did not move until the first fish had risen several times, after which the second fish rose to the bait slowly. After 2 or 3 such rises, the entire school of fish became quite active. It wasn't the food that necessarily triggered the feeding activity, but rather the feeding activity of other fish that prompted them to rise.

Despite ice-cold water and deep pools, grayling are often

difficult to find, especially during heavy fishing pressure, dog-day temperatures, or spawning salmon activity. I remember a June '83 trip with guide Jim Bailey of Stephan Lake Lodge. The air temperature was in the upper 80s and the cold mountain stream we were fishing was quite low. We had fished several deep pools that morning, and by mid-afternoon, had caught only 14 "runt" grayling. Jim knew the stream had a good grayling population, and that the big fish had to be somewhere. So we went on an exploratory hike. Half a mile downstream, we found a series of channels and pools just boiling with activity from both rainbows and grayling, yet the fish were small. The pool was about 5 feet deep, and almost 14 feet long. I had a hunch those big grayling were holding above bottom, so I tied on a small Mirro-Lure. The first cast retrieved directly under the surface brought outstanding results in the form of a thrashing, 15½-inch grayling. I hooked 3 more grayling—including a 16-incher—before the remaining anglers in our party found our hotspot. It wasn't long before I was loaning my rod and lure to Jim and the others.

I learned from this experience that grayling are primarily mid-depth and surface feeders. But above all, they are visual feeders. When a grayling sights food, it moves from side to side, bringing the item into its narrow cone of vision ahead of its snout where its binocular vision can be employed. With both eyes fixed onto its target, grayling can estimate distance better. Larger grayling, being more deliberate in their movements, are more efficient in taking food items from the surface of the water. This makes dry fly fishing one of the best ways to catch trophy grayling. Because of the grayling's social hierarchy, large fish are the first to sight an object and have plenty of time to intercept it. Smaller fish often chase around the pool for items that have drifted past the larger fish.

Rainy days and high water conditions have always been a problem for anglers pursuing big grayling. Studies of grayling stomach contents show that on rainy days they eat 1/3 to 1/4 less than on sunny days. Yet during periods of rain and high water, there can be five to ten times more drift organisms in a stream than normal for a sunny day. That grayling don't utilize a substantial food source available during periods of heavy rain confirms the belief that they are visible feeders.

While grayling fishing is often slow when its raining, I've

experienced noteworthy success using a large, fluorescent-red fly pattern rather than the standard black and brown patterns that work so well at other times. But this applies only to murky water where visibility is greater than one foot, and when the fly is fished within the first 6- to 10-inches of the surface.

Vascotto also noted that a lure worked directly across the bottom in high, murky water would catch fish throughout the day, while dry flies worked only from 1000 to 1800, with the peak activity occurring at 1600. I've found that ultralight spinning and light-action spinning lures will consistently take fish when fly offers turn cold. My favorites are: size 0 and 1 Mepps Black Furies, black Mister Twister grub lures, 1/4-ounce Chummin' Minnows, 1/64-ounce Fin-Chilla flies, small Panther Martins in black and orange, and 1/16- to 1/4-ounce spoons like the Fjord and Dardevle. Also, small drift lures such as Glo-Bugs work well with a small BB split shot attached 10 inches up the line.

Big grayling are smart feeders, and will shun a lure offering after several casts, especially if the angler has missed one or more strikes. Vascotto says about one experiment:

"Crushed mosquitoes, hookless artificial flies, and spruce needles were dropped in the pool. The grayling refused to rise or make investigational movements when the spruce needles were dropped. However, they rose and took the dry flies which they mouthed and dropped several times before allowing them to drift backwards to where other fish took them. Usually, these large fish rose to no more than 2 casts. After a 2 hour interval, the fish rose only to the first cast. When mosquitoes were dropped, the fish rose readily to them. However, many drifted past the first fish and were taken by others."

River or stream grayling feed in many different styles. One is to leap from the water and take the lure on the way down. Another is to snap it off the surface with a hefty splash of tail and dorsal fin. Or else they ease up to the lure, follow it downstream for a short distance, and take it with a slight dimple. I've also seen big grayling clear the water, strike a bait, and cause it to sink. Then they quickly swing around in the current and pick it up before it hits bottom. Because of these habits, the angler must be careful not to strike too soon, otherwise the bait could be pulled from the fish, possibly putting them into a non-feeding-attitude.

As the summer progresses, a change occurs in the grayling's feeding periods and activities. Vascotto noted that during the end of June when the water is high and murky, fish could be taken during most of the day, but only close to bottom. As the summer progressed, fish were taken much more readily on the surface than near the bottom. But, peaks in feeding intensity switched from mid-afternoon to midnight. In August, intensity of midnight feeding activity increased markedly until the nights began to get darker during mid-month. By September, night feeding had stopped completely and feeding activity took place only during a short period each day.

Fly Fishing

While grayling will normally take whatever food is available, they show strong preference to insects, both aquatic and terrestrial. A study of Interior Alaska grayling revealed that 65 percent of all material ingested by grayling in early summer consisted of aerial insects. Other studies support Ivlev's (1961) findings that as the availability of food increases the graylings' selectivity increases. In the stomachs of 278 Interior grayling analyzed by Vascotto, beetles, ants, small wasps and aquatic insects, both larvae and adult, were predominant.

However, sometimes grayling can be quite fussy about lures. Then the only way to catch them is to "match the hatch" as closely as possible. For example, studies showed that when dipterous larvae, especially Chironomids, were available in large numbers, this was often the only food taken by the fish. Other studies show that Caddis larvae compose the bulk of the grayling's diet in early spring, but less frequently as the season progresses. Grayling take Mayfly larvae year 'round, but adult Mayfly were uncommon. Fish eggs were found in grayling stomachs, but the study revealed that even during salmon runs, their prominence was slight. (In areas of high salmon spawning activity, the percentage of eggs in the grayling's diet is much higher.) Diptera larvae were common June through August. Alaska grayling seldom feed on fish, yet stomach content examinations do reveal a small percentage of fish and fish remains.

A considerable amount of vegetable matter was also

The silvery coloration of some grayling is due to the reflection of light from microscopic crystals of guanine embedded in each scale. This substance is used in the making of artificial pearls.

274

How to Catch
Alaska's Trophy Sportfish

When food items approach close or are floating on the surface of the water, grayling turn upward to keep a constant angle with the object. The fish keeps rising and engulfs the bait in a quick lunge before moving back to home center.

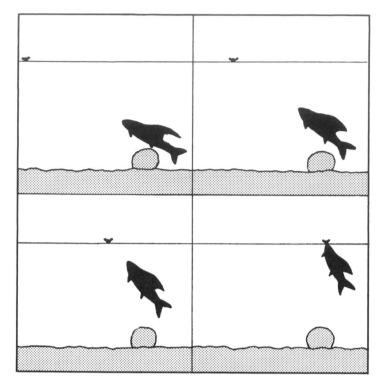

found in the stomachs of sampled grayling. Although this matter may have been ingested accidentally, the large quantity makes it appear otherwise. Several stomachs examined contained corn, rice, barley, and small seeds, probably discarded by people picnicking near the stream. Other forms of debris such as small sticks, bits of gravel, and silt were also common. Although it is not known if such vegetation was ingested selectively or accidentally, it suggests that grayling are also frequent bottom feeders. My personal catches indicate that the largest grayling were caught on lures or flies resembling fish or large insects such as stoneflies and leeches.

When my ultralight lures fail to produce, I follow guidelines based on Vascotto's studies of food preferences of Interior grayling. They are:

Ants, especially when they are swarming in July and August, are a significant food item. Black Ant patterns work extremely well when fished directly under the surface.

Mayfly larvae are usually the most numerous organism

How to Catch
Alaska's Trophy Sportfish

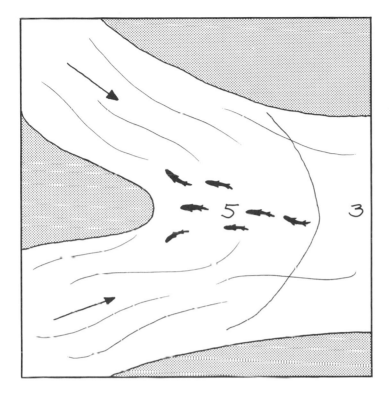

A prime hotspot for large grayling is a feeder creek emptying into a larger stream or river. Grayling will usually hold in the slower current at the mouth of the feeder creek or along the edge of fast water in midstream.

in a stream from the end of June through the first half of August. I have best success with a matching fly the first half of July when the hatch peaks. Later in the season, I like Green Mayfly patterns, preferring the hackled over the winged versions.

Stonefly larvae are a favorite grayling food item during August and September. Aside from the Woolly Worm, a Yellow Stonefly nymph pattern is my most productive fly in taking large grayling. Fish take this pattern best when it is crawled over the bottom.

Caddis and Midge flies are important food organisms for grayling, and fish will strike standard pupae and adult patterns. However, I've found that the small size of Midge patterns makes it unrewarding for me to fish them.

Salmon egg patterns work exceptionally well from mid-July through freeze up. Two-egg Marabou, Polar Shrimp, and similar flies used for trout will also take grayling.

It's important to fish each pattern through the entire structure. On occasion, grayling will disregard all laws and orders of hierarchy and follow a fly for yards before taking

Dan Rodey with a robust grayling caught on a float trip in the Lake Clark region. During periods of rainfall, it's possible to catch grayling every cast with a properly presented Black Ant, Woolly Worm, or Stonefly pattern.

it. Thus it's important to fish out each cast carefully, which includes the strip in. I've had grayling smash a fly as I was stripping it off the water, and smaller grayling attack a fly before it touched the water on my initial cast. Such go-getters may not be large fish, but they provide excellent sport. Vascotto commented on one four-inch grayling that chased a flying cranefly for 8 feet. It jumped out of the water 4 times in succession before capturing the insect on the last leap.

While grayling may be aggressive fish, when those to be released are not handled with care, they are subject to high mortality. When catch and release fishing, I always make it a point to crimp the barbs on my flies or single-hook lures. M.R. Falk's study, "Mortality of Angled Grayling in Great Slave Lake, N.W.T.," showed that grayling hooked on spinning lures suffered higher mortality rates than grayling caught on flies. The overall mortality rate for fish caught on barbed hooks was 11.8 percent compared to only a 5.1 percent for fish caught on barbless hooks.

How to Catch
Alaska's Trophy Sportfish

FRESHWATER INLET

Lake Fishing

Fishing for grayling in lakes is quite different than stream fishing. Oftentimes the lake surface is smooth as a pane of glass. Suddenly, as if someone turned on a biological switch, the surface can be shattered by the rings of feeding fish. I've yet to live through one of these experiences without a shaky hand and accelerated heart beat, especially when a dorsal fin as large as a hand cuts across the surface after a fly.

Such is the feeling of the trophy grayling angler fishing the Ugashik Lakes, which I consider the top grayling water in the state. Grayling here grow to dimensions that would put a pot-bellied stove to shame because these fish feed heavily on the readily available and nutrient-rich salmon eggs, smolts, and myriad insects common to the area.

Focus in on your trophy grayling hotspots on Ugashik—or for that matter, any lake—by choosing structure that best meets the needs of grayling. First, I've always caught more big grayling in that part of the lake with a mud or sand bottom than those sections with gravel bottoms. These mucky bottoms are home to multitudes of plankton and insect life, which in turn attract baitfish which attract grayling. It's been my experience that a BiVisible or Mosquito pattern will get a grayling to make its classic dimpled strike. On the other hand, they will often hit a spinner, plug, or spoon with twice as much vigor. I've watched grayling in clearwater lakes rise up 15 feet from the bottom to quickly eye and then inhale my

Inlets and springs are prime locations to find grayling throughout the year. Fish will usually be holding near bottom, except during a feed, when they will hold at mid-depth. A fly or lure fished slowly down with the current will take fish.

Homer Circle admires a large, Lake Clark grayling. To escape summer heat, large grayling will often congregate in the vicinity of snow-melt runoffs or springs rather than suspend in deep water. At this time, slowly work ultralight lures over bottom structure. Experiment with a variety of patterns until you find one the fish like.

lure. I've found that flashy lures, such as chrome and gold spinners or spoons, work well on sunny days in deep water, while shallow water fish favor the darker lures like a Black Fury or leech imitation.

In either situation, lures should be fished as slowly as possible. At midpoint, I like to impart a sudden, but slight, pickup in speed. This is usually enough to trigger the strike response in any large grayling following the lure.

Another tactic I employ when fishing for ice-out, lunker grayling is longlining what Tanada Lake Lodge manager Vince Guzzardi calls a "salamander." Originally meant for larger lake trout, this lure has since proven its effectiveness on big grayling. This prism-tape jig fly has a brilliant blue and white bucktail body and white eyes. Before Vince christened the lure with its amphibious name, I had intended it to resemble a grayling fry. I didn't much care what either one of us thought it should resemble, just as long as it triggered those big lakers in Tanada into striking.

I'm convinced the grayling thought the lure was so ugly
they smacked it just to get it out of the water. Nevertheless, it produced plenty of grayling in the 2½-pound
category, especially when it was longlined and twitched
through the depths about 50 yards from the boat in front
of stream outlets and marshy feeding areas. Success also
depended upon using 2- or 4-pound-test monofilament
line. Larger monos seemed to spook fish. And bright
sunlight and hot, humid days saw an overall decrease in
action, no matter what the lure. While the salamander
didn't catch the world-record grayling, I was on the right
track. Later that summer, 6-year-old Teresa Kardell
hooked a 19½-incher from Tanada using 4-pound-test
line. The fish had a mouth large enough to swallow three
salamanders.

Whether you're after a lively, mountain stream grayling
caught on a No. 16 Black Gnat, or the headstrong antics
of a "freshwater sailfish" from the Ugashik system, trophy

grayling fishing in Alaska offers an experience that not only deserves applause, but serious concern of sportsmen who want to keep this fish available in healthy numbers. Except for a trophy mount, serious sportsmen release all grayling unharmed so that others may enjoy the beauty and excitement this fish has to offer. Grayling fishing is a wilderness treasure that can uplift the soul like no other. It is worth every effort to keep around.

Where to go for Grayling

Southeast

Grayling were first stocked in these waters in 1962 and are now producing fish up to 2 pounds.

Juneau
Antler Lake

Ketchikan
Big Goat Lake
Manzoni Lake
Snow Lake

Sitka
Beaver Lake

Southcentral

The Talachulitna River is the top producer of large grayling in the Cook Inlet area. Here, late May through early June, and mid-September through mid-October are the best times for catching trophy grayling. Seventeen Mile, Harriet, and Long Lakes are stocked with grayling and offer fish up to 1¾ pounds, especially in May. Grayling are not indigenous to Kenai Peninsula waters.

In the Copper River area, Poplar Grove Creek is an excellent spring fishery, while the Gulkana offers grayling up to 18 inches throughout the summer months. Tanada Lake offers excellent grayling fishing for fish up to 19 inches in June and September.

Cook Inlet/Kenai Peninsula
Alexander Creek
Clear Creek
Coal Creek
Deshka River
Lake Creek
Paradise Lakes (Upper and Lower)
Talachulitna River
Twin Lakes

Copper River
Gulkana River
Poplar Grove Creek
Tanada Lake
Tolsona Lake

Southwest

Fish are available throughout this area, yet Ugashik grayling are unique. They are the largest found in Alaska, reaching weights of up to 4½ pounds. The best time to catch a trophy Ugashik grayling is during July and August. There are no grayling on the Pacific side of the Alaska

How to Catch
Alaska's Trophy Sportfish

Peninsula. The eastern boundary of the Bristol Bay watershed appears to be marginal habitat.

Grayling are not native to the Kodiak area. All fish are the result of experimental stocking programs. Lakes in the Kodiak region provide good fishing for 10- to 12-inch grayling.

Agulowak River
Alagnak System
Dream Creek
Goodnews River
Igushik River System
Itolitna River
Kijik Lake
Kokhanok River
Koktuli River
Kvichak River
Kvichak tributaries

Lake Clark
Lake Iliamna
Lower Talarik Creek
Mulchatna River
Naknek System
Newhalen River
Nushagak River
Ruth Lake
Stuyahok River
Tikchik Lakes
Togiak River

Ugashik Lake
Ugashik Narrows
Wood River Lakes

Kodiak
Abercrombie Lake
Aurel Lake
Cascade Lake
Cicely Lake
Long Lakes

Interior

Fish of up to 18 inches are frequently harvested early and late in the season at the headwaters of these watersheds. Tangle Lakes produces excellent trophies during June.

Chatanika River
Chena River
Delta Clearwater

Goodpaster River
Salcha River
Tangle Lakes System

North Central

Selby and Narvik Lakes are known to produce fish in the 18- to 21-inch class. However, all of the waters listed have the potential for trophy grayling. Grayling are also found throughout the watersheds of the North Slope, especially those with freshwater springs at their headwaters.

Brooks Range
Chandalar System
Iniakuk Lake
John River
Kobuk River
Koyukuk River (north fork)
Kugrak Lake

Narvik Lake
Redstar Lake
Selby Lake
Upper Noatak
Walker Lake
Wild Lake

Northwest

Some of the finest grayling fishing in this area can be had by driving the Nome Road System and fishing the various clearwater streams along the route. Grayling ranging from 14 to 19 inches can be found in most waters.

Fish River
Kobuk River
Nation River

Niukluk River
Noatak River
Sinuk River

Squirrel River
Unalakleet River
Wulik River

Northern Pike

Northern Pike

Northern pike are a strange lot. They don't have the throng of aficionados that the salmon or trout clan can claim; they don't exhibit the strength and cunning that steelhead anglers have come to expect from their quarry; and they possess a downright devilish mug that would make the scales of even an Irish Lord stand on end from fright!

Yet despite these failings, the pike is one of Alaska's most popular sportfish. Why? Because pike can be caught readily when salmon are not yet in the rivers, or when August Dog Days push trout into deepwater sanctuaries. The pike has captured the imagination of anglers young and old alike with its legendary appetite for waterfowl, muskrats, salmon, and even trumpeter swans. Tagged with this reputation, it's no wonder the northern pike is fast becoming a trophy many anglers are hanging on the wall nearest their prize rainbow or salmon.

However, while small pike, often known as "hammer handles," can be caught cast after cast in many of Alaska's backwater sloughs and lakes, larger pike come much harder. The big ones require the same forethought, planning and strategy given to any other trophy fish species.

Range and Description

The northern pike (Esox lucius) is also known as jack fish, waterwolf, and devil fish. The word *pike* is probably of Scandinavian origin, referring to the fish's long slender form—similar to that of a pike used in weaponry. However, the word could also be derived from the French

Big pike prefer quiet water sloughs with plenty of aquatic growth. There, the fish will wait to ambush mice, waterfowl, and forage baitfish. These food items are commonplace in late spring, which explains why topwater lures are so effective at this time.

285
Northern Pike

words pique and piquant, meaning to prick, and sharp or biting. These words aptly describe the pike's mouthful of needle-like teeth that often painfully wound the hands of careless anglers.

Several features make the pike easily recognizable. It has an elongated, flat, "duck-bill" snout. The vomer and premaxillary of the mouth are covered with several types of large, sharp teeth which are constantly being replaced. Its slender, elongated body has a single, soft-rayed dorsal fin located far back near the tail, and its caudal fin is slightly forked. The underpart of the fish is white or yellow. However, the overall coloration of a pike is extremely variable. A pike from a clearwater stream or lake is usually light green with irregular rows of yellow or gold spots accenting its sides. Pike from backwater sloughs or rivers are usually a dark brown, with darker side markings.

Pike are found in the numerous lakes, rivers and sloughs of Interior Alaska from the Canadian border to the Seward Peninsula, and from the Arctic coast southwest to the Bristol Bay drainages. Small populations of pike are in the lakes and rivers south of the Alaska Range, including the Susitna River drainage.

Spawning migrations of pike occur immediately after ice out. Most fish travel at night to reach the spawning grounds, which are usually shallow, marshy areas with emergent vegetation. Once water temperatures reach 43 to 48 degrees, spawning will usually take place in water no less than 20 inches. A 25- to 30-pound female can release up to 500,000 eggs. These are immediately fertilized by the much smaller male. The eggs will incubate wherever they fall, usually in aquatic vegetation, rocks and bottom debris. After the fry reach two inches in length, they immediately start a predatory lifestyle that has remained relatively unchanged for over 60 million years.

Perhaps the pike's almost unlimited diet has been indirectly responsible for its survival. Yet at the turn of the century, those eating habits nearly caused the pike's disappearance from many parts of the United States and Alaska. Old time Alaskans and commercial fishermen scorned pike and caught them by the hundreds to use as dog food because the fish was a cannibalistic bottomless pit that preyed upon so called respectable gamefish such as trout and salmon fry. But even mass harvesting was less threatening than a program of the Michigan Fish Com-

The author gills a 25-pound pike that struck a Hi-Lo plug. If possible, avoid gilling, as it is a dangerous way to capture large pike. Most anglers prefer a gaff, net, or tailer.

This is a 20-pound-plus pike taken from a slough adjacent to Lake Clark. The fish struck a large spoon fished along a shallow water breakline in early June.

missioners in 1875 aiming at complete extermination of this "devil fish." Many states followed suit. Not until the late 1930s was the importance of the pike's role in lake ecology universally understood. Then, limits were imposed, and anglers began to realize this "devil's" great potential as a sportfish.

Today, most large pike in Alaska are caught incidentally while fishing for other species. The current state record is a 38-pound fish taken from Fish Creek in 1971 by Rhoda Edwards. I have personally caught pike over 20 pounds, the largest a 25-pounder caught immediately after ice out, when the fish were moving into the shallows, laden with spawn. Several years ago, during the first week of June, I experienced a real workout with several northerns on a backwater slough near Lake Clark.

Guide Dan Rodey informed me that big pike had just entered the shallows of his "secret hotspot" to spawn. After we taxied up to a series of grass-lined sloughs emptying into a large river, I tied on a topwater plug while Dan tied on a Pixee spoon.

My first cast into the weedbed gracing the opposite shore resulted in an explosive strike. I struck back and the acrobatics of a young, 3-pound pike rewarded me. I quickly played and released it. While watching it swim back to its underwater sanctuary, I was shocked to see a large boil. The smaller pike had disappeared!

Both lures—Dan's and mine—found their mark near the gradually receding ripples. It was the wobbling action of Dan's spoon that enticed the killer pike to strike. During the next 20 minutes, the pike didn't once do what I expected: surface, thrash, or make a sizzling run out to the main river. But the fish did keep a dangerous arc in Dan's medium-action spinning rod by sounding to the bottom. He soon eased the fish into the grassy shallows, where I reached out with a trembling hand to gaff it. The "subdued" fish suddenly came to life, and it set out to splash all the water out of the slough, with most of it hitting me first. Minutes later, we watched the needle on the Deliar rest at 20 pounds.

During the next several hours, we proceeded to catch several more pike from 6 to 9 pounds on both topwater lures and spoons. One fish as large or larger than the 20-pounder smashed my topwater plug and spit it back to me with partially straightened hooks and several puncture holes.

Since then, I've learned that spring flood waters offer excellent opportunities for taking trophy pike. They are as much as 20 percent heavier at this time, and very territorial. For 7 to 10 days prior to actual spawning, pike feed aggressively on anything that moves, especially field mice, voles, and other displaced rodents skittering about, searching for food and cover. That's when I fish noisy topwater plugs such as the Jitterbug, Torpedo, Norman's Weed Walker, Injured Minnow, or a deer-hair mouse. Best are early mornings and late evenings, whenever the surface is relatively smooth. Then, pike can "hear" the lure buzz through the weeds.

Stealth is also extremely important at this time. Approach an area carefully by foot or boat, keeping well away from the water's edge. Watch for feeding activity or swirls caused by frightened baitfish. Place casts as close as possible to any visible structure such as trees, weed rows, flotsam, or undercut banks. It's critical to keep the plug motionless until the rings disappear, and then twitch it ever so slightly. Repeat this procedure through the structure. Heavy weed growth may dictate a fast retrieve across the surface, which can sometimes be extremely effective.

Stealth is important when stalking pre-spawning pike. Keep away from the water's edge and watch for feeding swirls or surfacing dorsal fins. Strikes are usually vicious at this time and often result in a series of acrobatics.

This technique is useful only for a brief period before mating. Pike lose interest in lures during spawning; just afterwards, when they have lost much of their weight, they are less desirable as trophies. But within several days to a couple of weeks later, they fatten up considerably. I remember a small duckling on a slough in the Minto Flats area that hugged the shoreline right after the pike

How to Catch
Alaska's Trophy Sportfish

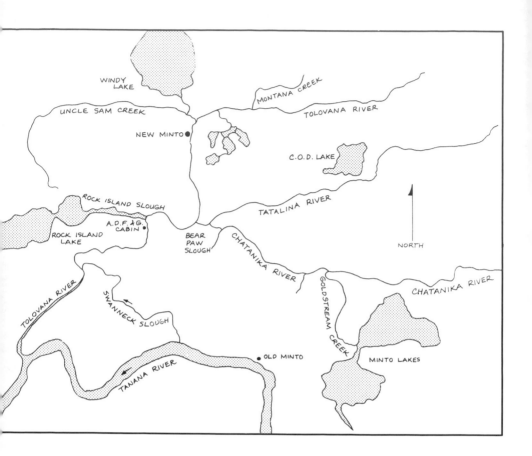

Minto Flats, located in Interior Alaska, offers good fishing for large pike throughout the year.

spawned. It tossed nervous glances out toward the water, and I assumed from the absence of the hen and other ducklings that this nervous youngster was the only one to survive the ravages of the hungry pike in the slough.

Trophy pike are found in watersheds with the best available forage food species. The large impoundments, watersheds, and sloughs—especially those with salmon, trout, and rough fish—produce the largest pike. Why? Because these waters are most likely to hold more of the large baits big pike feed on. Pike are smaller when their major food is other than fish (Cheney, 1971). A lunker northern relishes a prey that equals 10 to 20 percent of his own body weight. Occasionally, he will take on a potential meal that's well over 40 percent of his own size. So what does all this mean to the angler? An old angling adage sums it up: If you want a large pike, use a large bait.

How to Catch
Alaska's Trophy Sportfish

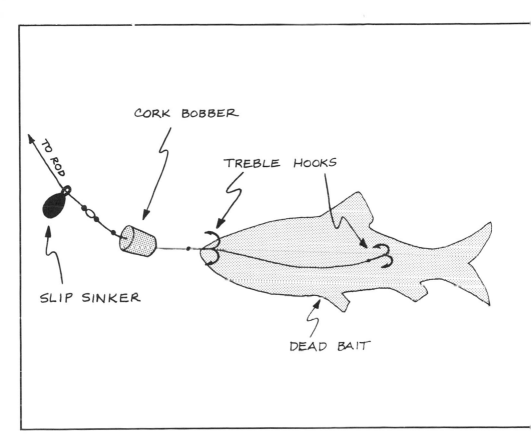

CORK BOBBER

TO ROD

TREBLE HOOKS

SLIP SINKER

DEAD BAIT

Bait Fishing

In Alaska, it's illegal to use live forage fish for bait. Therefore, the angler's preference and local conditions are what dictate whether to use dead bait or lures. For instance, in lakes where little weed growth exists, pike must prowl over greater distances for their food. Studies show one tagged pike in a large, weed-free lake traveled over 49 miles in a year's time. Under these conditions, pike rely heavily on smell to locate food. In relatively weedless lakes, herring, whitefish, and salmon scraps, especially salmon eggs, are ideal baits. Because they're very oily, their scent quickly permeates the water, drawing pike in, often from great distances.

Dead bait is also extremely effective in heavily fished waters where large pike are lure-wary. Most baitfish species in Alaska have an average life expectancy of five years.

A favorite dead-bait rig for trophy northerns is a double-hooked whitefish suspended from a float and fished along the edges of dropoffs and weedbeds.

This means that every year, approximately one fifth of a lake's baitfish population dies and sinks to the bottom, where pike, lake trout, and burbot feed upon the remains. Thus large lakes have a substantial tonnage of bottom food. There, large pike are accustomed to feeding safely on dead bait.

I prefer a slip-sinker rig when dead baiting for pike. Run the main line through a tear-drop sinker and then attach it to a ball-bearing swivel. On the swivel's other end is a 20-inch, 12-pound-test monofilament leader. This is connected to an 8-inch wire leader holding two No. 4 treble hooks that are partially buried in the bait: one in the midsection and one wired through the head. A small cork just ahead of the bait keeps it floating above bottom debris and in easy view of hungry pike.

Pickups vary, depending upon the type of bait. Strike immediately when fishing salmon eggs or cut bait, as pike generally ingest these deeply on the initial pickup. Pike like to take whole fish such as herring, smelt, or whitefish head first. Therefore, wait several seconds after the initial pickup to allow the pike to clamp firmly down on the bait. Then, reel in the slack and strike hard!

One last tip. Don't fish bait in water more than 25 feet deep. Studies show that pike prefer depths of 5 to 15 feet throughout the spring and early summer months.

Lures

Baitfishing is the preferred method for taking large pike. But bait anglers can't argue the fact that lures catch more, albeit smaller pike. However, Ol' Trophy Toothsome can be taken regularly on lures, especially if the proper techniques are employed.

First, lures should resemble the prevalent forage species as closely as possible. For instance, if you're fishing Interior Alaska's Chatanika River, it's almost a sure bet that whitefish are a favorite of pike in the area. Therefore, a gold-colored spoon fished in weedy sloughs and deep, shaded pools would be the ideal lure to use. But if a lake, such as Lake Clark on the Alaska Peninsula, incubates millions of sockeye salmon, a gaudy-blue bucktail and mylar fly or a chrome and reflex-blue spoon that best imitates a salmon smolt would be the lure to try first.

The importance of lure selection hit me strongly 6 years ago in the Brooks Range on a remote lake noted for growing bucket-mouthed pike. I was fishing a shallow, weedy bay with a sudden dropoff about 20 yards out. I knew large pike were congregated there, as they often are drawn to the security of a deepwater sanctuary.

I positioned myself so that my casts would be parallel to the dropoff. Yet several casts with a gold-colored spoon failed to produce a strike. I tried a chrome plug with equally dismal results. Finally, I tied on an elongated bronze spoon with a strip of Ripple Rind. The lure didn't sink more than a foot before my rod was nearly yanked out of my hands. I sharply set the hook and felt the heavy weight of a pike, first trying to work his way into the weeds, and then down into the depths of the dropoff. The fish rushed back and forth in runs of 10 to 20 yards as I pumped it up through the gin-clear water. Minutes later, I was muscling the fish into the shallows. As I was removing the hook from the 12-pound pike, it regurgitated a 14-inch pike and several pike fingerlings. Upon closer examination, I realized that the bronze spoon best imitated the side coloration of the smaller pike in this lake. And not only did the white rind match the belly color, but it also had the undulating action of a frantic pike fleeing for cover.

This incident taught me the importance of stocking a wide variety of spoons when fishing for pike. Unlike plugs that can get punctured by sharp teeth or spinner shafts distorted by the pike's cement-mixer gyrations, little can go wrong with a spoon. No other lure so effectively imitates the flash and action of a crippled baitfish unable to swim upright. My favorites include hammered and polished metallic finishes in silver, bronze, gold, and metallic green. To further enhance the appeal of these spoons, I apply oblong strips of prism tape to each side. These give the lure a scaled effect which I've found most effective in the clearwater tundra lakes where large pike are often particular about lure offerings.

Another good lure, especially in waters shared by salmon and pike, is the Pixee. It is a thick-bodied, hammered copper or silver spoon with a plastic, salmon egg cluster insert. Pike relish salmon and salmon eggs, and frequently feed upon dead salmon, especially females containing eggs. I've had exceptionally good luck with this lure on the Mulchatna River. There, it's not uncommon to see 15-pound pike following schools of sockeye salmon to their spawning beds. Whether the pike think the Pixee is

A salmon-egg imitating spoon, like this Pixee, is ideal for pike that follow migrating salmon to their spawning beds. Fish the lure slowly along the edges of sloughs and fast current in salmon spawning rivers.

salmon spawn, a crippled salmon, or baitfish, I don't know. But the Pixee is most effective with the fluorescent orange or red plastic insert. I like to fish it slowly over bottom near the bank's edge or along the outer edge of salmon schools.

If you lose a few lures or get hung up a lot in weeds, be encouraged. It means you're fishing where the pike are. Several years ago, I was dredging bottom with a large spoon when I hooked a 10-pound pike. Upon landing the fish, I was surprised to see a 7-inch mass of weed growth wrapped around the trebles, which were hooked deeply in the rear of the pike's tooth-lined maw. Since then I've landed several other pike that have hit lures with "weed" dressings. Only in areas with extreme weed growth do I recommend using weedless lures. Most anglers don't set their hooks with enough force—to sink the barbs through the weed guards and into the pike's mouth—to warrant their use. However, if you're a trophy king angler or plastic worm fisherman, you shouldn't have any difficulty hooking pike consistently with these lures. The Johnson Silver

How to Catch
Alaska's Trophy Sportfish

Minnow with pork-rind trailer is my favorite weedless spoon.

In heavily fished water or dense lily pads, a spoon is often inappropriate or just doesn't produce. This is when I generally switch to a soft-bodied grub lure with a leadhead and twister tail.

For instance, along deepwater dropoffs immediately before and after spawning, big pike will oftentimes approach a lure with caution and strike it tentatively. If a hard-bodied spoon or other lure is used, the pike may spit it out before the angler has a chance to react. The soft-bodied lures, on the other hand, feel like natural bait, and pike tend to hold on to them longer.

The best way to fish a grub is to let it sink to the bottom and then jerk it upward sharply in a 3- to 4-foot sweep of the rod. Maintain slight tension on the line as the lure sinks back to bottom, and repeat. I've found the large, soft-bodied, shad-type lures such as the Chummin' Minnow and Sassy Shad work well.

Plugs

Big pike are often extremely lazy, and even the slowest retrieved spoon or jig is often too fast to entice them to strike. This behavior calls for the versatility of plugs.

Plugs favored by Alaska pike are 5- to 8-inch, full-bodied models with a slow, wobbling action. While I feel wire leaders dampen the action of a plug, many anglers prefer to use a 4- to 8-inch, multi-strand, plastic-coated leader with a non-swivel clip. Rapalas, Flatfish, Tadpollies, and similar plugs in natural colors are my favorites.

I like to fish plugs in the Minto Flats lakes, sloughs and rivers. I've taken some big pike there, and the fishing strategy is rather simple.

First, search out the breaklines, especially those with a steep, sloping dropoff. These give pike two places from which to ambush their prey. Most popular among smaller pike is the weedbed itself. From here they can ambush mice, birds, and various baitfish while hiding from larger pike.

A big pike's ambush headquarters is just off bottom along the slope of the dropoff, usually in water ranging from 7 to 20 feet. These dropoffs usually serve as major migration routes for grayling, whitefish, and trout which stand little chance of surviving the sudden lunge of a

Large one-piece and jointed plugs are excellent lures for lunker pike. From the top, a mackerel finish plug, which is good in early spring; a silver and blue ABU Killer, which best imitates a salmon smolt; a brown trout pattern ABU Killer, which best imitates a young char or Dolly Varden; and a Hi-Lo plug, which has an adjustable lip for a variety of fishing conditions.

northern at close range.

Fish areas by parallel casting to structure with large plugs. Work the plug slowly and deeply, getting no further than 3 feet from the weedline or other structure. Every five feet or so, stop the lure for several seconds, allowing it to float toward the surface. Continue this retrieve-and-rise action all the way to the shore or boat. Pike will often follow and strike a lure when it is nearing shore or boatside. I've found it pays to leave the lure sitting motionless on the surface of the water for several seconds, just to be sure, before picking it up and making another cast.

You can also catch large pike successfully on plugs in rivers and streams. When fishing from the shore, cast a floating-diving plug—one with a large lip and capable of diving 10- to 15-feet—out into the current. Allow it to drift downstream. As the plug nears the shore, tighten your

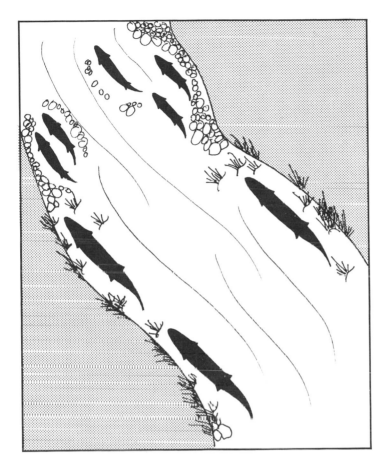

line, forcing your lure to dig for bottom. Work the lure slowly upstream by using your rod, not reel. Occasionally slacken your line for a second and allow the lure to flutter up in the slow, side current. If pike are in the area, the lure won't make it back without inducing a strike.

When fishing from a boat, use the same type of lure and technique. Instead of working the lure back with the rod, work the lure through a controlled drift. Known as power drifting, this technique requires using your motor to slow your downstream drift. Power drifting enables plugs to cover a wide area very slowly, which is extremely attractive to river pike. However, the drift must be done as slowly as possible, otherwise the plug won't maintain bottom contact. Break your drift occasionally with slow surges of power upstream. This causes the plug to wobble faster, imitating a baitfish scooting for cover.

A wire spreader is a useful device for unhooking lures from a pike's toothy maw. This fish struck an ABU Killer twitched along bottom structure.

Late Summer

During the summer months, large pike prefer the sanctuary of deepwater hideouts. However, rainstorms or overcast nights will draw these lunkers into the shallows like filings are drawn to a magnet. I remember fishing for pike at Minto Flats on one of those scorcher dog days commonplace in Interior Alaska. The temperature was in the 80s and my wife Adela and I had spent the morning hunting spruce grouse. Having bagged several birds by mid-day, we decided to spend the remainder of the afternoon pike fishing. We didn't expect to catch many fish, but several hours later, we hadn't even produced a single strike! Our tempers were building at the same rate as a layer of threateningly black clouds gathering nearby. While the sky darkened, we began catching several "hammer handles" which hit sinking Rapalas. Just before heading back to the cabin, Adela's rod snapped downward; mine followed suit. Hooplas and shouts for the net rang out as the rain pelted the water. The sun soon broke through the menacing clouds, but not before six pike between 8 and 15 pounds lay glistening in the wet grass. We fished for an hour afterwards, and caught nothing but small fish. We concluded that large pike took advantage of the weather to move into the shallows to feed, thus chasing out the smaller pike. When the large pike left after the rainstorm, the smaller ones returned.

Some of my late summer plugs for Alaska waters are: ABU Hi-Lo plugs with adjustable lip for either shallow or deep-water action in blue, silver, yellow or black; floating-diving, jointed Rapalas or ABU Killers in silver/blue or trout patterns; Model U-50 and U-20 Flatfish in bronze or gold; and Magnum Tadpollies in silver, gold, green and yellow.

Because of their brute strength and bulldog tenacity, plugs usually won't hold up to the maulings lunker pike dish out. It's not uncommon to have a lure look like a sieve after several fish. To keep a damaged plug in action, especially in wilderness areas, carry along a tube of quick-drying plastic cement for on-the-site repairs. Because the "lucky" plug may have an action identical plugs can't match, it's worth fixing.

I also like to ensure that each hook has a sharpened, three-sided edge. Three cutting edges are necessary to penetrate the bony tissues of a pike's jaw. A round,

Lures with sharp, stout hooks are necessary to survive the ravages big Alaska pike are capable of dishing out. Also carry a small tube of plastic cement to patch any plug that happens to get punctured by any one of a big pike's 700 teeth.

sharpened point won't do the job. Additional gear might include a gaff or net, wire spreader to keep the pike's jaws from clamping down on your hand when removing the lure, a tube of antibiotic cream for possible punctures or cuts, and a variety of snaps that balance with the plug you're fishing.

Trophy pike require stout rods with plenty of backbone, yet a limber tip. I prefer a 6-foot, medium-heavy action boron or graphite rod with a spinning or level-wind reel capable of holding 200 yards of 12- to 20-pound monofilament. Use the heavier line when large pike are in the weeds.

Pike fishing may not entice the angler with mountain-stream scenery and head-over-tail acrobatics, but it is a sport with a special aura of savagery that will sure to keep you coming back for more.

Where to go for Pike

Southcentral

Pike up to 10 pounds are located near Lake Creek in upper Cook Inlet. They are also found in the sloughs of the Yentna River up to Hewitt Lake.

Cook Inlet/Kenai Peninsula
Bulchitna Lake

How to Catch
Alaska's Trophy Sportfish

Southwest

Pike are found throughout the region from Mother Goose Lake northward into the Bristol Bay drainages. Most watersheds with a weedy shoreline or calm, backwater sloughs will hold pike.

Large northern pike are also scattered throughout the Kuskokwim drainage. However, they are not found in drainages south of the Ek River and generally not found in waters flowing into Kuskokwim Bay.

Chulitna Lake
Lake Clark
Long Lake
Pike Lake
Tikchik Lakes
Wood River

Kuskokwim
Aniak River
Holitna River
Innoko River

Interior

Pike are widely distributed throughout this region. Big pike up to 20 pounds are frequently caught in the tributaries and sloughs of the Chatanika and near Manley Hot Springs on the Tanana River. The Minto, East Twin, and Wien lakes and the lower Tolovana, Chatanika, and Tatalina rivers are some of the best trophy pike producers in the state.

Chatanika River
Chisana River
George Lake
Kantishna River
Lake Mansfield
Lake Minchumina
Lower Goldstream Creek
Minto Lakes
Moose River

Swan Neck Slough
Tanana River
Tatalina River
Tetlin Lake
Tolovana River
Twin Lakes (East and West)
Wien Lake
Wolf Lake

Northcentral

Pike are found in various lakes and rivers in the southern foothills of the Brooks Range. Walker, Selby, and Narvik are prime waters that receive little fishing pressure. There, pike can reach 25 pounds. Pike are not present in waters of the the North Slope.

Iniakuk Lake
Island Lake
John River

Kobuk River
Narvik Lake
Selby Lake

Walker Lake
Wild Lake

Northwest

Sloughs in these areas commonly produce pike in the 15- to 25-pound class. Fly-out is the main means of access.

Fish River
John River
Kobuk River
Kuzitrin River (lower section)

Noatak River
Pilgrim River (lower section)
Selawik Lake

Sheefish

CHAPTER 15

Sheefish

Sheefish are warriors. They are explosive, energetic, and extremely acrobatic—an Amazonian race of gamefish ready and able to do battle at any time. They've been known to strip drags, straighten split rings, and crimp the points on salmon-size hooks with gill-flaring, tail-twisting power. Nicknamed "tarpon of the north," the shee exhibits the tarpon's bone-hard mouth, large, silvery scales and aerial acrobatics, as well as the tenacity of a striped bass and the dark, lateral line and underslung jaw common to snook. Best of all, sheefish migrate up rivers and streams in staggering numbers, offering sportsmen literally "too much of a good thing."

With traits such as these, the shee should rank high on gamefish lists. Yet only since the early 1970s—when biologists began examining the life and habits of the shee, and air transportation allowed access to their wilderness habitat—have sheefish gained a foothold in the sport angling realm.

The sheefish (Stenodus leucichthys) is also known as Eskimo tarpon, connie or shovelnose whitefish. In Siberia, the vernacular nel'ma and belorybitsa (whitefish) are also used. The early French-Canadian explorers gave the fish its most common name, "poisson inconnu" meaning "unknown fish."

The shee is the only predatory member of the whitefish family in North America. Genetically, it is a young species, still in the process of range extension. Biologists theorize that the shee probably originated in Siberia and migrated to arctic and subarctic Alaska during or after the

Fred Ketscher with a 24-pound sheefish that struck a silver Krocodile in a Kobuk River tributary in early September.

There are seven distinct Alaska sheefish populations. They are:
1. Kuskokwim
2. Lower Yukon
3. Middle Yukon—Porcupine
4. Upper Yukon
5. Minto Flats
6. Koyukuk
7. Selawik—Kobuk
The latter has the largest sheefish found in North America.

Bering land-bridge era. The fish slowly evolved into an esturine-anadromous species, meaning it spends its winters in the brackish waters of delta areas, inlets, and tidal lakes of northern coastal Alaska, Canada and Siberia.

In Alaska, biologists have categorized the sheefish into seven populations according to their geographical distribution. These groups are the Kuskokwim, Lower Yukon, Middle Yukon—Porcupine, Upper Yukon, Minto Flats, Koyukuk, and Selawik—Kobuk. All of them are anadromous, except for the Minto Flats, Upper Yukon River and Porcupine populations, which are generally considered year-round residents.

Life History

Most sheefish begin their upstream migration to their spawning grounds immediately after ice-out. Lower Kobuk sheefish migrations may last as little as a few weeks, while Yukon River fish may spend over 4 months and travel over 1,000 miles to reach their spawning areas.

Sheefish spawn in late September and early October in clear, swift streams in water temperatures 40 degrees or colder. Spawning activity occurs in early evening and continues throughout the night. A female does not dig a redd or spawning nest. Instead, she swims rapidly under the sur-

How to Catch
Alaska's Trophy Sportfish

face, with her abdomen upstream, extruding eggs. The male swims through or above the eggs and fertilizes them as they sink. The slightly adhesive eggs lodge in the gravel. Unlike Pacific salmon, which die after spawning, sheefish survive the rigors of spawning, and afterwards, start a fairly rapid downstream migration to their wintering grounds.

Egg development is slow in the cold water, and can take up to 6 months before hatching occurs in early spring. The new-born fry are carried downstream with the spring flood waters to the delta areas of large rivers. Here they will begin a diet of plankton, and soon graduate to larger zooplankton and insect larvae. By the second year of life, sheefish are about 8 inches long and feed almost entirely on fish.

Age studies utilizing the scale-reading technique have shown that fish of each age group exhibit distinct growth rates, have a different life span, and reach sexual maturity at different ages. For instance, Kuskokwim and Minto Flats sheefish have the fastest growth rates. They reach 16 inches in length at age 2, and up to 30 inches and weights of up to 14 pounds at 8 years of age. In contrast, sheefish from the Selawik-Kobuk watershed grow much more slowly, weighing about 10 pounds at age 10, yet they can reach 60 pounds in 20 to 25 years.

Guide Lorrie Schuerch with a 30-pound sheefish caught from Selawik Bay in mid-June. The fish nailed a chrome HotRod fished slowly along bottom structure.

The Selawik-Kobuk watershed is the state's top hotspot for anglers wishing to catch a trophy shee. The current Alaska state record is a 53-pound fish taken from the Pah River of interior Alaska in 1986 by Lawrence Hudnall. I have caught over 100 sheefish over 20 pounds from the Kobuk. My own all-time record is a 30-pound, 8-ounce fish taken in 1979 near Selawik Bay.

During the first half of June, Selawik Bay and the mouth of the Kobuk offer the year's best sheefishing. Fish can be found off long, tapering points, along rocky sections of shoreline, and in the main river current, feeding on huge schools of smelt, which are also traveling upstream to spawn. Other top sheefish food items at this time include king salmon fry, least cisco, whitefish, lampreys, and sticklebacks.

Techniques

The only practical way to effectively fish this area is via a wide-bottomed riverboat. My first experience with large shee involved just such a craft. It was June 10th, and I had been dropped off at an isolated, yet cozy, houseboat at the mouth of the Kobuk River, an hour's flight by Super Cub from the village of Kiana. I was met by Lorrie Schuerch, the owner of Kiana Lodge and considered by many the top sheefish guide in the area. With him was Scott Key, a Juneau angler also after trophy sheefish. Since the main lodge was 60 miles upriver, the houseboat would serve as a "spike camp" to fish the sheefish populations entering the Kobuk. Our main means of transportation would be a 21-foot, extra-wide riverboat with a spacious fighting platform.

Within an hour, we were motoring down the murky currents of the Kobuk to a spot where Schuerch had earlier that week witnessed hundreds of shee literally boil the water while feeding on a smelt run. With our backs to the nippy arctic air, Scott tied on a bronze, 1-ounce HotRod while I chose a Stingsilda.

As we neared Schuerch's hotspot—a funnel of current emptying one section of bay into another—we both fired our lures into a small rip in the current. I felt my lure wobble slowly through several feet of current before it was walloped hard enough to teeter me on the fighting platform. I struck with enough retaliation to evoke a creak out

Scott Key battles a spunky sheefish at the mouth of the Kobuk River. It's not uncommon to catch over 30 sheefish a day before fish begin their upstream migration in mid-June.

How to Catch
Alaska's Trophy Sportfish

A split ring straightened by the fighting acrobatics of a 22-pound sheefish. Always replace standard hooks and swivels with extra-strong hardware.

of my heavy-action spinning rod, and hung on as a blur of silver and purple gyrated out of the water head over tail. I looked over at Scott, who was braced against the motor and also trying to tame a wild, acrobatic shee seemingly headed for Siberia. Lorrie just smiled at our battle stances, kicked back, and began to peel an orange. I quickly learned that harnessing a Kobuk sheefish takes time, grunt, and plenty of muscle.

After 15 minutes of battle, my shee was ready to net...or so I thought. I eased it up to the boat, and just as Lorrie reached out with his pliers to release it, the fish turned an inquisitive eye upward, caught a glimpse of Lorrie's outstretched hand, and wasted no time gaining its second wind. The muscular tail shot several gallons of water into the boat as the fish streaked across the surface. Without warning, the lure cut loose, and the sudden release of tension nearly caused me to take an unexpected swim. As Lorrie helped Scott release an equally belligerent sheefish, I examined my lure. The split ring between lure and hook had straightened. I feebly sat down and asked Lorrie for a piece of orange. It was going to be a long week.

During the remainder of that week, and in subsequent other trips to the Lower Kobuk, I learned that small shee can be caught on virtually any type of spoon or spinner. Yet certain lures seem to attract large shee with unerring consistency.

Silver and gold, one-ounce spoons with a broad surface area and a good action at slow speeds seem to outfish narrow-bodied spoons in Selawik Bay and at the mouth of

the Kobuk. If spring runoff is high, and water is murky, patterned spoons—such as the Five-O-Diamonds or chartreuse-bodied spoons—hook fish with brow-raising effectiveness, especially in the main waters of the Kobuk. A slow retrieve directly above bottom is usually most successful

When fish are feeding on top, or for more action but smaller fish, try buzzing a No. 4 or 5 Mepps Aglia or similar spinner within a foot of the surface. These seem to be the only conditions when spinners outfish spoons. Watching a sheefish strike a spinner in an explosion of spray and emerge with gills flared is sportfishing action at its finest.

Because a sheefish strikes a lure so savagely—the lure is in the back of its throat before the angler knows he has a strike—I recommend the use of single-hook lures. Not only do they minimize hooking injuries, to which sheefish are extremely prone, but single-hook lures enable you to keep a few more lures in the box, especially if you're fishing near the bottom where big shee like to hold.

Fly fishing for shee requires at least a 9-weight rod, a sinking or sink-tip line, 200 yards of 15-pound Dacron backing and a multiplier reel. The most productive flies are large, gaudy patterns tied on a 2 or 4/0 hook with plenty of mylar and tinsel. I prefer weighted versions and patterns with wings of blue, yellow, chartreuse, or green. A fly should be cast slightly upstream and slowly stripped in at various depths, starting from the surface. A butt extension is often helpful when battling early June fish.

Sheefish are called "tarpon of the north" because of their resemblance to the saltwater tarpon. And like their namesake, shee have bone-hard mouths that can easily curl the points of the sharpest flies or treble hooks.

Summer and Autumn

Large, chartreuse spoons work best for sheefish in murky water, while the chrome and Stingsilda types work well in clear water. Medium-action tackle is a must to fish either type.

Only in mid-July does freshwater fishing for sheefish actually take hold. By then, spring flood waters have emptied from most rivers, enabling the fish to locate lures and flies much more easily. Fish continue to feed prior to spawning, and will resume immediately after.

I tend to favor late August to early September sheefishing on the Middle Kobuk. The leaves have turned a dazzling yellow, wild berries abound, and the mountainous country offers a totally different feeling of wilderness than that experienced in the Kobuk-Selawik Bay lowlands. Streams and rivers are low and as clear as glass, chum salmon porpoise along the edges of the river and at the mouth of feeder streams, and grayling anxiously await to devour any fly or lure offering that hovers too close to their territorial domain.

Since sheefish are spread throughout the entire river system at this time, I've found the best way to indulge in top sheefishing—along with taking in the sights of an Arctic autumn—is to plan a five-day or longer float trip down the middle Kobuk.

Several years ago, I accompanied David Ketscher and some other interested anglers on a three-day float down a tributary of the Kobuk. We flew into a prime area where David has consistently caught big shee over the years, and set up a main tent camp. Afterwards, David flew us 12 miles upriver where we unpacked the Avon inflatables and began a leisurely float back to base camp, fishing every hole and run that looked as if it held sheefish. We weren't disappointed. Sheefish were seemingly behind every rock, logjam, and eddy throughout the river. In fact, the fishing was so good that after we returned to base camp, we asked David if he'd fly us back upriver for another float.

Several basic facts apply to catching river sheefish in late summer. First, sheefish are migrants. What may be a dead spot in the river one minute may be teaming with sheefish the next. Therefore it's important to fish an area thoroughly and patiently, and avoid any unnecessary wading or boat travel. I prefer to wade the shoreline shallows slowly, casting to the deeper runs of the river or behind obvious holding structure (such as mid-stream boulders, and quiet backwaters adjacent to the main current) where sheefish like to rest. After fishing an area for roughly 20 minutes, I'll climb onto shore, walk down to the next fishing spot, and re-enter the water. Usually, a member of the fishing party will float the raft and gear down after we've fished a half-mile stretch of water. Rafting doesn't spook fish nearly as much as unnecessary walking.

On bright days, ¼- to 1-ounce narrow chrome and gold spoons, such as the Fjord and Krocodile, seem to catch the largest sheefish. I've found that spoons with highly polished surfaces, rather than hammered or dull finishes, produce the most strikes. If a spoon's surface is dulled by abrading against bottom structure, a piece of prism tape will put the lure back in working order, often with more fish appeal than the lure originally possessed.

Retrieval speed is critical. Narrow spoons have a lazy wobble when fished slowly down and across current. This just happens to be the best retrieve for taking big sheefish. However, I've noticed that occasionally sheefish are suckers for a change in lure speed, especially when they are found in wide, flat sections of river. A jerk-pause retrieve, a surface-buzzed/slow-sink retrieve, or simply an erratic reeling method will oftentimes produce vicious strikes.

Another lure which I've found to be extremely effective on shee is the vibrating-type such as the Sonar or Gay Blade. I have never had a more exhausting workout from any other Alaska fish than fishing sheefish with smaller versions of these lures with ultralight gear. These lures emit sonic vibrations, triggering a sheefish kill response that must be experienced to be appreciated. Slow along the

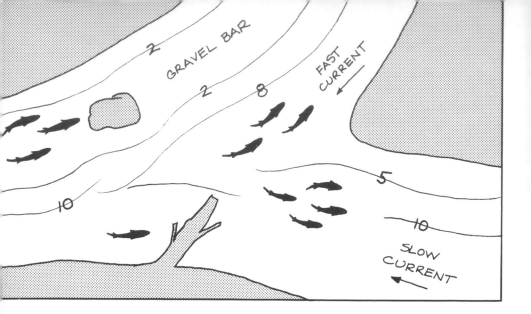

2

GRAVEL BAR

2

8

FAST CURRENT

10

5

10

SLOW CURRENT

Sheefish can be found throughout a river system, but especially in calm or quiet backwaters, behind mid-stream obstructions, or in deep channels with a gravel substrate.

bottom, jigged through the depths, or buzzed under the surface, these lures catch fish. I'm experimenting with various patterns, shapes, and colors to determine the most effective. Up till now, the gold, pearl, black, and chrome varieties have produced the most fish. On one trip I had to cut short my experimentation because the hooks on all my test lures were either busted or straightened out from rampant shee.

If using ultralight gear, expect to lose an occasional fish on the initial hookup because an ultralight rod doesn't have the backbone needed to bury the hooks firmly into the bony jaw of a shee. Thin wire hooks help, but you'll lose some fish—especially after a lengthy battle—from straightened hooks. If you're serious about pursuing shee on ultralight tackle, particularly if your goal is to set a world line-class record, it's good insurance to have a boat or raft ready to go at all times during the fight, just in case the fish decides to head for its wintering grounds early.

When using regular gear, anglers should replace standard factory hooks with extra-strong, 2/0 and 4/0 single hooks when using mono over 12-pound test. Thin, brass wire or nickel snap rings connecting lure to hook should also be replaced with heavy-duty steel rings, preferably one size larger. Use a medium-action spinning or casting rod with matching reel filled with 12- to 14-pound, abrasive-resistant, clear monofilament. I favor boron rods due to their sensitivity and strong backbone. Fly rodders should employ the same gear and flies recommended for lower

How to Catch
Alaska's Trophy Sportfish

Kobuk sheefish.

Due to the shee's delicate, white-flaky meat, anglers may be tempted to take home several coolers full. However, for this species, the consensus of sheefish anglers and guides has been catch and release. A particularly large shee to mount, and maybe one or two to eat, is a good policy. To take more counts as a cardinal sin against the beauty and wildness that is sheefish country.

The sheefish is not now, nor is likely to be in the foreseeable future, endangered by overfishing thanks to its remote and relatively inaccessible habitat. Yet with areas of the Lower 48 and even Alaska succumbing to the trends of crowded streams and rivers and stocked hatchery fish, it's encouraging to know a wild, spunky species of sportfish exhibits qualities and traits as unique as its surroundings. Sheefish are wilderness sportfishing's most stylish fighters.

Where to go for Sheefish

Southwest

Aniak River	Holitna River
Gweek River	Johnson River
Hoholitna River	

Interior

Sheefish can be found throughout the lower Yukon tributaries during July. The Koyukuk near Hughes is best in September. While it is possible to catch a 25-pound sheefish in any of these waters, most fish will run between 10 and 20 pounds.

Chatanika River	Minto Flats
Dall River	Nowitna River
Hess River	Porcupine River
Koyukuk (near Hughes)	Ray River
Melozitna River	Yukon River (Upper and Lower)

Northwest

The largest sheefish in the state are taken from the Kobuk-Selawik watersheds in early June. Fish are feeding aggressively and are easy to catch. Sheefish up to 40 pounds are not uncommon.

Kobuk River	**Selawik Bay**
Koyuk River	Hotham Inlet
Selawik River	
Tuklomarak River	

Whitefish

CHAPTER 16

Whitefish

If I had the opportunity to fish for either trophy coho or humpback whitefish, I would immediately start packing my ultralight jigs and spoons for whitefish. I estimate that fewer than 5 percent of Alaska sportfishermen go for whitefish. This is a sin. In my opinion, the whitefish is one of the strongest and most acrobatic fish in Alaska. The fish is solid muscle from mouth to tail, and its large, gold-colored scales give it the appearance of an armored torpedo. A hookup will trigger this fish into an explosive display of energy that can equal that of its salmonid cousins. And a whitefish will have plenty of reserve for a series of upstream surges that often leave a greenhorn angler's mouth agape in amazement.

Despite these trophy sportfish characteristics, there are two reasons why you'll rarely see a mounted trophy whitefish. First, the fish are extremely finicky about what they feed on, and reject all but the most carefully fished flies and lures on the lightest lines. Second, most anglers who've tasted whitefish can't bear to see a five-pound trophy go to waste in the form of a mount. Whitefish, with its flaky white and delicate flesh, is the "king of food fish."

In Alaska, there are several varieties of whitefish: the round, pygmy, least cisco, Arctic and Bering ciscos, and broad and humpback species. The last is considered a true whitefish and is especially noted for its sportfishing qualities. Humpbacks can reach weights of up to 8 pounds in Alaska waters. The current state record for whitefish is a 7-pound, 2-ounce fish taken from the Tolovana River in 1978 by Glen W. Cornwall.

Whitefish are widely distributed throughout Alaska; from lowland lakes to mountain streams, like the one this angler is fly fishing in the Talkeetna Mountains.

Favorite whitefish lures are
(from top): Woolly Worm,
Glo-Bug, white grub, and
Fjord spoon.

Little is known of the life cycle of Alaska's humpback or broad whitefish. Technically, the species is considered anadromous, yet this fish rarely ventures far into the sea, preferring brackish water areas. While spawning occurs in clearwater streams with a gravel bottom, little is known of its other habits. Biologists assume the life history is similar to that of the sheefish or other members of the whitefish family. After spawning, adults move downstream and over-winter in deepwater pools and intertidal areas. The young hatch in early spring and migrate quickly downstream, feeding along the way.

Humpback whitefish are cautious feeders. Clams, snails, aquatic insect larvae, and freshwater shrimp are their preferred food. Salmon and whitefish eggs are also big favorites in late autumn. While these food items can be closely imitated with a variety of lures on today's market, they don't trick the large humpbacks. You need to customize the type of lure and technique to the whitefish's lake or stream environment.

Techniques

Lakes

One of the most challenging aspects of fishing for lake whitefish is finding them. I've caught them in 50 feet of water while jigging for lake trout, and along flooded sections of shoreline in late May while fishing for pike. Piecing together all the facts from my 75-plus whitefish trips, I've come up with two observations that pertain to lake whitefish.

• Whitefish shun light. My best catches have always been in shallow water from early evening until dark. Rainy, overcast days also draw some fish into the shallows, especially after a rainstorm.

• Whitefish and grayling don't mix. I remember catching several 2· to 2½-pound whitefish one July afternoon near a stream emptying into Lake Louise. I probably would have caught more if it hadn't been for the grayling in the vicinity. They nailed the lure immediately after it hit the surface. The big whitefish holding a bit deeper didn't have a chance. I've found that with all factors,—i.e. temperature, location of fish in lake, etc.—being equal, grayling, being adapted for feeding at surface and mid-depth levels, will consistently beat a whitefish to the lure. The reverse holds true in streams; whitefish will beat grayling to a bottom bouncing lure almost every time. Therefore, it's necessary to fish structure that attract and hold only whitefish.

In my travels around the state, I've noticed that many lodges dump leftover remains of client-caught salmon into a lake to prevent bear trouble. If they dump in relatively shallow water, especially in a mud bay or narrows, whitefish will quickly home in on the remains and stay there indefinitely, feeding on the carcasses. Other fish, such as lake trout or burbot, will also home in on the salmon carcasses and feeding whitefish, making for additional sportfishing possibilities.

I first learned about this whitefish attractor method quite by accident when fishing out of Van Valin's Island Lodge on the shores of Lake Clark. Our party had just returned from an extremely productive day of sockeye salmon fishing, much to the dismay of the camp fish cleaners. However, they dutifully filleted each of the 21 salmon, and dumped the carcasses into the lake a hundred yards behind the lodge.

Still having the fishing itch that evening, I asked lodge owner Glen Van Valin where—within walking distance—I might catch a few fish. He explained that freshly dumped salmon carcasses always attract a few whitefish, some up to 6 pounds, but catching them would be difficult. This was exactly the challenge I was looking for, and I wasted no time threading my 2-pound-test line through the guides on my ultralight boron rod while walking out to the bay.

I rigged up with a 1/32-ounce ultralight jig enhanced with a drop of salmon egg oil. I fished the lure slowly across bottom, and despite the several "bumps" of striking fish, I failed to hook any. My efforts continued for at least a half hour, until I accidentally snagged a piece of salmon carcass. I closely examined the remains, and was surprised that the bones were nibbled free of the excess flesh often left after filleting. I cut off a chunk of salmon belly and threaded a small piece onto my ultralight jig, added a touch of scent, and cast it into the "honey hole."

I had no sooner begun to inch the lure along the bottom when my line twitched slightly. I snapped the rod to set the hook and was rewarded with an acrobatic display that was so energetic the fish threw the lure on the first head-shake.

After losing three more fish in a similar manner, I learned that I could barely apply the pressure to these fish because of their crappie-like mouths. I loosened the drag on my reel till it was almost free-spool, and it wasn't long before I had four, 1-pound fish and two 4-pounders laid out in the long, dew-wet grass near shore. When it became too dark to fish, I carried my prize catch back to the lodge and answered a barrage of questions. The next evening, the entire camp was lined along the shore fishing for whitefish. Several types of lures were used, yet it was the jig fly and salmon "appetizer" that consistently took top honors, producing the most and largest fish.

Since, I've narrowed my wide selection of whitefish jigs to a select few patterns. My favorite is a 1/32- to 1/64-ounce leadhead jig with a fluorescent pink head, black eyes, and a tinsel-wrapped body with a white marabou tail. Another good color combo is a red head, black chenile body and yellow marabou tail. The Fin-Chila jig flies work extremely well, as do the 1/80-ounce Trout Fuzzies in white and yellow.

It's necessary to "sweeten" these lures with an added at-

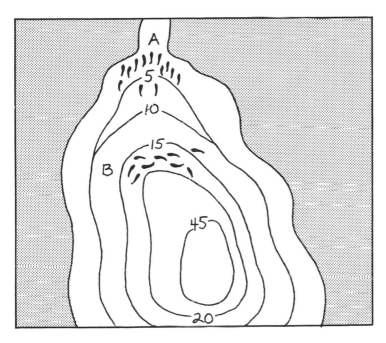

In lakes, look for whitefish at the inlets of streams in early morning and late evening (A). During midday, fish will often hold in deep water bordering their shallow water feeding areas (B).

tractor. I favor a small sliver of salmon attached to a piece of tough belly skin, threaded onto the hook of a jig so that it hides the barb and shank. A salmon egg is an effective substitute, especially in lakes with spawning salmon. However, whitefish are expert bait stealers and can pick a soft-skinned egg off a hook quite efficiently. Use boraxed or sugar-cured eggs or thread several eggs onto the barb and shank to keep the lure in operation. If no salmon or eggs are available, whitefish belly is an excellent alternative.

Never cast the lure directly into a school of feeding whitefish. Place the lure several feet beyond or to the side of the chumming spot and slowly work the lure into the area, swimming it fast enough to keep it just off bottom. It is often necessary to stop reeling and allow the lure to sit on bottom for a minute or two. At this time, the small whitefish that have been following and nipping at the lure will swarm around and try to inhale it. This activity attracts big whitefish. Strikes from large fish will usually occur when the lure is twitched into motion. Continue to work the lure without break to shore. I've had 4-pound whitefish follow a lure into less than a foot of water before striking it.

Streams and Rivers

It's often uncanny how an angler can be fishing a large, deep pool and catch grayling, Dollies, and rainbow on nearly every cast. Yet with a different fly tied on, whitefish will be the catch on every cast. With this in mind, you realize that it isn't so much finding stream whitefish that makes this sport challenging, but rather, figuring out exactly what bait, lure, or fly they will strike.

I've successfully caught stream whitefish on the miniature jigs mentioned above. However, it can often be difficult to get a 1/64-ounce lure down through the currents. A large split shot 12- to 16-inches ahead of the lure will usually resolve the matter.

Some of the best stream fishing for whitefish I've ever experienced has been during the months of September and October on the many streams and rivers in the Interior. Because whitefish are difficult to catch, the Alaska Department of Fish and Game has opened up a spear fishery for this species on most rivers. You can spear buckets of whitefish as they migrate upstream in large schools to their spawning beds. However, the ones that fall prey to anglers are the pre- and post-spawners that feed on the millions of free-drifting whitefish eggs washed downstream by the current.

A whitefish egg is a tad larger than a pin head, making it extremely difficult to imitate. However, my experience has shown that while it's important to keep the lure as small as possible, an exact imitation is unnecessary. Small jig flies in a whitish-yellow, imitating fertilized whitefish eggs, are very effective. I've also found that a yellow salmon egg attached to a single hook and fished with a piece of split shot on light tackle is another bait large whitefish can't refuse.

Proper presentation is the key to success. Because whitefish are bottom-hugging fish, and most streams are somewhat murky in late September and early October, you may have to fish the lure within several inches of bottom. One way of doing this is to cast as far upstream as possible to allow the lure plenty of time to reach bottom before working it through any fish-holding structure. In small streams, fish the lure along the edges of fast water, and fish slowly through eddies. On larger streams and rivers, dead drift an egg or lure through quiet backwaters at the edge of the current. Trees, large rocks, and logjams

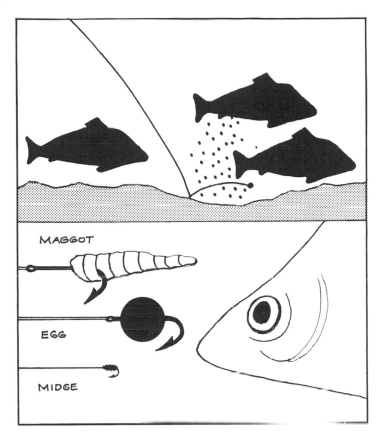

Trophy humpbacks feed heavily on whitefish eggs in September and October, when the fish are spawning in the upper stretches of clearwater streams and rivers. Tiny lures and flies are necessary to catch big fish at this time.

also create prime holding structure. Eggs tend to settle into the gravel at these points, attracting whitefish in large numbers. And don't overlook bridge pilings, islands, or the middle of a fast chute of water where migrating fish are heading upstream.

As whitefish are extremely wary of unnatural baits and presentations, it's important to keep a tight line and strike at the faintest tap or pickup. I like to use a lightly adjusted drag when fighting whitefish. If more drag is needed, I'll feather the spool with my fingertips.

Expect to lose plenty of lures when bouncing along a gravel bottom with 2-pound test. About every five casts, I check the line for frays and nicks, the main factors contributing to lost whitefish. Granted, changing line cuts into actual fishing time, but it's worth the satisfaction of knowing the tackle is A-OK when that 8-pounder sucks in the lure and heads upstream with the power of an Orca

Fresh-caught whitefish dipped in cornmeal and quick-fried over a stream-side campfire is gourmet eating at its finest.

pursuing a salmon.

On several occasions, I've run out of jig flies and have caught whitefish on tiny spoons and spinners. When using these lures, remember to keep the hooks sharp and hidden with hackle, marabou, or bait. Pieces of worm, beetles, and aquatic insects can also be used if nothing else is readily available. BiVisible, Mosquito, Black Gnat, Red Ant, Hare's Ear, Maggot, Scud, and Midge—tied on No. 14 or 16 hooks—have all produced whitefish for me when fished with a 6X to 7X leader.

Whitefish are not for the average angler. It takes skill, patience, and refined tackle to catch the smallest specimens, let alone the trophies. Granted, whitefish are not blessed with the dazzling colors typical of a rainbow or char. But they are, without question, a symbol of an angler's acquired skill and sportfish knowledge. An angler who can consistently catch trophy whitefish is indeed an expert fisherman.

Where to go for Whitefish

Note: Whitefish are distributed throughout most lakes and river systems in Alaska. The following is a list of my favorite places.

Southcentral

Whitefish are distributed throughout upper Susitna watersheds and in many lakes north of Palmer.

Cook Inlet/Kenai Peninsula
Alexander Creek
Deshka River
Little Susitna
Montana Creek
Susitna River

Copper River/Upper Susitna
Eyak Lake
Mentasta Lake
Slana River

Southwest

Most watersheds in this area have populations of whitefish. The largest trophies are lake resident fish, especially the humpback whitefish population in Lake Clark.

Lake Clark   **Kuskokwim**
Illamna Lake   Found throughout

Interior

The Chatanika offers an excellent spear fishery for whitefish. However, large humpbacks are extremely susceptible to bait during the autumn months, and flies throughout the summer months.

Broad Pass Lakes
Chatanika River
Delta Clearwater River
Lake George
Medicine Lakes
Tanana River tributaries

Northcentral

Found throughout

Northwest

Found throughout

Halibut

CHAPTER 17

Halibut

Without a doubt, Alaska's offshore heavyweight champ is the Pacific halibut. All too often, anglers will hook into this largest member of the flatfish family, hoping for a quick, tug-em-up battle and into the ice chest. They soon learn, however, that trophy halibut are not easily fought nor landed. These fish, often called barn-door halibut—a term that literally describes their-size—require a boatful of luck, plenty of grunt, and lots of prayer just to muscle them off the bottom! Battles lasting up to several hours are not uncommon. Even if an angler is lucky enough to land one, his work is cut out for him back at the boat dock. There, big halibut must be off-loaded with an overhead crane and weighed on a scale with springs large enough to support a half-ton pickup!

But despite these scare tactics and the halibut's bigger-than-life reputation, the best way to prepare for a bout with the champ is to become familiar with its life history and habits, along with a strenuous mental workout reviewing techniques and fighting strategy.

Life History and Habits

The Pacific halibut (Hippoglossus stenolepis) originally received its name from Scandinavians who named its cousin, the Atlantic halibut, "halleflundra" meaning "a fish that can be found in deep holes." From this, the English derived the word "holibut" meaning "the fish to be eaten on holy days." Today, modern names for the fish include northern halibut, right halibut, and albato.

The Pacific halibut is more elongated than other flat-

This angler is proud of his 315-pound Kachemak Bay halibut caught from the "Char Dan" out of Homer. The battle from hookup to gaff lasted over an hour. The fish had to be dispatched with a shot from a .38 pistol before it was boated.

fishes: Its width is about one-third its length. They are highly migratory fish; adult specimens travel more than 2,000 miles and to depths of 600 or more fathoms. However, many halibut can frequently be found in the relatively shallow, food-rich waters near their spawning grounds off the Alaska coast.

Halibut generally spawn between November and March along the continental shelf. Depending on her size, a female lays from 2 to 3 million eggs annually. The eggs hatch after 15 days, and become free-floating larvae. Ocean currents then transport them hundreds of miles along the Pacific Northwest coast.

During the next six months, an astonishing change takes place. The larva's fish-like form begins to flatten, and its left eye migrates to its right side. At this time, juvenile halibut migrate to shallow water to begin their bottom life, feeding on shrimp, baitfish, and other small crustaceans. After a minimum of five years, they'll move off into deeper water.

The growth rate and size of halibut depend upon sex, location, food availability, and other habitat conditions. Female halibut are larger than male halibut, weighing 300 to 400 pounds and living 35 to 45 years. The current Alaska record for sport-caught halibut is a 440-pound female caught near Point Adolphus in 1978 by Joar Savland. In contrast, males rarely exceed 40 pounds and live a maximum of 25 years. Female halibut also are more numerous than males, a fact that should make the sport angler quite happy.

Both males and females can be found along most of Alaska's coastline from Ketchikan to the Bering Strait. Halibut coloration tends to resemble the ocean bottom, varying from dark brown to gray, with light or starry-like spots on the top side and white on the blind or bottom side. This color adaptation allows a halibut, feeding at mid-depth, to escape detection from bottom-feeding predators by blending in with the sky.

Records indicate that more lunkers are caught from mid-May through June, when the fish are indulging in a feeding frenzy in the shallow coastal waters. The Cook Inlet-Kachemak Bay fishery is one of the most popular and productive at this time, with anglers catching 100-pound and larger halibut while trolling for migrating salmon, or simply by jigging bait and lures within several miles of

A 340-pound Kachemak Bay halibut. These fish are often called "barn door" halibut, a term that literally describes their size. (Alice Puster photo, courtesy of the Anchorage Times.)

How to Catch
Alaska's Trophy Sportfish

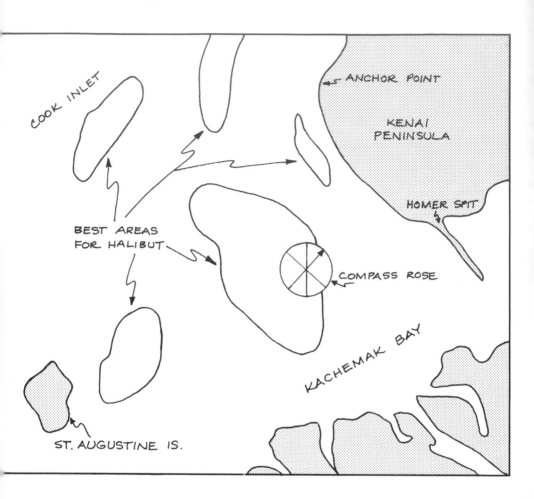

COOK INLET

ANCHOR POINT

KENAI PENINSULA

HOMER SPIT

BEST AREAS FOR HALIBUT

COMPASS ROSE

KACHEMAK BAY

ST. AUGUSTINE IS.

The Cook Inlet—Kachemak Bay area has an abundance of halibut structure scattered throughout the area. The best hotspots are in channels running the length of Anchor Point and Deep Creek, throughout Compass Rose, near Mount Saint Augustine, and in select areas 25 miles west of Homer Spit.

shore. I've found the best depth for halibut varies from 10 to 20 fathoms over sandy bottoms, tidal-induced depressions, and major channels emptying upper Cook Inlet into Kachemak Bay. Such areas are numerous off the shores of Deep Creek and Anchor Point, and remain hot for trophies until mid-July, when the halibut move into deeper water. Tidal rips, reefs, and channels 25 miles out from Homer Spit seem to produce the most lunkers during the remainder of the year.

Finding and fishing these areas is generally hit and miss unless you're equipped with a sonar recorder and hydrographic map. Charter operators equipped with a LORAN system, a navigation aid that can put them within 10 feet of any charted or previously recorded hotspot, have a definite advantage. This is why many

How to Catch
Alaska's Trophy Sportfish

anglers without similarly equipped cruisers patronize the charter operators. However, I've found that by scouting with a graph recorder, marking my fishing successes on a large hydrographic map, and using marker buoys properly, it's possible to locate and hook big halibut from a small boat on a regular basis.

If you don't own a boat, or the water is extremely rough, you can oftentimes catch halibut from shore. The local tackle shops often buzz with such fish stories. One lucky angler managed to wrestle a "slab" halibut into the surf off Deep Creek; another hooked into a big halibut from the Homer Spit and was about to lose all his line from the rampaging fish when a boater picked up the angler, ran down, and subsequently landed the 200-pound flatfish. I discovered there is no secret to catching halibut from

shore. Richard Gardner and I did exactly that one June day when a storm forced us to head for cover on an island in Resurrection Bay.

Wanting to get in as much fishing as we could, we walked out to a rocky point stretching out into a semi-protected bay of the island. Tying on a 6-ounce Sebastes jig, Rick lobbed the lure into the whitecaps and allowed it to sink. After a 45-second wait, he jumped the lure off bottom and allowed it to flutter back. On the second jump, he began an erratic retrieve to the surface when the lure hung on what he thought was a piece of kelp. Forcefully, Rick began to crank on the level-wind reel, hoping to bust it through the vegetation. It was then that the "kelp" sounded for bottom.

For the next 25 minutes, we gambled away all our worldly possessions betting on what Rick had hooked. Finally, the brown and white silhouette that signals halibut popped into view. It seemed Neptune was on our side, as the winds settled to a light breeze and the seas calmed to a roll. Rick worked the fish to a sandy stretch of beach and managed to plane the halibut to shore on an incoming wave. He fell on his prize in the surf, and quickly dragged it to higher ground. It was a sleek, 42-pounder, an average fish for Resurrection Bay waters. Using the same technique from shore, we managed to hook two more, both under 20 pounds.

While surf fishing for halibut is fun, it can't match the big-water excitement or action of a bait-induced strike from a 200-pound fish that is intent on dragging the boat to China!

Techniques

Bait

Catching large halibut is a science, and both novice and veteran anglers can't get a more scientific education than that provided by some of the halibut skippers operating out of Homer. I've spent several hundred hours under the tutelage of Frank Kempl, who has landed more 100- to 300-pound-plus halibut than most skippers read about in a lifetime.

Kempl stresses that the proper bait is of paramount importance for large halibut. Herring is his favorite, and it must be firm, with shiny scales and a uniform shape, never

Surf casting for halibut is possible in areas with steep sloping dropoffs in water from 150 to 300 feet deep. Large, shiny jigs are best, especially when worked slowly above sand, mud, or clay bottom structure.

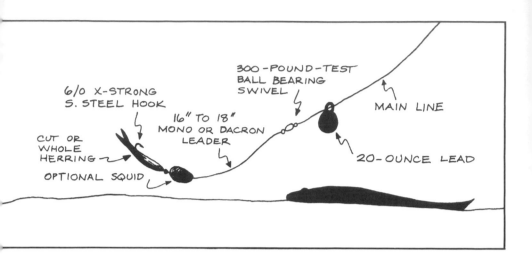

6/0 X-STRONG
S. STEEL HOOK

300-POUND-TEST
BALL BEARING
SWIVEL

MAIN LINE

16" TO 18"
MONO OR DACRON
LEADER

CUT OR
WHOLE
HERRING

OPTIONAL SQUID

20-OUNCE LEAD

*A slip-sinker rig is a fav-
orite for halibut in heavy
currents. Add a chunk of
squid in areas where bait
thieves are a problem.*

soft, mushy or waterlogged. If obtainable, "starved her-ring" is undoubtedly the best. This is a name for specially conditioned herring kept in huge vats without being fed for several days to a week. The starved herring have uti-lized their body fat to survive, thus becoming firm and ex-tremely streamlined. They are then electroshocked and carefully packaged, preventing damage to their scales. The end product is a prime herring bait no trophy halibut can pass up.

Kempl likes to maintain the bait's appearance by keep-ing the herring frozen before and during use. He fishes it on a special slip-sinker rig that is rather simple to tie up. First, a 20-ounce teardrop, cannonball or triangle sinker is threaded onto a mainline of 80- to 120-pound test. This is sufficient weight for slack tide. (When fishing Cook Inlet during a tidal flow, you need to double this amount to keep the bait on the bottom. This area is renowned for having the second highest, and subsequently strongest, tides in the Northern Hemisphere.) To the main line is tied a X6R, 300-pound-test Sampo or similar swivel. En-sure the swivel does not pass through the eyelet of the weight or become hung up in any way. Next, attach a leader of either 120-pound-test Dacron or two strands of the same test monofilament to the swivel. Use a Trilene knot for securing the line to the swivel, and to the heavy-duty, 9/0 or 10/0 stainless-steel hook. Next, run the barb through the operculum of the herring, turn the point toward the tail of the fish, and bury it into the mid-section

How to Catch
Alaska's Trophy Sportfish

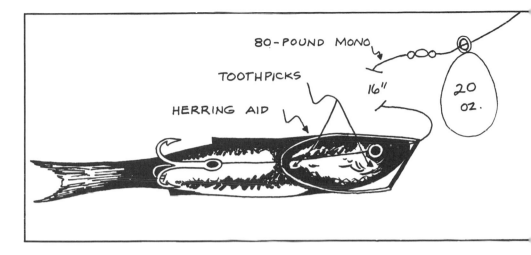

80-POUND MONO

TOOTHPICKS

HERRING AID

16"

20 OZ.

of the bait. If using half herring, bury it into the midsection of the piece, with only the point of the hook protruding from the other side. This is important as halibut usually grab a baitfish by its mid-section.

At times, large halibut can be picky about herring, especially if ol' Clampjaw has several hook/leader combos hanging from his trophy maw. Under these conditions, I prefer my herring to spin lazily in the current. And there's no better way I know of to accomplish this than a technique I discovered while trolling for king salmon off Deep Creek

It was an incoming tide, and the kings were out a bit further than usual: about 200 yards from shore in 45 feet of water. I rigged up a Herring Aid with a large, 9-inch herring, added a three-ounce weight, and began trolling in a zig-zag pattern. I hadn't trolled more than 100 feet when my rod slammed down, and stayed down!

I motored around, thinking that I was hung on an old commercial fish net. Then I felt the fluttering sensation that signals only one thing...big halibut! I took an easy half hour to wrestle the 80-pound-plus fish to the surface. As the fish neared the surface, I slowly reached for my .410 shotgun. Big halibut must be shot before bringing them into the boat, otherwise they can cause serious personal injury or boat damage. Just as I was ready to shoot the fish, it shook its head twice across the mono leader and broke free.

Two weeks later, while loading the boat for a halibut

A Herring Aid, modified with 80-pound mono and an extra-strong treble, is an excellent rig to use when drifting for halibut.

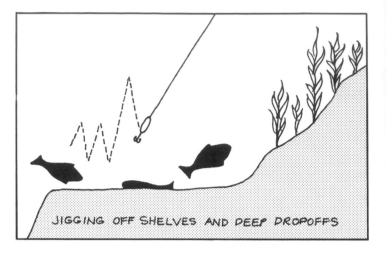

JIGGING OFF SHELVES AND DEEP DROPOFFS

trip, I remembered what that lunker had been trying to tell me. So instead of tying on a standard 9/0 hook, I threaded the plastic Herring Aid onto an 80-pound-test leader and a number 8/0, extra-strong treble, and sweetened the rig with the largest herring in the bait box. My rig looked formidable, and it brought a few laughs from my fishing buddies. Later that afternoon, with a 52- and 83-pound halibut in the boat, I had the last laugh. I finally succumbed to a variety of bribes and rented out the rig to my once-doubtful buddies. Since then, I've found this rig works best when drifting with 6 to 10 ounces of lead, or anchored in moderate tidal flows with 20 ounces of lead.

Despite what method you use, fishing during slack tide requires the bait to be lowered to the bottom slowly and then raised up about a foot. Occasionally hitting bottom whenever the boat rocks from a swell is a good indication that your rig is staying within this strike zone. I lift the bait slowly every 10 to 20 seconds to impart added appeal and to prevent the crabs from stripping the hook.

When the tide is running full bore, your rig will seldom stay on bottom, even with 40 ounces of weight. This is when you must "walk the bait." Once you feel the sinker lift off bottom in the current, strip out or free spool about four feet of line while lifting the tip of your rod to about a 70-degree angle. Now slowly tap your weight along bottom by working your rod in an up and down motion. This keeps your bait "walking" along bottom until your rod is horizontal. Then you must strip out another four feet or

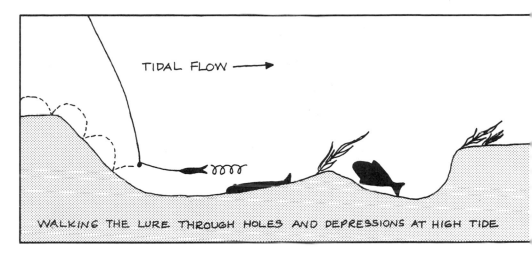

TIDAL FLOW ⟶

WALKING THE LURE THROUGH HOLES AND DEPRESSIONS AT HIGH TIDE

more of line, raise your rod tip, and repeat the procedure.

After you've "walked" the bait about 100 yards, reel in and check the bait. Using this technique with 40-ounce weights during a full-bore tide is the most exhausting type of halibut fishing. But it is the only effective way to fish for halibut under these conditions.

In areas with minimal tidal fluctuations, anglers often must contend with bait thieves. An added enticer that is also a bait-thief deterrent is threading a walnut-size chunk of squid onto the line ahead of the herring. Even if thieves steal your herring, your rig will still remain effective, as I've yet to find a bait thief that can remove a piece of squid from a hook. Also, the feeding frenzy of the thieves around the squid can attract larger halibut which simply move in and inhale the bait.

Stomach analyses of large halibut have shown they frequently feed at mid-depths, especially during slack tide. Under these circumstances, "the bigger the bait, the bigger the fish" theory holds true.

One of the most effective methods of catching trophy halibut under these conditions is to bait up with a whole salmon head. Millions of salmon migrate through prime Southeast and Cook Inlet halibut grounds, and Belugas and killer whales leave plenty of remains after their ambushes through the salmon schools. I've found that baiting with an entire head several feet off the bottom during heavy tidal flows, and at least 10 or more feet off the bottom during slack tide, will catch more trophy halibut than

In heavy tidal currents, "walking the bait" is the best way to keep a herring near bottom, where big halibut like to hold.

Jigs are excellent lures to use for halibut. This 20-pounder struck a 6-ounce Wolfer with an Uncle Josh Big Boy pork rind trailer.

any other "big bait." Of course, a salmon head is usually large enough to keep the smaller 30- to 50-pounders off the hook, so don't expect much action. But when you do get a strike, you can bet your fishing buddy a king crab dinner that the halibut will near or exceed 100 pounds.

Lures

In the hands of an experienced halibut angler, a metal jig is the most effective lure available for trophy halibut. Chrome, silver, or nickel-plated models such as the Vi-ke, Krocodile, and Diamond Jig in 8, 16, and 32 ounces are the most popular. Sportfish tackle dealer Roland Cusson of Soldotna has the best success with a white, 14-ounce Krocodile when driftfishing for Cook Inlet halibut. In bays indirectly affected by heavy tidal action, I prefer a 6-ounce Sebastes jig with fluorescent orange and yellow skirt with an Uncle Josh Off-Shore Big Boy pork rind teaser.

Jigging is best done immediately before, during, and immediately after slack tide. In many of the protected coves and bays in Southeast Alaska, where tidal action is not as pronounced as in the Cook Inlet-Kachemak Bay area, jigging is good anytime. In these calmer waters, the lure has a chance to flutter in a dying baitfish-like manner and can cast a reflection great distances in the clear water. However, when fishing near kelp beds, I prefer a leadhead jig: The single hook helps minimize snags, and is extremely effective in hooking and holding large fish.

I prefer to fish both types of jigs in an irregular pattern: I use three-foot jumps off the bottom, followed by a few seconds to allow the lure to flutter back. Remember, halibut will invariably strike an artificial while it's settling, or before you snap it off bottom. So keep a tight line at all times. And unlike bait fishing, there is no mistaking the strike of a halibut on an artificial lure. This is one of the main reasons I favor this type of fishing so much. The strike can best be described as a hard "chomp". The angler's response should be a brutal hookset. And if the fish is 100 pounds or larger, it's best to have a good brace against the railing or a rope around your mid-section, as it will definitely yank back. My wife Adela became involved in such a tug-o-war with a lunker halibut while fishing out of Waterfall Resort near Ketchikan, Alaska.

We were fishing a half-mile-wide shelf on the Pacific side of Bucareli Bay in late June. Adela was jigging a 16-ounce Vi-ke about 15 feet off bottom in 160 feet of water, and perhaps giving each upward jig a bit more "oomph" than required. Just as she was about to begin her third upward sweep, a huge halibut grabbed the lure just in time to receive the full brunt of her savage technique. The halibut responded wildly, nearly pulling her 5-foot, 2-inch, 105-pound frame over the boat railing. Not wanting the halibut to think it got the best of her, she slammed the hooks home again. Her fish responded in kind, which again caught her off balance. The slug-out lasted for 45 minutes before the halibut broke off. Somewhat disappointed, Adela reeled up her lure with its mangled treble hook. A 4-inch section of metal was stripped from the center of the lure, and the hook eye was partially straightened. Disappointment quickly turned into excitement as she tied on another Vi-ke and continued her eye-crossing technique.

However, the fun part is over when the fish nears the boat. If the halibut is large, you could be facing a potentially dangerous situation. It's imperative to dispatch the trophy in the water. Boat damage, broken legs and tackle have resulted to those who failed to respect the power this heavyweight can dish out.

The excitement of catching big halibut is best summed up by the comments of an elderly woman who had just disembarked from a tour bus while we were unloading a day's catch of halibut. The woman shook her head as she gazed upon a 60-pounder waiting to be cleaned. After asking numerous questions about the fish and fishing, she returned to her husband, who was taking pictures of the boat dock.

"Elmer," she said in an enlightened voice. "We're going to cash in these sightseeing tickets and go halibut fishing."

From what I understand, the couple left Homer with a 124-pounder and a promise to return the following year.

How to Catch
Alaska's Trophy Sportfish

Where to go for Halibut

Southeast

This area of Alaska offers some of the best halibut fishing found in North America. Charter boats for halibut operate out of most Southeastern cities. If fishing on your own, look for trophies on underwater shelves near steep dropoffs in 90 to 250 feet of water.

Admiralty Island
Barlow Cove
Doty's Cove
Favorite Reef
Piling Point
Point Arden
Point Retreat

Juneau
Aaron Island
Auke Bay
Barlow Cove
Echo Cove
Icy Point
Lena Point
Lincoln Island
Marmion Island
Middle Point
North Pass
Outer Point
Point Bishop
Point Hilda
Point Retreat
Point Salisbury
South Shelter Island
White Marker

Ketchikan
Bell Island
Blank Inlet
Bucareli Bay
Chasina Point
Clover Pass
Grant Island
Grindall Island
Point Alava
Point Sykes
20-Fathom Bank
Vallenar Point
Yes Bay

Petersburg
Cape Straight
Frederick Sound
Security Bay

Sitka
Chatham Straight
Peril Straight
Sitka Sound

Wrangell
Greys Pass
Wrangell Harbor

Southcentral

Mid-May through June is the best time for large halibut in Cook Inlet-Kachemak Bay. In Resurrection Bay, large halibut can be found on occasion near the shipping buoys by Rugged Island or in water from 180 to 300 feet deep.

Cook Inlet/Kenai Peninsula
Anchor Point Kelp Beds
Bluff Point
Compass Rose
Double Falls
Flat Island
Happy Valley
Homer Spit
Kachemak Bay
Resurrection Bay
Saint Augustine Island

Kodiak Island
Chiniak Bay
Middle Bay
Monashka Bay
Shelikof Straight

Yakutat
Yakutat Bay

Rockfish

Rockfish

Mention rockfish to anglers, and chances are you'll be swamped with a deluge of stories about "fish" that were fought but never landed, busted treble hooks on 8-ounce lures, and snapped, 120-pound-test lines caused by this "species." Of course, the "rockfish" most anglers refer to are just that: rocks or snags on the bottom of a stream, river or ocean. A hookup with such an opponent might have an angler fighting it for minutes before realizing his mistake. Because this type of "fish" is responsible for thousands of dollars in lost tackle each year, it is greatly scorned by most anglers.

Yet for years, the various species of true bottomfish (which for the purposes of this chapter are rockfish and ling cod) were also scorned by anglers. The reason was not because of lost tackle, but because the species were considered bottom dwellers and scavengers, unchallenging fishes unworthy of an angler's time. Opinion was only a fool or novice would fish for them, while people of class and reputation would pursue the coho and chinook existing in large numbers in the very same waters!

While the salmon still ranks tops with many anglers, the varied species of bottomfish are rapidly gaining popularity. They are fish worthy of trophy consideration due to their size, fight, and oftentimes dazzling coloration. But most of all, they can be caught when there are few salmon, when halibut waters are too rough to venture out upon, and when fail-safe fishing action is necessary for that young angler or visiting relative who may not have the patience to wait hours for a salmon or trout to strike.

This 15-pound yelloweye rockfish inhaled a 3-ounce Wolfer jig fished in 75 feet of water. Medium-action tackle and 20-pound-test monofilament helped bring this fish to shore.

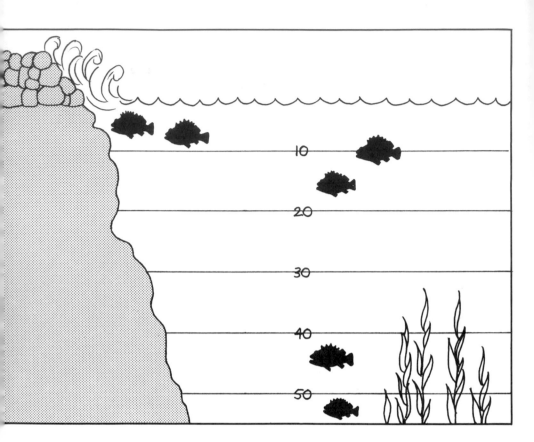

Trophy rockfish are typically found along tidewater breaklines, suspended from 5 to 20 feet below the surface, or hugging bottom structure, especially near weedbeds.

Rockfish belong to the genus Sebastes, and are members of the family Scorpaenidae, or scorpion fishes. They are appropriately named, as the prickly spines emerging from their dorsal fin contain a mild toxin that can cause painful discomfort to the angler unlucky enough to get pricked by one. Rockfish are also known as rock bass, black sea bass, kelp bass, and rock cod. There are over 60 varieties found along the Pacific coast, with the black, quillback, China, and canary rockfishes most common to Alaska waters. The yelloweye or red rockfish, also common to Alaska waters, is erroneously called red snapper by many charter boat operators. True red snapper are native only to Atlantic and tropical waters.

Rockfish grow slowly in Alaska waters. A 10-year-old fish averages 16 inches and weighs almost 4 pounds, while a 20-year-old fish averages 20 inches and weighs about 7 pounds. Any rockfish over 5 pounds should be considered a trophy.

Techniques

Lures

Trophy rockfish can be found in two kinds of areas. First, during the winter months and immediately after, rockfish can be found in water 125 feet or deeper. Deepwater jigging is usually quite effective, provided you can tolerate the inclement weather common to Gulf of Alaska waters during this time of year.

During the summer months, however, rockfish are often in water less than 100 feet, and usually directly under the surface, feeding on herring and needlefish. Under these conditions, 3-ounce lures can be fished at virtually any depth quickly and effectively.

With these points in mind, along with the battlesome nature of rockfish, its easy to understand why light tackle is the only way to pursue these "Denizens of the Deep."

I prefer a medium-action, 6-foot spinning or level-wind

This quillback rockfish struck a chrome Vi-ke fished with a sharp, jigging action above a sandy bottom in Valdez Harbor. Be careful when landing these fish, as the dorsal spines contain a mild toxin which can cause painful inflamation.

rod and matching reel filled with 17-pound-test monofilament line for large, shallow water rockfish. Not only do I need a rod with plenty of backbone to properly set the hook into their bony mouths, but also to compensate for the stretch in the monofilament line when jigging at depths greater than 25 feet. Limber, light-action rods simply won't hook fish on a consistent basis.

I've experimented with hundreds of lures over the past 10 years on rockfish from Resurrection Bay to Prince of Wales Island, and have yet to find a better producer than a leadhead jig. I favor the 1- to 3-ounce Flowering Floreos with a fluorescent red head and a yellow, crinkled nylon tail—or a Sebastes jig or Wolfer in fluorescent orange, red, and yellow. I highly recommend a 4- to 8-inch, rubbery, twister-type tail attached to the single hook. The undulating action of the tail while sinking and swimming drives rockfish wild. However, rockfish like to chomp and chew on the tails, and I've gone through as many as 26 in a single afternoon. After that experience, I switched to Uncle Josh's Ripple Rind in yellow and white. The rind is virtually indestructible, it stays on the hook well, and is equally effective as twister tails for putting fish into the boat.

For deepwater rockfish, the 6- to 16-ounce Vi-ke, Krocodile, and Diamond jigs are the most effective. They have the weight needed to get down to the fish fast, and a fluttering action that reflects light off their polished sides in all directions, thus attracting fish to the area.

Finding good rockfish habitat is a matter of using your eyes and a quality graph recorder. One of the most popular rockfish waters in the state is Resurrection Bay. Here, there is an abundance of visual structure that can clue you in to large rockfish habitat. Such structure includes, but is not limited to, kelp beds, rocky outcroppings, rocky beaches, and the faces of rock cliffs and points of islands washed by the tide.

This trophy yelloweye rockfish, caught by Adela Batin in Southeast Alaska's Bucareli Bay, struck an 8-ounce Vi-ke jigged above a kelp bed in 130 feet of water.

Structures which usually require a graph recorder to locate are: underwater reefs, shoals, deepwater kelp beds, shelves, wrecks, and rocky, shallow water areas bordering steep dropoffs.

I always make it a point to fish from shallow water to deep. If near shore, I cast to visible structure and bottom-bounce the lure back to the boat. In the middle of bays, I frequently locate rockfish suspended within 10 feet of the

How to Catch
Alaska's Trophy Sportfish

Richard Gardner with a 3-man catch of Resurrection Bay rockfish and halibut. These fish were caught on a 6-ounce Sebastes jig with a chartreuse skirt and white twister tail.

surface. In cases like this, it's just a simple matter of lowering the jig over the side and holding on to the rod! Waterfall Resort manager Russell Chun and I caught over 50 rockfish from such a school one afternoon. The fish were suspended above a kelp bed, and as long as we remained directly above the weedy stuff, our rods remained doubled over with fighting rockfish. But once we drifted 20 or so yards off to one side, the action quickly subsided.

Another major factor to consider is tidal flow. Avoid fishing during extreme fluctuations in tide. I've had best success fishing waters sheltered either directly or indirectly from the tide. For instance, on an incoming tide from the south, I fish the northern bays, points, and other structure removed from, but near, the major tidal flow. Current flow around these islands produces backeddies, which trap food. On many occasions, I've watched rockfish dart out into the current, grab a mouthful of shellfish, and dart back to their rocky lair.

There are several ways to fish both the metal and leadhead jigs. The most effective for me has been an erratic

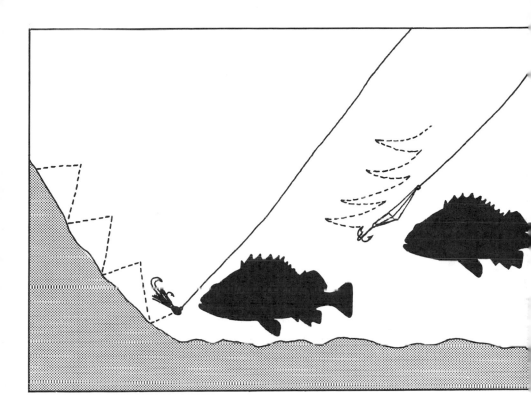

retrieve or jigging motion. Always add a "twitch" to the main swimming or jigging action of the lure. If a strike is missed, slowly work the lure in place with one-inch twitches of the rod. The second strike is almost always more forceful than the first, so hold on and set that hook hard enough to cross the fish's eyes!

Summer rockfishing results in plenty of youngsters that are often released. Remember that winching up a rockfish from the depths with heavy tackle will usually result in the fish experiencing the "bends." A fish with the "bends" is not a pretty sight. Their air-filled stomach protrudes from their mouth and their eyes bug out. This is the result of rockfish having an air bladder with a closed system. Unlike salmon and halibut that have a bladder allowing them to release air and adapt quickly to changes in depth, rockfish must absorb any excess gas into their system before they can ascend or descend. An angler can minimize possible damage or death to these fish by slowly reeling them up from the depths. Such an action will ensure healthy rockfish populations for years to come.

Leadhead jigs are popular lures for structure-holding rockfish, while metal jigs are a favorite for deepwater and mid-depth fish.

Ling Cod

Ling cod are popular fish for two reasons: They can attain weights of up to 60 pounds, and their flesh is an epicurean delight. They are related to the rockfish family, but lack the spiny head. They are somewhat elongate in shape and have large, pike-like teeth. They can be caught from shallow water down to 1,400 feet.

The ling is a voracious predator and feeds mainly on other fishes. While the leadhead and metal jigs used for rockfish commonly take ling, the largest specimens are consistently caught on bait.

Rockfish and ling inhabit the same territory; therefore, an angler can use no better bait than a freshly-caught rockfish. By using the methods described previously for catching rockfish, you can have a fresh and effective bait whenever necessary. For bait, I favor rockfish in the 1- to 3-pound class.

Bait

After catching a rockfish, trim the caudal fin, much the same way a crappie angler trims the tail of his minnows to give them a wounded or crippled appearance. Next, run an 8/0 halibut hook through the rockfish's top and bottom lips. This is important as lings always swallow rockfish head first. Attach the hook to an 18-inch wire leader, clipped on via snap to a 3-way swivel of at least 60-pound test. Attach a 1- to 3-ounce pyramid sinker via a dropper line to the bottom eyelet of the 3-way swivel, and attach the main line to the remaining ring. I like to use a heavy line, preferably 40-pound-test Dacron. That's because after hooking a ling, it often likes to wedge itself between rocks and can be extremely difficult to break free. Also, the heavier the line, the more resistant it is to the abrasive effects of submerged rocks and the raspy teeth of a ling.

Once rigged, lower your bait to within several feet of a rocky bottom, slightly higher over kelp beds. With its tail trimmed, the rockfish bait will swim in a crippled manner, and the short leader will prevent it from hiding in nearby cover. Occasionally lower the rod tip and let the sinker tap the bottom. Lings are especially noted for homing in on wounded fish, and the added noise of your sinker hitting bottom will help attract a ling to the bait.

Ling cod are voracious predatory bottomfish that offer excellent sport in addition to being superb table fare. This ling was caught on a Flowering Floreo with a pork rind attractor in 135 feet of water.

When a ling has taken your bait, open the bail and slowly pay out line. A large ling will use its long, needle-like teeth to paralyze the rockfish before spitting it out and re-ingesting it head first. Once the line begins to move out slowly, reel in any slack, lower your rod tip to the water, and strike with every ounce of strength you can muster. A ling won't waste any time showing how much of a sport-fish it can be.

While bottomfishing for lings and rockfish may not, at first, conjure up the feelings of excitement and challenge experienced in a match with a silver salmon, give it a try when action is slow or upon returning to the boat harbor some afternoon. A few bouts with these hard-striking welterweights will have you convinced there's not a more willing and cooperative sportfish in the North Pacific.

Where to go for Rockfish

Rockfish can be found off almost any rocky shoreline from Southeast Alaska to the Alaska Peninsula. Anglers should have no trouble finding trophy rockfish in any area. However, do keep in mind that trophy rockfish are often found at depths of 300 or more feet.

Southeast

Admiralty Island
Barlow Cove
Doty's Cove
Favorite Reef
Point Arden
Point Retreat
Pybus Bay

Juneau
Aaron Island
Lena Point
Point Bishop
Point Retreat
South Shelter Island
White Marker

Ketchikan
Bell Island
Bucareli Bay
Caamano Point
Chasina Point
Clover Pass
Mountain Point
Point Sykes
Vallenar Point
Yes Bay

Petersburg
Cape Straight
Security Bay

Wrangell
Grey's Pass

Southcentral

Cook Inlet/Kenai Peninsula
Resurrection Bay
Seldovia

Copper River
Port of Valdez
Prince William Sound

Southwest

Kodiak Island
Kizhuyak Bay
Monashka Bay
Ugak Bay
Women's Bay

Planning
Your Trip

Planning Your Trip

A successful Alaska trophy fishing trip doesn't "just happen." It is the direct result of long hours of advance preparation. You must study the area thoroughly, and attempt to calculate the arrival of peak migrations with algebraic precision. Tackle and equipment must be purchased, and long hours of studying individual fish habits are necessary for success. Yet before doing any of these activities, conduct an honest self-examination. Recognize your angling abilities and needs. If you're basically a lake fisherman, an unguided float trip down a wilderness stream—requiring strategic techniques for low-water trout and knowledge of stream structure—may not be right for you. Or if you're after trophy salmon for the freezer rather than the wall, you don't want to fish a catch-and-release area or those with restrictive bag limits. An honest look at your abilities and goals will allow you to plan a trip that either requires a guide for instruction or just the bare basics for you to challenge the fish on a one-to-one basis.

The next consideration is financing your venture. The overall price will depend upon many variables. I find it helpful to first break down the support costs. These are expenses in addition to those paid to the lodge or charter operation such as accommodations at the base city, transportation, hotel, meals, souvenirs, fish processing, taxidermy work, licenses, special gear, and any expenses not included in the actual fishing process. These should be totalled and kept separate from the actual fishing costs. This prevents you from making the mistake of allowing for just the fishing trip price. A bush village is no place to be

A competant fishing guide does more than offer fishing advice on the stream. He knows the area, its wildlife, and is woods-wise enough to prevent a direct confrontation with brown bears or any other potentially dangerous situation.

A *riverboat charter is an inexpensive alternative to
reach distant fishing
waters. They operate in
weather that keeps aircraft
grounded, have virtually no
weight restrictions, and cost
a fraction of the price for a
fly-out trip.*

stranded because you didn't figure enough in the overall trip for additional hotel fare due to inclement weather delaying the trip.

Time of year is another important factor to consider. Contrary to belief, you can't catch a trophy fish at just any time in Alaska waters. There are hundreds of different salmon runs in the state, each with their own timetable. The individual actions of non-anadromous fish can also vary greatly. If your goal is a trophy rainbow, you'll have to plan for early October when the fish are following the sockeye salmon upstream. This fishery doesn't exist any other time of year. A good rule of thumb to follow for individual species is this: Always plan your trip to coincide with the peak of the run in the area you'll be fishing. If you're unfamiliar with the locale, extensive communication with the guide or outfitter is necessary. If your goal is variety as well as size, July and August are the best months to plan for.

Once you have a budget and know what species you want to pursue, start your homework. Query different lodges and charter services listed in travel or outdoor magazines. Specific questions about their services will usually solicit specific replies. There are a variety of trips, one for every budget and taste. The following is an overall view of what you can expect.

Do-It-Yourself (Unguided)

Car: Alaska has a variety of good fishing waters accessible by highway. The Kenai offers excellent king salmon fishing, the Anchor River and Ninilchik prime steelheading, and the Russian River is a favorite for sockeye salmon. The lakes and streams of the Interior offer a wide selection of roadside waters containing lake trout and grayling. A car-topper or trailered boat, 12 feet or longer, is necessary to safely fish most of these larger rivers and lakes. In certain areas, boat rentals are available. However, unless you're familiar with Alaska's rivers, leave the riverboating to the charter operators. An error in judgement or equipment failure on many of these glacial-fed waters can be deadly.

Although waters accessible by road are often productive, they can also be elbow-to-elbow fishing, especially in the high-density salmon areas such as the Russian River. Some of the crowds can be avoided by fishing early in the morning and during the weekdays.

Hike-In Fishing: The backpack and pack-rod method is often good in early spring and late fall, and often during the salmon season. The general rule of thumb is to hike at least a mile up or down the river from where the road crosses the waterway. Fish are generally more plentiful away from the heavily fished roadside areas. But be prepared. Mosquitoes and Devil's Club are two painful reasons why people fish close to the road.

Lakes accessible only by trail often have excellent fishing for rainbows, grayling, and lake trout. A small, one-man backpack raft will greatly increase your chances of success by allowing you better access to structure-holding fish.

Charter Boat: Many of Alaska's prime salmon streams in the Susitna, Copper, and Talkeetna fisheries are reached only by riverboat. These craft are specially built boats with large engines and jet drive units that can handle Alaska's glacial rivers. Riverboat operators generally serve as a taxi service only. They'll drop you off and pick you up at a predetermined time and place. And there is no time limitation on how long you can stay in an area. This is an inexpensive way to experience semi-wilderness fishing. Prices can range from $50 on up to several hundred, depending upon the distance travelled. However, some of the most popular fishing locales accessible only by

A do-it-yourself fishing trip can be productive, providing the angler is thorough in all aspects of pre-planning, from researching the best fishing areas to packing the right fuel canisters for the propane stove.

riverboat can transform into miniature cities with shoulder to shoulder fishermen during holiday weekends.

Railroad: This transportation means is an inexpensive, yet practical way to leave the crowds behind and experience good fishing. The railroad has scheduled runs between Anchorage and Fairbanks and back, stopping at whatever stream or river along the way to drop off fishermen, hikers, and adventurers. Once you're done fishing an area, simply flag the train down, load your gear, and you're off to your next fishing spot or back to civilization. The prime fishing areas lie between Anchorage and Cantwell. A round trip ticket is approximately $70.

Air Charter: Air travel is expensive, yet it's the best way to access true wilderness fishing. Most of the state's trophy fish areas—such as the Wood River, Bristol Bay, Iliamna, and Gates of the Arctic—are accessible only by floatplane.

You have two basic options when hiring an aircraft charter: Outfit yourself and pay just for flying time, or pay for both charter time and use of the operator's equipment. Rates are reasonable and most have all the equipment necessary to outfit a full-scale fishing expedition. Tent camps, cabins, boats, motors, and rafts are also available from many operators.

If packing your own gear, pack lightly. Many anglers show up at dockside with over 400 pounds of gear, food, and booze, all for just a simple weekend trip. They have no

How to Catch
Alaska's Trophy Sportfish

concept how much gear a floatplane can safely carry. It's always best to contact the charter operator, but as a general rule, figure on 1,000 pounds of people and gear in a Cessna 206, and 1,800 pounds of people and gear in a DeHaviland Beaver.

The use of an aircraft or river charter is no guarantee you'll experience super fishing away from the crowds. The Deshka River, accessible by aircraft or riverboat only, can be a madhouse of boats and planes during the king salmon season. So again, plan your trip accordingly. Voice your preferences to the air charter operator well in advance. Many have secret spots that have excellent fishing at various times of the year. But as a general rule, if you want true wilderness fishing, be prepared to pay for the transportation to reach it.

Guided

There are a variety of guided fishing options. The most popular are the fishing lodges. There are three basic catagories:

• **$1800 to $2500 per week:** These lodges are invariably situated in trophy wilderness fishing areas and cater specifically to people desiring luxury and a large variety of sportfish.

You'll generally fish an average of 8 hours per day, with the remainder spent relaxing and enjoying the lodge's other features such as a bar, sauna, pool table, or fireplace.

The reason many of these lodges don't fish longer is because travel to and from the fishing areas is usually conducted via floatplane. Depending upon the location of the lodge, it may take an hour or more to reach many of the prime fishing locations in the Lake Clark/Wood River/Iliamna area. Add time spent for meals, trip preparation, and eight hours of sleep,—not to mention time allocated for enjoying the exquisite meals and added features of the lodge—and there's not much time left for additional fishing. However, many of these lodges are located within walking distance of prime fishing waters. Lake trout, whitefish, pike, grayling, and rainbow can often be caught within minutes from the lodge's front door.

These lodges are extremely popular with couples who like to fish without roughing it in any way. Executives and professional types also book with these lodges for conferences, making it a tax-deductable expense. And last but not least, you'll find a variety of people here from all walks of life pursuing that "trip of a lifetime" in terms of numbers and variety of fish caught.

To stay in business, these lodges must gear up for volume. This means a high turnover of people from week to week. It's not uncommon to dine with as many as 14 or more other guests at the same meal. However, all these lodges have support personnel to handle large groups, with a moderate amount of personal attention. In addition, private rooms and baths are the norm here, usually in the form of separate cabins apart from the main lodge. Again, you're paying for the quality of the experience and the transportation to various trophy fish areas.

• **$1000 to $1600 per week:** These lodges are more popular among avid anglers due to their price range and close proximity of fishable waters to the lodge. The main factors influencing the price reduction here are generally fewer fish species available, a few less luxuries (such as pool table and sauna) and the use of surface or boat transportation rather than aircraft to reach fishing areas. Accommodations can be either separate or shared.

Also in this mid-price lodge category is the outfitted or guided float trip. These are geared for the angler who wants to sample a variety of fishing, see some country, and still be pampered with all the luxuries possible on such an excursion. A good portion of the fee is applied toward transportation to and from the area to be floated. Your guide takes care of erecting camp, preparing meals, and handling the inflatable from hotspot to hotspot. This is usually a fine choice for a first Alaska fishing trip, or for the angler who is challenged with catching fish under a variety of stream conditions.

• **$875 to $1400 per week:** These are often considered "low-price" lodges, but don't let them fool you. They can either consist of the bare basics or rank with the full-service lodges in terms of numbers of fish caught and quality accommodations.

This type of lodge is usually located on the bank of a river or lake. Fishing is within walking distance or done by boat. This type of lodge may only have 3 to 6 species of fish to offer its clients, or it may specialize in one particular species, such as king or silver salmon. Accommodations can range from tent camps to modern bunk houses with

How to Catch
Alaska's Trophy Sportfish

three full meals a day. It pays to thoroughly investigate lodges in this catagory before making any deposit. These types of lodges are excellent choices if they have the particular fish species you desire. Why pay extra for the opportunity to fish for other species that don't interest you?

• **Day Trips:** There are numerous guided, fly-out and charter boat day trips. Here, the guide or operator will stay with you throughout the day, taking you to the best fishing spots where you're most likely to catch fish. Halibut and salmon charters are the most popular among trophy fish anglers.

Here are a few air travel tips to keep in mind.

Commercial Airlines: Double-protect rods by packing them in crush-proof tubes. I usually pack my rod in its original metal tube and pad that inside a larger adjustable type such as a rod caddy. You can never have too much protection. A fishing buddy had both of his "airline proof" metal rod cases, and the graphite fly rods within, delivered to him at the airport in a U configuration. On another occasion, I witnessed the wind blow my rod case off the baggage cart and send it tumbling down the taxiway before a mechanic caught up with it.

Also, try to pack equal portions of clothing and tackle in separate bags. This way if one gets lost, you'll still be able to fish.

Float or Bush Plane: The Alaska wilderness is not a place for suitcases. Pack all gear into soft duffel bags. Rods should be two piece and broken down. One-piece rods can

A fly-out fishing trip is a good investment of time and money for the angler who wants quality fishing away from shoulder-to-shoulder fishermen. However, be sure to check out any flying service thoroughly by asking for references several months prior to your trip.

Planning
Your Trip

be easily damaged in a crowded plane. Boarding and un-boarding a floatplane is easier if you're wearing hip boots. Carry whatever you need during the flight in your pocket, including camera, film, and ear plugs (for sensitive ears). It's often impossible to reach your gear once you're air-borne.

Overall, the safest way to plan your trip is to contact the outfitter or lodge directly. Ask for an exact list of the items you'll need for your fishing trip. Many places supply everything except personal hygiene items, while others provide only basic transportation and shelter and you sup-ply the food, gear, equipment, etc. The old saying, "Let the buyer beware!" is most appropriate here.

Nevertheless, half the fun of experiencing an Alaska fishing trip is in the planning.

We've fished miles of water since the beginning of this book, have become intimately familiar with fish life history and lore, and shared in a variety of exper-iences—some thought-provoking, others humorous—that have hopefully given you a proper perspective of Alaska's one-of-a-kind trophy fisheries.

In closing, keep in mind these last thoughts. Treat Alaska's fish with care, as if they were your own, because they are. Practice catch and release to help perpetuate populations of trophy fish. And most important, take kids fishing. Teach them respect for the fishery resource. Because once they have that respect, the rest will fall into place. Automatically. See you on the water.

How to Catch
Alaska's Trophy Sportfish

What to Bring

Proper clothing is important for an enjoyable fishing adventure. Pack for any and all weather conditions. Water resistant duffel bags with handles are the most convenient to use.

Personal Equipment
☐ Sweater
☐ Windbreaker
☐ Down or fiberfill jacket
☐ Gore-Tex or quality raingear with hood
   (3/4 length—No ponchos)
☐ Lightweight wool long underwear
☐ Wool socks (several pair)
☐ Waterproof camp shoes
☐ Lightweight gloves
☐ Corduroy pants
☐ Flannel shirts
☐ Hat with visor
☐ Headnet (optional)
☐ Daypack
☐ Felt inner soles for hip boots and camp shoes
☐ Extra eyeglasses (prescription)
☐ Ear protection (for fly-out trips)
☐ Personal hygiene items

Fishing Equipment
☐ Polarized sunglasses
☐ Ankle-fit hip boots/waders
☐ Insect repellent
☐ Fishing vest
☐ Antibiotic cream
☐ Ultralight spinning or casting rod
☐ Medium-action spinning or casting rod
☐ Heavy-action spinning or casting rod
☐ 7-weight fly rod
☐ 10-weight fly rod
☐ Fillet knife
☐ Hemostat or needlenose pliers
☐ Line clipper
☐ Sharpening stone
☐ Scent or soap
☐ Small, metal fly or lure boxes (no tackle boxes)
☐ Extra reel spools
☐ Extra line
☐ Lures

Index

How to Catch
Alaska's Trophy Sportfish

Alaska Angler® Editor Chris Batin Will Teach Your Fishing Club or Group the Secrets of How and Where to Fish Alaska Successfully

Now you can benefit from a wealth of fishing information by scheduling one of Chris Batin's Advanced Alaska Angling Programs, and make money for yourself, your club or organization at the same time.

This simple plan yields big results for everyone.

First, when your recommendation results in a seminar booking, you personally receive 10 percent of Chris' honorarium, which can mean as much as $500 for you.

Second, your organization can make money from this workshop. The Pasadena FlyCasting Club sold enough of Chris' award-winning books at his workshop to receive his multimedia flyfishing seminar free of charge!

Third, Chris Batin's Alaska Angling Seminars and Workshops are content-rich, stimulating events that are specially designed to meet the informational and trip-planning needs of your group. Chris' outstanding photography and enthusiastic stage presence will entertain and educate your audience for an hour, a day or a weekend. His seminars are perfect for:

- flyfishing banquets and sportfish meetings
- business or professional groups
- national and regional sport shows
- Instructional seminars at your lodge

Call today and take advantage of this opportunity for you or your group to tap into one of the most knowledgeable minds in Alaska sportfishing. Chris Batin became successful by helping others achieve their Alaska fishing dreams beyond their wildest expectations. He then shaped these individuals into Alaska angling success stories with his follow-up technique and strategy seminars. Call now for your opportunity to benefit from his two decades of Alaska fishing experience, and 14th successful year of Teaching Alaskans How To Fish™.

For more information, write or call Chris at:
Alaska Angler/Alaska Hunter Seminars
P.O. Box 83550A, Fairbanks, AK 99708
(907) 455-8000

Ask about our special rates for personal or group instruction on our complete line of Alaska Hunter® seminars and workshops.

Author Christopher Batin with a rainbow trout caught in the Talkeetna Mountains.

About the Author

Over the last two decades, Christopher Batin has emerged as one of Alaska's most well-known and influential sportfishing writers. He is the author of the best-selling, 'How to catch Alaska's Trophy Sportfish' as well as 'Fishing Alaska on Dollars a Day,' 'Hunting in Alaska: A Comprehensive Guide' and is co-author or contributor to three other books. He is editor-in-chief of The Alaska Angler® , a publication that provides a comprehensive look at current research in Alaska sportfishing techniques, lodge and guide reviews, do-it-yourself fishing opportunities, and 'inside information' on Alaska sportfishing.

He has served as Alaska Editor for many national and regional magazines and newspapers. His byline has appeared in Sports Afield, In-Fisherman, Western Outdoors, Outdoor Life, Trout, Saltwater Sportsman, Petersen's Fishing and many others.

Along with his wife/fishing partner, Adela, the couple enjoy widespread, nationwide exposure for their work in promoting Alaska sportfishing. In the last 10 years, they have appeared on the covers of over 20 national and regional publications and have received recognition in numerous articles, radio talk shows and tv appearances.

Chris' dedication to producing quality work has won him over 50 national and regional writing and photography awards. These include several first-place awards for his book, 'How to catch Alaska's Trophy Sportfish' considered by many to be the bible on how to fish Alaska. *Field and Stream magazine* reviewed it as "Alaska Fishing Book Unparalleled." He is also the recipient of 32 trophy fish certificates sponsored by various state and national organizations.

Far from being an 'armchair outdoor writer,' Chris spends from 150 to 180 days per year traveling throughout Alaska. Much of that time is spent personally researching various tips and techniques that help anglers catch more fish. He has hiked into volcanoes, rafted glacial rivers, climbed wilderness mountains and survived Alaska's worst weather to search out and experience the state's unique and undiscovered, as well as most popular, sportfishing opportunities. Chris and Adela's photo file, which contains over 45,000 Alaska sportfishing transparencies, is a testimonial to this continuous quest.

The International Gamefish Association appointed Chris to be their Alaska representative. He helps promote the conservation goals of the organization and assists in verifying world-record fish. In 1986, the Alaska Outdoor Council honored Chris as their Conservationist-Sportswriter of the year.

When he isn't fishing some remote area of Alaska, he is in great demand for his fishing seminars and instructional classes. He is now entering his 14th year of teaching the extremely popular 'Advanced Alaska Fishing Techniques™,' an intense, eight-hour seminar designed to help anglers increase their skills in Alaska sportfishing. Since 1984 he has been a featured speaker at the Great Alaska Sportsman Show, where hundreds of people fill the bleachers to hear his dynamic presentations.

His fishing experience extends beyond Alaska. He has fished throughout Canada and the Lower 48, Mexico, Sweden, Germany, Hawaii, Japan and Russia. He says he has yet to find a place that offers the variety and quality of sportfishing that Alaska offers.

While he fly fishes for personal enjoyment and research, Chris frequently uses other types of gear to 'learn whatever is necessary to increase my knowledge about fish and fishing, and pass this information on to my readers.' He is equally adept at catching lunker halibut on deep-sea rigs as he is bottom-bouncing drift lures for salmon or dancing mini-jigs on a five-foot ultralight for lake trout. He is a strong advocate of catch and release.

Chris lives on a five-acre homesite outside Fairbanks, Alaska with his wife, Adela, their dog Tiger Lily, yellow-naped Amazon parrot, Juliet and sun conure, Cilantro. Chris is always interested in hearing about his readers' fishing adventures in Alaska. Write him at P.O. Box 83550, Fairbanks, AK 99708.

The Alaska Hunter®

Dear Alaska Hunter:

Before you make another Alaska big game hunt, heed this warning: **The hunting crowds are getting worse.**

...In many areas, game animals are not as large as they used to be.

The market is flooded with incompetent guides out to make a quick buck.

Statistics show that guides typically harvest 8-foot bears because they lack the skill and knowledge to find larger bears for their clients.

And do-it-yourself hunters who don't have an insider providing them with Alaska hunting information seldom enjoy the areas they are in, or the fruits of a successful hunt...

However, now YOU can regularly receive the inside scoop on:

■ Where the largest big game animals are taken,

■ The undiscovered, do-it-yourself trips that offer near 100 percent success rates;

■ The guides with high success rates for big bears, trophy moose and caribou.

These successful hunters all have one thing in common. They subscribe to **The Alaska Hunter®** .

With **The Alaska Hunter®** as your guide, you become one of the state's most knowledgeable hunters. Why? Because with each issue, you receive the most current reports and analyses necessary for success.

You can look elsewhere for this information, but don't expect to find it. Conventional sources of information offer you fluffy stories with no substance. Rarely do these stories satisfy the informational needs of knowledgeable hunters who demand specifics such as harvest figures, game densities, access corridors, and information on guides and outfitters offering outstanding trips, or do-it-yourself hunts with high success ratios.

The Alaska Hunter provides you with all this information...and more.

We cater to you, the experienced hunter who wants the very best. And with **The Alaska Hunter®** , you receive specific answers to your Alaska big game hunting questions.

In each issue, you can expect...

At least a dozen new contacts necessary for a successful Alaska hunting trip...outfitters, guides, air charter operators, biologists, hunting experts. Save valuable time and money by allowing us to do the legwork for you. Just the contacts and references you receive each month are worth the yearly subscription price in money saved from expensive long-distance phone calls!

With **The Alaska Hunter®** , you receive the facts without bias from booking agents, bribed writers or advertisements.

Our only allegiance is to you.

We receive no commissions for the trips or contacts we report. No gun reporting or adventure stories. Only unbiased objective reports on Alaska hunting. You won't find this information anywhere else. Pure and simple.

In each bi-monthly issue, you receive specific answers to your Alaska big game hunting questions. You'll receive:

Do-It-Yourself Alaska Hunter
A special page with complete where-to, how-to information on planning your Alaska big game hunt, by yourself or with a group. Prices, logistics, transportation, chances of success, special equipment, game populations, best ways to ship home trophies and meat, companies that rent float hunting gear.

Hunt Reviews
The best and worst do-it-yourself and guided hunts for every species of Alaska big game. In future issues, discover Alaska's best trophy moose area, where record-book bulls are dying of old age...read where the current, world-record brown bear is living, and why hunters haven't been able to bag him...how two-plane hunts offer 80 to 100 percent success ratios...the story behind the rip-off $400 fly-out hunt special, and more.

Hunt Area Specifics
In-depth reports on a specific game management units, what's available, type of terrain, weather, success figures for each species of big game animals, and more. This is information that would take you weeks to acquire on your own.

The Best of the Best
Alaska hunting guides and outfitters who are providing the very best guided trophy and do-it-yourself hunts. In-depth profiles on the guides whose clients are regulars in the Boone and Crockett, Pope and Young and Safari Club record books.

Secrets of Alaska's Hunting Guides
Tips gleaned from veteran guides with decades of field experience. Their observations and tips can spell the difference between success and failure.

Alaska Hunter News Updates
The most current news of the Alaska hunting industry, disciplinary actions, outfitter problems, USFWS sting operations on registered guides and renegade outfitters, new hunt openings, hunt closures, and Department of Fish and Game management decisions.

Marine Mammal Coverage
Ready for walrus, seal or polar bearhunting? The Alaska Hunter will keep you up-to-date on the status of the Marine Mammal Protection Act, and who the top guides will be so you'll be ready when the seasons open.

Guide/Outfitter Issues
The inside stories behind the guides' push for dominance in the hunting market. How Alaska's big game populations are in trouble from unregulated hunting by renegade outfitters. The detrimental effect some air taxi operators are having on your hunting success.

Political Forum
Up-to-date reports on important political decisions and actions that affect you and your Alaska hunting plans. This is especially important as Alaska moves toward deregulation of guide areas, Native Sovereignty, 1991 amendments, and removal of prime hunting lands by the National Park Service.

Discounts
- Last minute hunt cancellations
- Special hunt openings
- The best registration hunts
- Waterfowl/big game hunts
- Fishing/hunting combos and more

The information you'll receive each month is an unbeatable combination of experience and knowledge.

It's created for hunters like you by year-long resident Alaska hunters and writers. And they are directed by Chris Batin, one of Alaska's most experienced hunting writers and editors.

Batin is author of the award-winning, "Hunting in Alaska: A Comprehensive Guide," and former editor of Alaska Outdoors magazine and The Alaska Professional Hunter newsletter. He has received over 30 awards for his reports in national and regional publications, including the Journalist of the Year from the Alaska Professional Hunters Association and Sportswriter of the Year from The Alaska Outdoor Council. With over 15 years of experience covering the Alaska hunting scene, Chris is both as an active participant and veteran journalist. He is considered by many of the country's top outdoor writers as one of Alaska's most knowledgeable hunting editors.

Compare us with other publications on the market. A year's subscription is only **$49**, which includes first-class postage to your home or office.

If you want the very best of Alaska big game hunting, you can't afford to be without a subscription to The Alaska Hunter.

Don't miss a single issue. Send in the attached order form or call toll free today and be among those who benefit from **The Alaska Hunter**®

The Alaska Hunter.........$49 per year.

Hunting in Alaska
A Comprehensive Guide

By Christopher Batin

"(Hunting in Alaska) is the standard by which other Alaska hunting books will be judged."
Bob Robb,
Petersen's Hunting

Hunting in Alaska is a rich source of Alaska-tested hunting ideas & strategies that work!
■ 416 information-packed pages, 138 photos, many award winning
■ 51 maps & illustrations
■ Expert advice on hunting sheep, bear, moose, caribou, waterfowl, and more!
■ Detailed, where-to-go information and harvest statistics for each species in each Game Management Unit

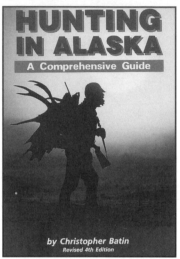

HUNTING IN ALASKA
A Comprehensive Guide

by Christopher Batin
Revised 4th Edition

ISBN 0-916771-11-3

For years, successful guides and hunters have known that it takes scientific knowledge and specific strategies to successfully harvest Alaska's most coveted big game trophies. Now, for the first time, **Hunting in Alaska: A Comprehensive Guide** offers you over 1,000 of these hunting secrets and tips. Master guides and big game experts provide decades of first-hand experience, ensuring your Alaska hunt is a complete success.

Based on 15 years of Alaska hunting experience and research, "Hunting in Alaska: A Comprehensive Guide" **provides you with a wealth of never-before available information on:**
■ High Bush and Low Bush Thrashing: Tactics scientifically proven to call in trophy moose.
■ Specifics on hunting Kodiak and Alaska Peninsula Brown Bear
■ Scientific data on the habits of full-curl Dall sheep, where they're found and how to hunt them, including interviews with guides who regularly take record-book sheep.
■ 10-year trends on game populations, hunter statistics and harvest totals that give you pre-hunt knowledge of your chances for success in each of Alaska's 26 Game Management Units.

■ Detailed maps and Game Management Unit descriptions that will familiarize you with Alaska's wilderness hunting hotspots and game concentrations.
■ Planning a do-it-yourself hunt.
■ Secret bear hunting techniques used by one guide who is nearly 100 percent for big brown bear, and who has put several in the record books, including a 30-incher.
■ Criteria for choosing an Alaska big game guide.
■ Learn secrets of taking wolves along salmon streams
■ Understanding seasonal migration habits of big mountain goats and goat hunting methods that have helped one guide bag over 40 trophy goats for his clients.
■ Specialized equipment needs for guided, unguided, backpack and float hunts.
■ Over 1,000 listings of where you can hunt Alaska's big and small game and waterfowl.
■ Care of trophies and meat.
■ How to hunt ridges, over bait, berry patches, and tidal flats for trophy black bear.
■ Extensive chapters on duck, goose, sea duck and crane hunting, small game, grouse, ptarmigan.
■ Four award-winning stories on Alaska Hunting Excitement, Ethics, Camaraderie, and Adventure.
■ Big game behavioral and natural history information of special interest to you as a hunter. Historical synopses of Alaska big game species, including transplants and current distribution information.

Hunting in Alaska:
A Comprehensive Guide
Softcover....$25.95 (Canada.....$27.95)
Hardcover........$45 (Canada.........$47)

Fishing Alaska on Dollars a Day

A Comprehensive Guide to Fishing & Hunting in Alaska's National Forests

by Christopher and Adela Batin

A seven-day stay at a premier Alaska fishing lodge will cost over $4,000, a price beyond the financial reach of many anglers.

However, if you can row a boat, cook your own meals and handle cast-after-cast excitement for feisty, fresh-from-the-sea salmon, you can enjoy comparable Alaska sport-fishing for only dollars a day. **Fishing Alaska on Dollars a Day** reveals Alaska's best angling hideaways where you can catch trophy steelhead, salmon and trout. The book is the result of years of research and travel to some of Alaska's best fishing hotspots.

All the information you need for planning your trip is in this one book, saving you hundreds of dollars in research time and phone calls.

This 352-page book provides you with:

■ **Specific details on over 200 wilderness cabins,** exact locations, how to get there, free boats for your personal use, free cabins and shelters, and where you'll find the best wilderness sightseeing, wildlife photography and adventuring opportunities, as well as pages of alternate contact sources for more information.

■ **Available for the first time are the names and locations of over 375 Alaska steelhead streams.** Discover where you can average 8 to 12 steelhead per trip; choose from over 200 cutthroat waters, many located in Alaska's finest scenic mountain wilderness, or the best intertidal areas where fly fishermen catch over 20 silver salmon per day!

3rd Edition

Fishing Alaska On Dollar$ A Day

A Comprehensive Guide to Fishing, Hiking & Outdoor Recreation in Alaska's National Forests

By Christopher and Adela Batin

ISBN 0-916771-26-1

■ **Detailed USGS topographic maps and fishing charts** help you pinpoint the best fishing and hunting areas. If purchased separately, these maps alone would cost you over $150. These maps are **FREE** with the book, and are invaluable in helping plan your trip.

■ **Specific advice on flies and lures,** as well as 100 photos to prove these recommendations work!

■ **With this book you'll also learn where you can inexpensively hunt** for moose, goat, brown and black bear, wolf and Sitka blacktail deer, as well as waterfowl. You'll have the comforts of a wilderness cabin to enjoy at the end of a successful day's hunt.

The book is profusely illustrated with over 150 maps, photographs and charts. When used in conjunction with our award-winning book, "How to catch Alaska's Trophy Sportfish", you have all the information you need to plan a complete and successful Alaska fishing adventure.

"An excellent book that is essential for anyone considering making the trip."
San Francisco Examiner

"If you've dreamed about an Alaska adventure but can't afford the $2,000 to $4,000 price tag for most outfitted trips, this book is the answer."
Allentown Morning Call

"A comprehensive guide destined to become dog-eared by dedicated anglers. Written by Chris Batin, perhaps the best-known fishing authority in Alaska."
Akron Beacon

Fishing Alaska on Dollars a Day....$24.95
Canada............$26.95

Each Issue of The Alaska Angler® Provides You With 10 Benefits:

Lodge Reviews

You don't need to spend $4,000 to discover if a lodge has a four-star rating or whether it's a fly-by-night operation. We visit the lodges and provide you objective reports on the number of fish you can expect to catch, accommodations and compare it with other lodges. We take the risks, you benefit from our experience.

Do-it-Yourself Alaska Angler

Tired of fishing with the crowds? Receive inside information on affordable trips you can enjoy, both from the road system and fly-out trips. You receive everything necessary to duplicate our successes: names of air taxi services, contacts, detailed maps, what to use and how to fish it: First-hand information because we've been there, and want to share these great fisheries with you!

Advanced Alaska Angling Techniques

With each issue, you become an instant expert with a crash course on a specific angling situation you're likely to encounter while fishing Alaska. You'll be on the cutting edge of the most popular and effective fish-catching techniques as well as field-proven flies, lures and equipment. The result? You'll be catching fish when others are not.

Guide Review

In a recent field survey, over 60 percent of the fishing guides we fished with were judged to be

incompetent. Why fish with a guide who will catch you five fish, when you can fish with a guide who can help you catch 20 fish, and larger ones at that? I review the best guides, investigate their success ratios and score them against the industry's best.

Alaska Angler Field Notes

Bringing a loved one to Alaska, or looking for a trip that caters to women? Perhaps a secluded cabin you can rent for dollars a day, away from the crowds but in the thick of the salmon? Or specific technical data on water flow, speed, substrate, forage fish and hatches on streams? I tell you the specifics, and the best patterns you need to catch the big ones. I know because I've been there, having earned more than 30 trophy fish certificates and awards, so that you can benefit from this experience, NOW.

Alaska Angler Field Reports

Read about the successes or failures of other anglers who fish Alaska as they rate the best and worst of Alaska fishing...valuable information that will help in taking home personal experiences of catching and releasing trophy fish...not just stories of the catch someone else made last week.

Short Strikes

Brief news notes on items that will enhance your fishing knowledge, making you a better angler. Some recent topics include "Techniques for finding and catching trophy gray-

ling"; "Forage fish preferences of Alaska rainbow trout"; "Three steps to catching 10-pound-plus fish when all else fails"; and "When do fish feed during Alaska's 24 hours of daylight".

Alaska Angler Notebook.

Trip discounts, last-minute fishing closures, and field notes regarding Bush travel, suppliers of inexpensive, quality flies for Alaska fishing, uncharted steelhead fishing and more information on how you can fish Alaska on a shoestring budget.

Custom Trip Consulting

Planning on making a trip soon? Subscribers can take advantage of our low-cost information service on lodges, guides, resorts or areas you plan on visiting in 1991. We'll tell you what to expect, and if you'll be better off going elsewhere! We provide harvest statistics, success ratios, lures, tackle equipment for specific areas and contacts over the telephone if you need them in a hurry or by mail if you want to share them with friends.

Special Reports

Discover the behind-the-scenes story major magazines won't publish, stories that will change how you view so called "blue ribbon" fisheries. In the past, we've covered the problem of Alaska's widespread incompetent guide problem, the demise of the Iliamna watershed fishery, the advertising hype surrounding the Brooks River fishery, and more.

Not Available in Stores!

The Alaska Angler® is available only by subscription...it is not sold on newsstands or to libraries. Thus, our information stays among our close-knit network of subscribers.

If our bi-monthly reports were made available through newspapers, magazines and tv, the good fishing I reveal would cease to exist. But I'm willing to share this information with you, a fellow sportsman who cares about Alaska's fishery resources.

Why You Need to Act Now!

The Alaska Angler® has become the information source for anglers who

want the very best in Alaska sport-fishing. Here's what our subscribers have to say:

"Informative, concise, well worth the investment." Dr. R.T., New York, N.Y.

"Excellent information on Alaska sport-fishing. We have planned trips because of articles in The Alaska Angler."
I.H., Anchorage, Alaska

Receive over 60 pages of special reports and information a year...the cost of a couple flies or a fishing lure per issue. And the price includes first-class postage to your home or office.

The Alaska Angler......$49 per year.

Chris Batin's 20 Great
Alaska Fishing Adventures

by Christopher Batin

The greatest adventures in Alaska sportfishing that you can experience today!

Frustrated by shoulder-to-shoulder crowds... mediocre Alaska fishing opportunities...and fish that are small and too few in number?

If so, get ready to fly into a glacial-rimmed volcanic crater and fish nearby streams where you will land 50 salmon a day... a wilderness mountain retreat where you catch 11 different species of sportfish in one week... or discover a remote river where anglers catch several, 10 to 17-pound rainbow trout each day!

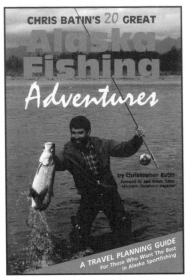

CHRIS BATIN'S 20 GREAT
Alaska Fishing Adventures
by Christopher Batin
Foreword by Jack Brown, Editor Western Outdoors magazine
A TRAVEL PLANNING GUIDE
For Those Who Want The Best in Alaska Sportfishing

ISBN 0-916771-09-1

Free information on contacts, charter pilots, lodges, road-access routes, telephone numbers...everything you need to plan your Great Alaska Fishing Adventure THIS YEAR!

It's an adventure book you won't want to put down!

This book is also chock-full of Alaska wilderness fishing adventure stories and anecdotes that not only entertain, but inform. Only a handful of anglers experienced in the world's best fishing have known about many of these areas.

At your fingertips is everything you need to duplicate the author's successes...as well as specific travel details necessary for you to plan one of Alaska's 20 finest fishing adventures NOW.

Many fisheries are so remote, only a handful of anglers visit them each year!

This book has over 150 photos and maps...showing you what you can expect first-hand. See the rivers...country... fish...and the adventure you can expect on each trip!

This book offers you detailed information on where to find fish at each location...forage fish and hatch information...and personal observations on the habits of these sportfish so you can make outstanding catches...and releases... of trophy fish Alaska is famous for.

A comprehensive listing of the most productive flies for each area, based on actual field tests.

"In 20 Great Alaska Fishing Adventures, Chris Batin captures the spirit and excitement of Alaska sportfishing adventure!"

Jack Brown, Western Outdoors magazine

"In recent years, Chris and Adela Batin have become synonymous with and trusted sources for Alaska fishing information.

Twenty Great Alaska Fishing Adventures stresses the best in Alaska sportfishing and details trips that qualify in that 'adventure of a lifetime' category. The book also offers a commendable emphasis on catch-and-release fishing."

The International Angler

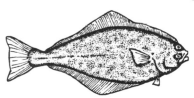

Chris Batin's 20 Great Alaska Fishing Adventures.................$19.95

How to catch Alaska's Trophy Sportfish

By Christopher Batin

"Alaska Fishing Book Unparalleled" *Rich Landers*
Field and Stream magazine

Over 30,000 anglers around the world have benefited from this advanced guide.

Anyone can catch four-pound rainbows or 12-pound salmon. But if you want to catch 60 to 80-pound Alaska king salmon, 300-pound halibut, 20-pound silvers, 30-inch rainbow trout, trophy grayling and steelhead, **"How to catch Alaska's Trophy Sportfish"** is your must-have, on-stream guide.

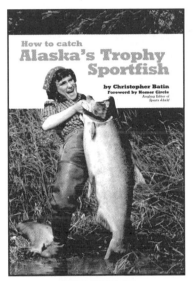

ISBN 0-916771-04-0

This Book Gives You A PH.D. Crash Course In Alaska Fish Habits and Biology Necessary for Success

"How to catch Alaska's Trophy Sportfish" translates volumes of biological data into terms every angler can understand and use to catch trophy sportfish.

You'll learn about:
- aggravation responses that catch 70-pound salmon,
- social hierarchies that tell you where to find fish before you reach the water,
- stream equations necessary for catching the largest trout and char.

We show you how each species of Alaska trophy sportfish respond to stimuli, and how you can duplicate those responses through our proven field tips and techniques. If you order NOW, you can have this knowledge today...at your fingertips.

Use this book when you go shopping for flies and tackle.

You receive sixteen full-color pages showing the different sportfish and the best flies and lures you need for success, all of which have earned the highest marks for catching trophy sportfish in 10 years of testing.

With this advice, you'll spend your time catching fish, rather than wondering what to catch them on.

This book is also a must-have volume to fully understand the author's fishing recommendations in "Fishing Alaska on $15 a Day."

"Batin's long time on Alaskan waters (over 30,000 hours) gives his new book singular value. What fisherman wouldn't pay for a decade of experience condensed into plain English? The author's experience shows. No matter what the species being sought, Batin's book is a great place to start." Joe Bridgman
The Anchorage Times.

This book can make your Alaska fishing trip a success with its:

- 368 pages and 120 action-filled photos showing you the fish-catching secrets that has enabled the author to catch and release thousands of sportfish.

- Fly fishing techniques for Alaska's lakes and streams.

- Detailed information, life histories, and feeding habits for all of Alaska's 17 major sportfish species.

- Over 500 specific areas in Alaska where you can catch your trophy sportfish.

- 16 full-color pages identifying Alaska's trophy sportfish plus color charts of the most effective lure and fly patterns.

- Detailed charts and illustrations showing you where to find trophy sportfish.

- Fish-catching secrets of over a dozen guides and biologists.

"If you plan to go to Alaska, or already live there, read this book thoroughly and you fish it better. Chris Batin IS Alaska fishing."
Homer Circle
Angling Editor, Sports Afield magazine

How to catch Alaska's Trophy Sportfish

Softcover....$25.95 (Canada.....$27.95)
Hardcover-Limited Edition.............$45
(Canada..........$47)

Best Recipes of Alaska's Fishing Lodges

by Adela Batin

A unique addition to your cookbook collection. This book tells it all...the lodges and accommodations, the cooks and their recipes, photographs of scenic Alaska, fishing and food. Everything you've wanted to know about Alaska's fishing lodges.

An excellent travel planning guide, you'll learn what it's really like to be there!

Best Recipes of Alaska's Fishing Lodges is more than just a cookbook—It's a celebration of a wilderness lifestyle that many of us dream about, but few live.

Best Recipes
of Alaska's
Fishing Lodges
Adela Batin

ISBN 0-916771-10-5

■ 190 kitchen-tested recipes, home-style to gourmet: Fish, meat, poultry, soups, salads, breads and desserts.

■ Delicious ways to fix your Alaska catch of salmon and halibut, moose or caribou. Plus the perfect accompanying dishes to make a complete meal.

■ 140 photographs showing the food, fishing, accommodations and activities at the lodges.

■ Three-color format, 6'' x 9'', 320 pages, complete recipe index.

Each chapter is seasoned with photos and descriptions of 16 of Alaska's finest lodges, garnished with cooks' profiles and frosted with anecdotes on Alaska that inform as well as entertain.

This book gives you a variety of lodge experiences. Each lodge is unique in its location, the type of fishing it offers, the way meals are prepared, the type of food served, and the ambiance created by owners and personnel.

Each year, thousands of anglers pay up to $4,000 a week to enjoy the services and partake in the sensational meals served at these world-famous lodges.

Best Recipes of Alaska's Fishing Lodges gives you the opportunity to sample the many wonderful flavors of Alaska.

Delight family and friends with this taste-tempting assortment of **190 best recipes** that include: Alaska Sourdough Pizza, Savory Dill Salmon, Smoked Halibut Spread, Kulik Cream Cake, Stuffed Kvichak Chicken, Icy Strait BBQ Halibut and Strawberry Island Bread.

Best Recipes of Alaska's Fishing Lodges, was recently honored as the "Best Outdoor Book" by the Northwest Outdoor Writers Association, winning first place in design and editing. It makes the perfect gift for anglers and cooks alike.

Novice and gourmet cooks—as well as anyone interested in Alaskana—will cherish this book.

This book is your link to the Alaska lodge experience. If you've stayed at one of these featured lodges, these recipes may help you savor those memories. If you've never been to Alaska, allow this book to be your guide.

Best Recipes of Alaska's Fishing Lodges (softcover)..........$24.95
(Canada....$26.95)

Bear Heads & Fish Tales

By Alan Liere

Patrick F. McManus, internationally recognized humorist, book author and columnist for Outdoor Life magazine, has this to say in the foreword of Alan Liere's recent book on Alaska outdoor humor entitled, "**Bear Heads & Fish Tales**":

"What's funny? Nobody knows for sure, but I would venture to say that it's that tiny, gritty bit of truth that produces the pearl of laughter. I do not mean to imply that author Al Liere in any way resembles an oyster. The man is a funny writer, which is the best thing you can say about a humorist. I personally plan to buy a gross of Bear Heads & Fish Tales. If we have another Great Depression, people will need something to cheer them up, and I figure a copy of this book will be as good as gold in the marketplace."

Bear Heads & Fish Tales is a collection of zany outdoor stories written by Alan Liere, Alaska's ambassador of mirth and humor to the funny bone. Learn the techniques for smoking fish, Alaska-style, by burning your neighbors garage; what words to say to your oil pan while sleeping under your car, tips on preparing wilderness gourmet meals such as Chicken Noodle Salmon or Humpy Rainwater Soup, how to stuff a mature bull caribou into the cargo space of a Subaru hatchback and much more.

"This book is for anyone who has ever wielded a fishing rod, a shotgun, or a wiener stick," says Liere. "It's for those who experience deflated air mattresses, rubber rafts, and egos— sometimes all on the same outing. **Bear Heads & Fish Tales** is for anyone who believes in that fine line between tragedy and comedy and knows with all their heart that maturity is highly over-rated."

"*Alaska Outdoor Humor At Its Best!*"

Bear Heads & Fish Tales

By Alan Liere

Foreword by
Patrick F. McManus

ISBN 0-916771-05-9

The 13 stories in this 139-page book are based on Liere's real-life personal misadventures and hilarious insights. In "King Tut's Revenge," Liere expounds on his childhood phobia regarding mummy-type sleeping bags. "Thanks, Aunt Judy" reveals tips on how Liere has learned to survive Alaska mosquitoes through such evasive tactics as "The Screamin' Exit" and the liberal use of garlic. And with a humorous eye, he examines that glossy, hope-inducing product of creative writing and adjective overuse known as "The Alaska Outdoor Brochure."

Each story is illustrated by outdoor cartoonist Jeff Schuler. The combined efforts of both author and cartoonist effectively capture the side-splitting antics and foibles of sportsmen in the Alaska outdoors, the Northcountry's grandest comic playhouse.

Bear Heads & Fish Tales $9.95

Alaska Angler® Information Service

Want to know the best rivers to catch all five species of Pacific salmon? Anxious to discover the Top 10 do-it-yourself trips for wild, 8 to 10-pound rainbow trout? Or a listing of Alaska's five-star lodges that serve you early-morning coffee in bed and at night, place European chocolates on your pillow?

The answers to these and other Alaska sportfishing questions can be answered by calling the **Alaska Angler® Information Service**.

The Information Service provides "answers for anglers" who are planning a fishing trip to the 49th state.

"There's a common misconception that Alaska fishing is good year-round, no matter where or when you go," says Chris Batin, editor of **The Alaska Angler®** "Alaska has over 3 million lakes and 3,000 rivers covering a land mass one-fifth the size of the continental United States. Planning is crucial for success. A miscalculation of several days can have anglers staring at fishless water rather than a stream filled with salmon."

He stressed the information service is not a booking agency.

"Objectivity is the key to the Alaska Angler® Information Service," Batin said. "We do not receive any remuneration or benefit from recommending one stream or fishing service over another. This ensures that our customers receive objective information on fishing opportunities, guides and lodges that surpass industry standards for service, quality and professionalism. We can provide all the information anglers need, from the best flies for a particular watershed, water conditions to expect, type of hatches, and even the flora and fauna in the area."

Travel agents and booking agents are often unfamiliar with Alaska's myriad sportfishing options.

"Many travel agents sell a limited selection of trips that offer the best commissions for them," he said. "It's not cost effective for them to recommend quality, inexpensive trips, even though it may be perfect for the angler's needs. The Alaska Angler® Information Service provides unbiased information so the angler can personally decide whether to spend $25 or $4,000 for a trip.

The crew of **The Alaska Angler®** spends over 180 days a year fishing Alaska, searching out the best do-it-yourself and full-service adventures for the company's information service, periodicals and books.

The cost is **$30** for **15 minutes of consultation**. Before consultation begins, callers provide a Mastercard or Visa credit card number. To expedite matters, have ready your list of questions. To benefit from the Alaska Angler® Information Service, call **1-907-455-8000** 10 a.m. to 6 p.m. Alaska Standard Time, Monday—Friday. You may also fax your list of questions to Chris Batin at **(907) 455-6691.** Include your credit card number, name, address and phone number and the best time to return your call.

Send $1 for your Alaska Angler Resource Guide that includes our entire selection of Alaska fishing books and periodicals that ensure your success on the stream!

Ship to:_____

Address: _____

City _____

State _____ Zip _____

Daytime Phone( )_____

Send order to:

Alaska Angler® Publications
P.O. Box 83550-HTC
Fairbanks, Alaska 99708
Or call (907) 455-8000
24 hours a day, 7 days a week

Quantity	Item	Price	Total
_____	Bear Heads & Fish Tales...................................	**$9.95**	_____
_____	Best Recipes of Alaska's Fishing Lodges...................................	**$24.95**	_____
_____	Chris Batin's 20 Great Alaska Fishing Adventures........................	**$19.95**	_____
_____	Fishing Alaska on Dollar$ a Day...	**$24.95**	_____
_____	How to catch Alaska's Trophy Sportfish, softcover........................	**$25.95**	_____
_____	How to catch Alaska's Trophy Sportfish, Limited Edition, hardcover........	**$45**	_____
_____	Hunting in Alaska, softcover..	**$25.95**	_____
_____	The Alaska Hunter® newsletter (one-year subscription).................	**$49 ppd**	_____
_____	The Alaska Hunter® custom binder..	**$14 ppd**	_____
_____	The Alaska Hunter® ceramic mug (great for the office).................	**$14 ppd**	_____
	Circle color: Cobalt blue Black Both have microwaveable gold trim		
_____	"Alaska Hunter® " wool hunting cap, one size fits all....................	**$16 ppd**	_____
	Color: Black with hunter green brim		
_____	"Alaska Hunter® " cotton hunting cap, one size fits all..................	**$14 ppd**	_____
	Circle color: Black with hunter green brim or Green Woodland Camo		
_____	The Alaska Angler® newsletter (one-year subscription).................	**$49 ppd**	_____
_____	The Alaska Angler® custom binder..	**$14 ppd**	_____
•_____	The Alaska Angler® Field Staff ceramic mug (great for the office)....	**$14 ppd**	_____
	Circle color: Cobalt blue Black Both have microwaveable gold trim		
_____	"Alaska Angler® " poplin leisure cap, one size fits all....................	**$14 ppd**	_____
	Circle color: Teal Green Red		
_____	"Alaska Angler® " leisure cap, one size fits all............................	**$16 ppd**	_____
	Circle color and fabric: Teal Green Red Corduroy Ripstop Nylon		

Gift Section

Book(s) personalized to: (please print)

Name _____

Title of book(s) _____
_____

Book(s) personalized to:

Name _____

Title of book(s) _____
_____

Book(s) personalized to:

Name _____

Title of book(s) _____
_____

Book Shipping Charges

Priority Mail delivery (1 to 2 weeks)......$6. _____
each additional book Priority Mail...............$3. _____
Newsletters, binders, apparel postage paid....0.
Canada, add to above charges................$3. _____
Foreign countries, Airmail, per book....$15. _____
Airmail, per newsletter subscription..........$20. _____

ORDER AND SHIPPING TOTAL _____

Payment Method

Enclose your personal check, money order or credit card info.
☐ **Check**   ☐ **Money Order**   ☐ **VISA**   ☐ **Mastercard**

Card Acct. Number_____

Exp. Date — Signature _____

For money-saving discounts on our books and publications that help ensure your success in the Alaska outdoors, send $1 to:

Alaska Angler/Hunter Publications
P.O. Box 83550, Dept F3
Fairbanks, Alaska 99708

You can obtain any Alaska Angler® or Alaska Hunter® book in print by ordering directly from the publisher. See the order form on page 383 in the back of this book.